KT-458-708

SEMANTICS
AND
COGNITION

Current Studies in Linguistics Series
Samuel Jay Keyser, general editor

SEMANTICS AND COGNITION

Ray Jackendoff

The MIT Press
Cambridge, Massachusetts
London, England

This book was set in VIP Baskerville by Village Typographers, Inc., and printed and bound in the United States of America.

Library of Congress Cataloging in Publication Data

Jackendoff, Ray S.
  Semantics and cognition.
  (Current studies in linguistics series; 8)
  Bibliography: p.
  Includes index.
  1. Semantics. 2. Cognition. 3. Categorization (Psychology) 4. Meaning (Psychology) I. Title. II. Series.
P325.J29 1983   415   83–881
ISBN 978-0-262-10027-4 (hard)
ISBN 978-0-262-60013-2 (paper)

20 19 18 17 16 15 14 13 12 11 10

Contents

Contents

Series Foreword

We are pleased to present this book as the eighth volume in the series Current Studies in Linguistics.

As we have defined it, the series will offer book-length studies in linguistics and neighboring fields that further the exploration of man's ability to manipulate symbols. It will pursue the same editorial goals as its companion journal, *Linguistic Inquiry,* and will complement it by providing a format for in-depth studies beyond the scope of the professional article.

By publishing such studies, we hope the series will answer the need for intensive and detailed research that sheds new light on current theoretical issues and provides a new dimension for their resolution. Toward this end it will present books dealing with the widest range of languages and addressing the widest range of theoretical topics. From time to time and with the same ends in view, the series will include collections of significant articles covering single and selected subject areas and works primarily for use as textbooks.

Like *Linguistic Inquiry,* Current Studies in Linguistics will seek to present work of theoretical interest and excellence.

Samuel Jay Keyser

Preface

The need to write this book arose out of work I was doing during the mid seventies on the generalization of grammatical and lexical form over various semantic fields of verbs and prepositions. As the great scope of these generalizations gradually became evident, it dawned on me to ask why they should exist. Surely, I thought, there is no reason intrinsic to *grammar* that explains why the verb "keep," for instance, can express maintenance of position ("keep the book on the shelf"), continued possession ("keep the book"), maintenance of a property ("keep Bill angry"), and coercion ("keep Bill working"). Lacking a grammatical explanation, the only alternative I could imagine was that such generalizations arise from the structure of the *concepts* the lexical and grammatical systems express. If my guess was correct, then, this sort of analysis yielded a striking approach to the age-old dream of using linguistic structure to uncover the nature of thought.

But I found myself frustrated at every turn in trying to incorporate my findings into existing theories of semantics. There simply was nothing in the frameworks I had encountered that accorded any significant force to my form of argumentation. In fact, some conclusions that followed rather naturally from my work ran directly against received practice in formal logic. So I began to explore the unstated intuitions behind my arguments, hoping to find where I diverged from other frameworks.

This book represents the fruits of that exploration, emphasizing the role of semantics as a bridge between the theory of language and the theories of other cognitive capacities such as visual perception and motor control. From this view of semantics follow a number of important consequences. First, the notion of "individual," often taken to be a logical primitive, is cognitively complex; moreover, the kinds of individuals that must be countenanced by semantic and cognitive theory include not only objects but also such entities as places, paths, events, actions, and amounts (chapter 3). Second, in order to express adequately the relationships among these entities, a formal syntax of concepts must be established that is in some ways much richer and in some ways much more constrained than standard logic. Chapter 4 presents the essentials of such a system. Chapters 5 and 6, the heart of the book, explore the fundamental cognitive process of *categorization*. These chapters demonstrate that, once a theory of cognition has sufficient formal power to account for nonlinguistic categorization, it also can account for linguistic inference, the domain of traditional semantic theory. This means that there is no justification for a "semantic" capacity independent of cognition; it also means that when we are studying semantics of natural language, we are by necessity studying the structure of thought.

In the course of chapters 3 to 6, several arguments develop concerning the nature of word meanings. In particular, it is shown that none of the three most popular alternatives in the literature—systems of necessary and sufficient conditions, prototype templates, and meaning postulate systems (or their variant, associative networks)—adequately accounts for the role of lexical items in categorization. Chapters 7 and 8 amplify these arguments and develop a more satisfactory theory of lexical decomposition. This theory crucially involves the notion of a *preference rule system,* a computational mechanism that has appeared implicitly in the psychological literature for over half a century but has not previously been recognized, except by the Gestalt theorists, as a pervasive characteristic of natural computation.

Perhaps the most fundamental consequence of the approach adopted here is that the standard notions of truth and reference play no significant role in natural language semantics (chapter 2). Though this is likely to be the most controversial aspect of the book, and probably deserves a book of its own, I think that the alternative view of reference developed here is amply supported by the psychological literature and by the way it overcomes some of the more important impasses of contemporary semantic theory.

The end product of the investigation is a psychologically plausible formal framework in which to study both meaning in natural language and the structure of concepts. The potential applications of this framework to psychological concerns are numerous. For instance, the study of perception can be enriched by a more thorough understanding of the conceptual information that the perceptual systems must deliver. Similarly, a formal theory of concepts may provide a way of stating more explicitly certain problems of conceptual development; for example, when a child comes to achieve "object constancy" in a certain experimental situation, it should be possible to ask what formal properties (if any) have changed in his conceptual system.

The applications I discuss here, however, are to the problems of linguistic semantics that motivated this study in the first place. Two of these—the analysis of expressions of spatial position and motion (chapter 9) and the generalization of this analysis to other semantic fields (chapter 10)—have received only sporadic attention in the literature. The third (chapter 11) involves the venerable problem of belief-contexts, for which I develop a solution radically different from and considerably more general than traditional approaches. Each of these areas has deep consequences for the nature of language and cognition alike; I have therefore tried to present them in a fashion accessible to nonspecialists.

In the course of working out this material, I have incurred many intellectual debts, which it is now my pleasure to acknowledge. I have benefited greatly from conversations with numerous students and colleagues; among the most prominent in my mind are Dick Carter, Len Talmy, Jane Grimshaw, Janet Fodor, George Miller, John Goldsmith, Erich Woisetschlaeger, Sparky Jackendoff, and particularly John Macnamara. Dick Oehrle, Fred Lerdahl, Georges Rey, and Noam Chomsky provided detailed comments on earlier versions of the manuscript, helping me smooth over many rocky areas.

I have presented many incarnations of this work at colloquia and conferences, and I have profited from everyone's comments and questions. Most valuable to me were the opportunities to develop the material at length: courses at Brandeis University in spring 1980 and fall 1981; a lecture series at McGill University in summer 1977, arranged by Glyne Piggott; a course at the 1980 LSA Linguistic Institute, organized by Garland Bills; a lecture series at Sophia University, Tokyo, in fall 1980, at the most gracious invitation of Felix Lobo and Akira Ota; and a mini-course at the University of Ottawa in winter 1982, arranged by Shalom Lappin.

For a number of years, Jim Lackner and I have taught a course together called "Language and Mind." Through Jim's part of the course, I came to appreciate the importance of abstractness, creativity, and innateness in cognitive capacities other than language, particularly in the neglected but crucial area of motor control.

Concurrently with the writing of the present book, Fred Lerdahl and I were working on our *Generative Theory of Tonal Music.* While I don't recommend to anyone the experience of writing two major books at once, these two works have had a salutary mutual influence. This will be most noticeable here in my occasional references to problems of musical cognition and musical performance, and most crucially in the motivation of preference rule systems in chapter 8. But the music theory also had the effect of forcing me to think about nonlinguistic generative theories, and of prompting me to learn more about vision. Thus many aspects of this book are indirectly due to Fred, without whom the music theory could not have come to pass.

If there is any one person responsible for the intellectual climate in which this book could develop, it is of course Noam Chomsky. To him is due the mentalistic viewpoint of this work, as well as two fundamental arguments: from creativity to the need for rule systems, and from poverty of the stimulus to innateness. (I was once told that my views on sense and reference push Chomsky's approach to its logical extreme. I took this as a deep compliment, even if it was intended as quite the opposite.) In addition, Chomsky's notion of polycategorial (X-Bar) syntax, introduced in "Remarks on Nominalization," provides the inspiration and motivation for the polycategorial semantics developed here in chapter 4.

My ideas on conceptual structure were sharpened by Jerry Fodor's *The Language of Thought,* George Miller and Philip Johnson-Laird's *Language and Perception,* and John Macnamara's unpublished paper "How Can We Talk about What We See?" Jeffrey Gruber's *Studies in Lexical Relations* is the source of much of the theory of thematic relations presented in chapters 9 and 10. My views on nonverbal cognition and its relation to semantics were stimulated by Macnamara's *Names for Things,* Wolfgang Köhler's *The Mentality of Apes,* Michael Polanyi's *Personal Knowledge,* and Frederick Perls's *Ego, Hunger, and Aggression.* Robert Pirsig's *Zen and the Art of Motorcycle Maintenance* had something to do with it too.

For a work like this, at the intersection of linguistics, psychology, philosophy, and computer science, a full mastery of the relevant literature is far beyond someone with my lifestyle. If I had tried to read everything I should have, the book would never have been finished.

Nevertheless, while my biases as a linguist inevitably show through, I believe I have avoided parochialism more than most of my predecessors. To all those who, through haste, oversight, or ignorance, I have still failed to insult adequately, my apologies.

I was granted the unusual favor of three semesters' leave from Brandeis by Jack Goldstein, then dean of faculty, permitting me the luxury of educating myself in psychology while drafting much of this and the music book. The National Endowment for the Humanities made the leave financially possible through a Fellowship for Independent Study and Research. The completion of the book was supported in part by Grant IST–8120403 from the National Science Foundation.

Elise, Amy, and Beth are what give life meaning beyond just reading another book, giving another talk, or writing another paper. Elise has never known me without this book on my mind. I hope now I can give her a real vacation.

Throughout the past eighteen years, Morris Halle has been an inspiration to me as a devoted and lucid master of his craft. I flatter myself to think that some of his way of approaching linguistics has rubbed off on me. More than anyone else, Morris has constantly encouraged me to ask the right questions and to pursue them regardless of currently reigning intellectual fashion. I would like to dedicate this book to him in gratitude.

Part I

BASIC ISSUES

Chapter 1
Semantic Structure and Conceptual Structure

1.1 Ideology

This book is intended to be read from two complementary perspectives. From the point of view of linguistics and linguistic philosophy, the question is: What is the nature of meaning in human language, such that we can talk about what we perceive and what we do? From the point of view of psychology, the question is: What does the grammatical structure of natural language reveal about the nature of perception and cognition?

My thesis is that these two questions are inseparable: to study semantics of natural language *is* to study cognitive psychology. I will show that, viewed properly, the grammatical structure of natural language offers an important new source of evidence for the theory of cognition.

While the idea that language mirrors thought is of great antiquity, current philosophical practice does not on the whole encourage us to explore it. The tradition of semantics in which most of us were educated traces its roots back to mathematical logic—Frege, Russell, and Tarski, after all, were primarily interested in mathematics. As a result, this tradition shows little interest in psychological foundations of language, nor much concern with finding a particularly enlightening relationship between semantics and grammatical structure. The burden of this book is that psychological and grammatical evidence *must* be brought to bear on the issues of semantics addressed by traditional linguistic philosophy, and that this evidence leads to a theory of semantics considerably richer in both formal and substantive respects than standard logical approaches.

This chapter will place the investigation in the context of psychological and linguistic theory, and frame the goals of the inquiry in terms more conducive to a formal approach.

1.2 Modes of Description in Psychology

To clarify the sense in which I understand this study to be a contribution to cognitive psychology, I must distinguish five broad modes of description available to psychological theory: phenomenology, physiology, functional architecture, process, and structure.

Phenomenology deals with the character of experience. Most of modern psychology has of course been motivated by an attempt to go beyond this mode of description. Except in radical behaviorist circles, though, it still remains an important goal of psychological theory to explain why things seem to us as they do. At the same time, this mode of description is crucially involved in the production of data: where would we be without subjects' saying things like "I see it now," "They look the same," "It's ungrammatical," and the like, or responding to such judgments by pushing a button? On the other hand, phenomenological description provides us with no theory about how we can talk about what we see, for example. From the introspective point of view, we just *do* it, virtually without effort.

At the other end of the spectrum is *physiological description,* which deals with brain structure and function as such. A great deal is known about overall functional localization in the brain and about details of various small areas, but this mode of description is at present of little help in answering the question of how we talk about what we see. For example, we haven't the slightest idea how speech sounds are encoded neurally—only that Broca's area has something to do with it. (In this respect the theory of language is much worse off than the theory of vision, some low-level aspects of which have received fairly detailed physiological description.)

In trying to explain the relation between brain states and experience, much of traditional cognitive psychology (for instance, Neisser (1967)) abstracts away from the brain as a physical structure and couches its descriptions in terms of what might be called *functional architecture:* the kinds of information-processing facilities that must be available to account for the organism's functioning as it does. In answering how we talk about what we see, this mode of description might speak of information flow from iconic to short-term visual memory, thence to propositional memory, and so on. Much important work has been done within this paradigm on memory capacities, processing times, interference effects, rates of learning, and so forth. But these results are not very helpful with specific questions such as: How does one decide to say that this thing is a dog and that one is Uncle Harry? That is, specifying certain capacities for processing information is not the same as specifying what the information *is*.

The *process* and *structure* modes of description are more explicit about treating the brain as an information processor. They attempt to identify not just the conduits for encoding and transferring information, but also the formal properties of mental information and of the processes it undergoes. In response to the question of how we talk about what we see, a description in structure mode will present formal characterizations of visual information, of linguistic information, and of the relationships between the two. A description in the process mode will add to this a characterization of the algorithms involved in computing such information in real time.[1]

These five modes of description are not mutually exclusive, nor are the distinctions among them hard and fast. Clearly a full theory of mind will require descriptions in all five modes, relating information structure, algorithms, and processing capacities to each other and especially to brain states and to experience. On the other hand, current practice has shown that one can usefully operate in any of the modes with a certain degree of independence from the others. In fact, a premature demand for unification (such as the Gestalt theorists' attempts to identify their principles of perceptual organization with electrical field phenomena in the brain) can have the effect of stultifying research.

Let me concentrate on the distinction between structure and process modes, for here lies an ideological matter of some importance to the present work. The distinction has appeared most clearly in theories of language. Linguistics is the study of grammatical structure— what Chomsky (1965) calls *linguistic competence*. Psycholinguistics is the study of the strategies employed in processing grammatical structure in real time—*linguistic performance*. Obviously these two inquiries have a mutual influence. On the one hand, a theory of language processing presupposes a theory of linguistic structure; on the other hand, one crucial test of a theory of linguistic structure is whether it can be integrated into a theory of processing. Moreover, many phenomena are amenable to either structural or processing description, and it is often an interesting question how to divide up the power of the theory between the two domains.[2]

In practice, though, the direction of influence in the theory of language has always been predominantly from linguistics to psycholinguistics. The most interesting work in psycholinguistics has been that stimulated by and dependent on theories of linguistic structure, whereas much important work in grammatical theory makes virtually no use of psycholinguistic evidence. This may be simply a function of our present depth of understanding in the two modes of description: syntactic and phonological theory nowadays typically investigate phenomena far more complex and subtle than we know how to study experimentally. On the other hand, this direction of influence is to a certain extent inherent in the nature of the problem: without a theory of structure, we cannot know what a theory of process has to explain.

An illustration from recent phonological theory may make this point clearer. Liberman and Prince (1977) argue, and it has been widely accepted, that phonological representation is not just a string of speech sounds analyzed into distinctive features, but a hierarchical *metrical structure* quite distinct from the familiar syntactic trees. If this is the case, it has drastic consequences for the theory of phonetic perception, since the end product of processing must now be a tree rather than a string. Liberman and Prince's theory is motivated solely on structural grounds such as stress placement in English; in fact, it is hard to imagine how our present understanding of phonological processing could be brought to bear in any detail on the correctness of the proposal.

This example is not yet widely known, and it has not had the effect it should eventually have on the theory of processing. But I could equally well cite the impact of generative syntax on psycholinguistics in the 1960s: a major change in the nature of processing theories stemmed from a new theory of linguistic structure (see Fodor, Bever, and Garrett (1974, especially pp. 221ff.)).

All this discussion is in justification of my methodological decision to pursue a theory of cognition primarily in the structure mode, contrary to most current practice in psychology and computer science. In attempting to investigate how we talk about what we see, I will develop a theory of *conceptual structure*—the information shared by visual and linguistic modalities—without much concern about how this information is computed, what resources are available for computing and storing it, or how neurons manage to encode it. I believe that a strong theory of information structure is vital to the construction of theories in the other modes of description.

The utility of such a theory is explicitly disputed by Kintsch (1974), who disparages the notion of linguistic competence and announces his intention to develop a theory of language that integrates structure and process. Nevertheless, before turning to processing, Kintsch devotes a chapter to presenting a theory of linguistic structure, based rather uncritically on Fillmore's (1968) case grammar. Similar chapters appear in Anderson and Bower (1973) and Anderson (1976); and most work on processing in semantic memory begins by stating a theory of semantic structure (see Smith (1978)). In other words, description in the structure mode is indispensable to psychological theory, but concern with processing considerations has obscured its importance, and very little attempt has been made to justify such descriptions on language-internal grounds. From a psychologist's point of view, then, the present work may be seen as an attempt to state the purely structural constraints on a theory of cognition, leaving it to others to work out the consequences for processing.

Keeping processing and physiological considerations in the background is of course not the same as disregarding them altogether. In particular, one must always remember that a theory of mental information structure must eventually be instantiated in a brain. This imposes two important boundary conditions on the theory: (1) the resources for storing information are finite; (2) the information must somehow get into the mind, whether through perception, learning, or genetic structure. We will make frequent use of these constraints; it is surprising how rich their consequences can be.

1.3 Semantics in Generative Linguistic Theory

Having briefly discussed how the goals of this work relate to traditional concerns of philosophy and psychology, I want to touch base with the discipline out of which this work grew most directly—generative linguistics.

The goal of generative linguistic theory is a description, in structure mode, of what a human being knows (largely unconsciously) that enables him to speak a natural language. This knowledge is described in terms of a *grammar,* a finite set of formal principles that collectively describe the infinite set of structures that a speaker judges to be sentences of the language. In order to explain how children manage to learn a particular language rather rapidly from rather fragmentary evidence, it is of great importance to extract from grammars of particular languages a theory of *universal grammar,* that aspect of linguistic competence which is due to the human genetic endowment and which therefore need not be learned. It is in principle desirable to maximize the contribution of universal grammar, since one can then claim that the choices a language learner has to make are relatively limited. On the other hand, of course, the choices left to the language learner must be sufficient to differentiate all known human languages.[3]

It would be wonderful if we could further divide universal grammar into aspects specialized for language and aspects used in common with other cognitive capacities.[4] At present, however, we know so little about other capacities (not to mention universal grammar) that such a division seems premature. As Chomsky (1975) puts it, to attempt to reduce all mental functions to general principles, without understanding them individually to some extent, would be like trying to reduce all physiological functions to general principles without first knowing what the heart does, what the liver does, what the eyes do, and so forth.[5]

Since the appearance of Katz and Fodor's paper "The Structure of a Semantic Theory" (1963), it has been accepted that part of the goal of describing linguistic knowledge is to describe the mapping between surface form and meaning. The problem of incorporating an account of meaning into linguistic theory can be separated into two major issues: (1) What sort of formal object is a meaning? (2) How are meanings related to syntactic form?

Katz and Fodor proposed that meanings are expressed by a formal level of linguistic description, distinct from syntactic structure, called *semantic representation,* here to be called *semantic structure.* This level of linguistic structure is related to syntactic structure by a set of rules which Katz and Fodor called *projection rules,* and which will be called here *correspondence rules.* Although it is often assumed that the correspondence rules are the only determinant of semantic form, it makes sense to posit an additional rule component that characterizes those aspects of semantic structure that are independent of syntactic structure: at the very least, the inventory of semantic primitives and the principles for combining them. We will call this rule component the *semantic well-formedness rules* (WFRs).

With this conception of semantic theory, the overall structure of a grammar can be represented roughly as in (1.1). (Rectangles represent rule components and stored lexical information; ellipses represent types of structure creatively generated by or affected by rule systems.)[6]

(1.1)

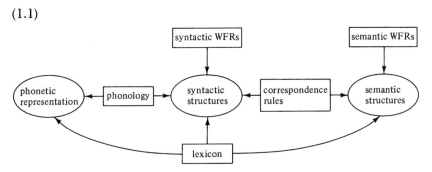

The syntactic well-formedness rules include phrase structure rules, transformations, and any further syntactic rules such as output constraints. The lexicon includes a list of the words in the language with their syntactic, semantic, and phonological properties, plus rules of word formation that both account for morphological and semantic relationships among lexical items and allow for creation of new lexical items (cf. Halle (1973), Aronoff (1976), Jackendoff (1975a)). The syntactic well-formedness rules and the lexicon together determine a set of syntactic structures, where each member of this set is to be thought of as a complete derivation from underlying (deep) structure to surface structure. The phonological component, which maps syntactic structures into phonetic representations, needs no comment here; the semantic well-formedness rules and correspondence rules are as discussed above.

In terms of this theory, the question of what meanings are like can be rephrased as the question: What are the semantic well-formedness rules like? The question of how meaning is related to syntax can be rephrased as: What are the correspondence rules like? Within the purview of the first question lies research on the structure of word meanings, on the type of quantification necessary to express sentences of English, on the nature of presupposition, and so forth. Within the purview of the second lie such issues as what level of syntactic derivation is most directly related to semantic structure, whether there are levels of representation intermediate between syntactic and semantic structure, and, most crucially, how syntactic structure makes it possible to construct a meaning for a sentence from the meanings of its words.

Among generative linguists, the most hotly contested of these issues has been how the correspondence rules apply to the syntactic derivation. In one current of thought, including the original Katz-Fodor theory and now Montague grammar (Partee (1975)), the correspondence rules compose semantic structure on the basis of the application of rules in a syntactic derivation: for each syntactic rule application, there is a corresponding semantic rule application. Thus rules of syntactic and semantic composition stand in a one-to-one relationship.

The predominant view, however, has been that the correspondence rules apply to particular levels of syntactic derivation. In the "standard theory" of Katz and Postal (1964) and Chomsky (1965), the correspondence rules compose semantic structure from the information present in underlying (deep) structure.[7] Various inadequacies of the standard theory led to two divergent schools of thought: generative semantics (see note 6) and the "extended standard theory" developed by Chomsky (1972), Jackendoff (1972), and others. The extended standard theory posited that the correspondence rules can be differentiated into discrete types, each of which concerns a particular aspect of semantic structure. Some of these types of rules read their information off of deep structure, and some off of surface structure. In more recent work, such as Chomsky's (1975, 1980, 1981) "revised extended standard theory" and Bresnan's (1978, 1982) "lexical-functional theory," there remains the differentiation of correspondence rules into types, but all types apply to surface structure. In each case, revision of the theory has been motivated by the desire to constrain the possible variation among particular grammars, so as to limit the choices the language learner must make.

In the present work I will not be concerned with this particular issue, since, for most of the syntactic phenomena to be discussed, the syntactic input to the correspondence rules will be essentially the same at all levels of syntactic derivation. For convenience, I will assume some version of the extended standard theory and its derivatives.

1.4 Constraints on Semantic Theory

A number of requirements on semantic theory have been widely assumed in the literature. This section will mention four; the next two sections will add two more constraints which have been generally less prominent but which I take to be of utmost importance.

Expressiveness: A theory of semantic structure must be observationally adequate; it must be able to express all the semantic distinctions made by a natural language. In practice, of course, no theory can be tested on all possible sentences, but everyone assumes that some significant fragment of the language must be accounted for.

Universality: In order to account for the fact that languages are (largely) intertranslatable, the stock of semantic structures available to be used by particular languages must be universal. Where literal translation of a sentence of one language into another is possible, the two sentences must share a semantic structure. On the other hand, this does not mean that every language is necessarily capable of expressing every meaning, for a language may be limited by its lexicon, grammatical structure, or correspondence rules.

Compositionality: A semantic theory must provide a principled way for the meanings of the parts of a sentence to be combined into the meaning of the whole sentence. This requirement may be taken more or less strongly, depending on whether or not one requires each constituent (as well as each word) of a sentence to be provided with an independent interpretation. Russell (1905), for example, espouses a very weak form of compositionality in which noun phrases do not receive unified interpretations: "The phrase ['the author of Waverley'] per se has no meaning, because in any proposition in which it occurs the proposition, fully expressed, does not contain the phrase, which has been broken up." Montague grammar, by contrast, requires every constituent to receive a well-formed interpretation. Chapter 4 will present a position intermediate between these, though much closer to the strong form.

Semantic Properties: Semantic theory should be able to account formally for so-called "semantic properties" of utterances, such as synonymy, anomaly, analyticity, and presupposition. In particular, the notion of "valid inference" must be explicated.

I should also mention a constraint I wish not to adopt. In artificial intelligence circles it is commonly taken as a requirement on a theory that it be expressible as a computer program, preferably a running one. Two sorts of justifications are usually given. The first is methodological: the need to write a fully specified program is seen as a way of keeping the theorist honest. In my experience, though, there are always aspects of one's theory that one hasn't any idea how to formalize, whose formalization is not germane to understanding the matters at hand, but whose effects are excluded from the analysis at one's peril (section 8.3 discusses one such case). I think it is altogether legitimate to offer a promissory note in such a situation; but a computer requires instead a trick that evades the problem. I don't want to waste my time with tricks, and I trust my colleagues to keep me honest.

The other justification of computer modeling is a formal one: it is frequently said that anything describable can be computed by a Turing machine and hence can be computer simulated. This argument is often reinforced by citing the McCulloch-Pitts (1943) proof that a neural network consisting of "all-or-none" neurons has a computational capacity within that of a Turing machine. Hence the brain can be thought of as a kind of computer.

The trouble with this argument as justification of computer modeling is that the character of mental computation is not just a matter of computing power. Rather, it depends heavily on the particular specialized structures that have evolved to perform different sorts of computations—and these may not be especially congenial to presently available computer technology. For a blatant example, it appears that the brain achieves its speed largely through massive amounts of interactive parallel processing, a kind of computation difficult (if not impossible) to simulate in real time with contemporary hardware.[8] Moreover, the McCulloch-Pitts result depends on the idealization to neurons with discrete (i.e., digital) states. If the information conveyed by neurons has any nondiscrete properties—say, if rate or pattern of firing is significant, as I am led to believe—the argument loses some weight. At various points in this book we will encounter response patterns of a continuously graded character. These can of course be simulated digitally, but perhaps it is worth asking whether to do so misses the point. For reasons like these, to set programmability as a criterion on a theory may well unwittingly bias research in a totally misguided direction.

By these remarks, I do not mean to reject computer modeling altogether. It certainly plays an important role in research. I submit, though, that it is hardly the sine qua non of cognitive theory that it is sometimes claimed to be.

1.5 The Grammatical Constraint

Important though the criteria of expressiveness, universality, compositionality, and semantic properties are, they do not bear directly on how the syntactic form of language reflects the nature of thought. In order to address this issue, two further criteria on semantic theory are necessary, which I will call the *Grammatical Constraint* and the *Cognitive Constraint*.

The *Grammatical Constraint* says that one should prefer a semantic theory that explains otherwise arbitrary generalizations about the syntax and the lexicon. As one motivation for this constraint, consider the task of the language learner, who must learn the mapping between syntactic form and meaning. It appears that the language learner cannot acquire the syntax of a language without making use of the correspondence rules: he must be independently guessing the meaning of utterances from context and putting it to use in determining syntax. In fact, under certain assumptions about the nature of syntax, Wexler, Hamburger, and Culicover have proven that syntax is formally unlearnable unless the learner makes use of information from the underlying structure of sentences, which they take to be derivable from the meaning (see Wexler and Hamburger (1973), Wexler and Culicover (1980)). Reinforcing this result, Macnamara (1982), Gleitman and Wanner (1982), and Grimshaw (1981) show the fundamental importance of innate aspects of meaning in the very early stages of language acquisition, and how they help shape the development of syntax. Similarly, Miller (1978) points out the advantage of formal relations among apparently distinct readings of a polysemous word, since these would make it easier for the language learner to acquire one reading, given another. From a different angle, one of the major points of Jackendoff (1972) is that many apparently syntactic constraints follow from semantic constraints, so that once a language learner has learned the meaning of the construction in question, the observed syntactic distribution will follow automatically.

The force of the Grammatical Constraint is addressed by Fodor's (1975, 156) speculation that the resources of the inner code are rather directly represented in the resources of the codes we use for communication. [If true, this] goes some way toward explaining why natural languages are so easy to learn and why sentences are so easy to understand: The languages we are able to learn are not so very different from the language we innately know, and the sentences we are able to understand are not so very different from the formulae which internally represent them.

Note that Fodor's suggestion goes beyond language learning to include facts about language universals. Under the reasonable hypothesis that language serves the purpose of transmitting information, it would be perverse not to take as a working assumption that language is a relatively efficient and accurate encoding of the information it conveys. To give up this assumption is to refuse to look for systematicity in the relationship between syntax and semantics. A theory's deviations from efficient encoding must be rigorously justified, for what appears to be an irregular relationship between syntax and semantics may turn out merely to be a bad theory of one or the other.[9]

This is not to say that *every* aspect of syntax should be explainable in semantic terms. For instance, it is well known that the notion of grammatical subject cannot be reduced to expression of agent or topic, though the subject often does play these semantic roles. Similarly, the grammatical category *noun* cannot be identified with any coherent semantic category. The point of the Grammatical Constraint is only to attempt to minimize the differences of syntactic and semantic structure, not to expect to eliminate them altogether.

For a familiar example of a theory that violates the Grammatical Constraint, consider traditional quantificational logic. The sentence "Floyd broke a glass" translates into (1.2a) or, in the notation of restricted quantification, (1.2b).

(1.2) a. $\exists x(\text{glass}(x)\ \&\ \text{break}(\text{Floyd}, x))$

b. $\exists x_{\text{glass}(x)}(\text{break}(\text{Floyd}, x))$

In either case, the syntactic constituent "a glass" does not correspond to any semantic constituent; rather, its interpretation forms several discontinuous parts of the logical expression. In addition, the logical translation severely distorts the embedding relations of the sentence, since the existential quantifier, the outermost operator in the logical expression, is a semantic contribution of the indefinite article, the most deeply subordinate element of the sentence. (In the passage quoted in the previous section, Russell (1905) points out this lack of correspondence with a certain glee; since then tradition has sanctified it.)

Naturally, there are good reasons for adopting the formalism of quantificational logic, having to do with solving certain aspects of the inference problem. Yet one could hardly expect a language learner to learn the complex correspondence rules required to relate quantificational formalism to surface syntax. The logician might respond by claiming that this aspect of the correspondence rules is universal and thus need not be learned. But then we could ask on a deeper level why language is the way it is: Why does it display the constituent structure and embedding relations it does, if it expresses something formally so different?[10] In short, the Grammatical Constraint does not permit us to take for granted the use of quantificational logic to model natural language semantics. A competing model that accounts for the same inferences but preserves a simpler correspondence of syntactic and semantic structure is to be preferred.[11] (This argument will be amplified in chapter 4.)

Nor are logicians the only offenders. A sizable segment of the artificial intelligence community (for example, Schank (1973, 1975), Wilks (1973)) seeks to process natural language—to relate texts to semantic structures—without especially detailed reference to syntactic properties of the texts. While I agree that syntactic structure alone is insufficient to explain human linguistic ability, and that human language processing is not accomplished by doing all syntactic analysis first, I do not agree that syntactic structure is therefore a trivial aspect of human linguistic capacity, merely incidental to language processing. One reason such attempts may have seemed plausible is that the syntax of the texts used as examples is invariably rather trivial, and little attempt is made to explore the grammatical and lexical generality of the patterns used for analysis. That is, this work is concerned on the whole only with the observational adequacy of the system and with such descriptive adequacy as the system fortuitously provides; explaining linguistically significant generalizations is subordinate to getting the system to work, on-line. Thus the Grammatical Constraint is met only occasionally and by accident.

It is my contention that the Grammatical Constraint must be imposed on semantic theory for semantics to be an empirically interesting enterprise. Linguistic research has shown that syntax is not the chaotic, unprincipled mass of facts it was once thought to be; rather, it is a system of remarkable complexity and subtlety. Its organization is not predictable in any simple way from general principles of cognition, semantics, pragmatics, communicative convenience, or ease of processing. In studying natural language, one ignores (or denigrates) syntax at the risk of losing some of the most highly structured evidence we have for any cognitive capacity. It is the Grammatical Constraint that sanctions the attempt to extend this evidence into the domain of semantics. Without it, one will never even try to discover anything of interest in the relationship between form and meaning.

1.6 The Cognitive Constraint and the Conceptual Structure Hypothesis

The Grammatical Constraint, however, is not sufficient for constructing an argument from grammatical generalization to the nature of thought. A further constraint is needed, one that has received attention recently through such works as Clark and Chase (1972), Fodor (1975), and Miller and Johnson-Laird (1976). This constraint has been occasionally acknowledged by linguists and in certain kinds of work in artificial intelligence; but it has not played a significant role in recent philosophical discussion or in most artificial intelligence work on text processing.

I will call this constraint the *Cognitive Constraint:* There must be levels of mental representation at which information conveyed by language is compatible with information from other peripheral systems such as vision, nonverbal audition, smell, kinesthesia, and so forth. If there were no such levels, it would be impossible to use language to report sensory input. We couldn't talk about what we see and hear. Likewise, there must be a level at which linguistic information is compatible with information eventually conveyed to the motor system, in order to account for our ability to carry out orders and instructions.

Notice that a satisfactory theory of psychology obviously requires interfaces between nonlinguistic modalities as well. For instance, to use vision to help tell it where to go, the organism must incorporate a visual-motor interface; to know that visual and auditory sensations occur simultaneously or are similarly localized, it must incorporate a visual-auditory interface; and so forth.

It is reasonable to make a simplifying assumption that, if true, places interesting constraints on the theory of mental processing.

The Conceptual Structure Hypothesis
There is a *single* level of mental representation, *conceptual structure,* at which linguistic, sensory, and motor information are compatible.

I emphasize that there is no logical necessity for the existence of such a unified level—as there is for the existence of individual interfaces between modalities. At worst, however, the Conceptual Structure Hypothesis is a plausible idealization; at best, it is a strong unifying hypothesis about the structure of mind.

As Fodor (1975) observes, conceptual structure must be rich enough in expressive power to deal with all things expressible by language. It must also be rich enough in expressive power to deal with the nature of all the other modalities of experience as well—no simple matter. In order to give some formal shape to the problem, I will assume that the possible conceptual structures attainable by a human being are characterized by a finite set of *conceptual well-formedness rules.* I will further assume that these rules are universal and innate—that everyone has essentially the same capacity to develop concepts—but that the concepts one actually develops must depend to some extent on experience.[12]

The position that conceptual well-formedness rules are innate contrasts with what I take to be the strongest version of Piagetian developmental theory, which could be construed in the present framework as a claim that certain conceptual well-formedness rules, such as those having to do with measurement and amounts, must be learned. Fodor (1975) argues, to my mind convincingly, that in order for hypotheses about the world to be formulated, the relevant conceptual dimensions must already be available to the learner. For instance, one could not learn color distinctions if the mind did not provide a conceptual dimension in terms of which color distinctions could be mentally represented. It is the existence of such conceptual fields, not the precise distinctions within them, that must be innately specified by conceptual well-formedness rules.

Where there is development in the child's conceptual ability, then, it must be attributed to increasing richness and interconnection of concepts and, more significantly, to the growth of either well-formedness rules or computational capacity, over which the child and the environment have little control. The kind of growth I have in mind is akin to the growth of bones and muscles: the environment must of course provide nourishment, and one can stimulate growth by exercise, but these inputs hardly can be said to control the interesting aspects of structure. As Chomsky (1975) points out, the same nutrients build bird wings and human fingers; it is the innate structure of the organism that determines which of these actually develops. There is no reason not to suppose that the same is true of the brain.

The Cognitive Constraint, then, is a specific statement of the psychological reality of linguistic information, and it serves as a link between linguistic theory and cognitive theory. Thus the two relatively novel constraints on semantics, the Grammatical Constraint and the Cognitive Constraint, serve to make semantic theory responsible to the facts of grammar and cognitive psychology respectively. It is just these two constraints which are lacking in the traditional philosophical program of research on semantics of natural language, and which are necessary in evaluating a theory that purports to use linguistic evidence to study the nature of thought.

We can understand why the Grammatical Constraint played little or no role in semantics in the days of Frege and Russell, when so much less was known about grammar than now. Today it is harder to condone a semantic theory that lacks proper attention to syntax. Similarly, it is perhaps excusable that little serious attention has been paid to the Cognitive Constraint, even by those who espouse a mentalistic theory of language, because it is so difficult to see how to apply it usefully. Our notions of the information conveyed by nonlinguistic peripheral systems are if anything feebler than our understanding of linguistic information. But while there is little useful theory of the end product of visual perception, there is certainly a great deal of highly organized evidence available that can be brought to bear on such a theory, and, given the Cognitive Constraint, on semantic theory as well.

1.7 The Connection between Semantic Theory and Conceptual Structure

Let us see how the Cognitive Constraint and the Conceptual Structure Hypothesis potentially affect semantic theory. There are in principle two ways that conceptual structure could be related to the linguistic system, within the overall conception of grammar laid out in section 1.3. First, conceptual structure could be a further level beyond semantic structure, related to it by a rule component, often called *pragmatics,* that specifies the relation of linguistic meaning to discourse and to extralinguistic setting. This is the view of Katz and Fodor (1963) and Katz (1980), and it was more or less the view that I assumed in Jackendoff (1972). (1.3) illustrates this hypothesis.[13]

Alternatively, semantic structures could be simply a subset of conceptual structures—just those conceptual structures that happen to be verbally expressible. This view would claim, then, that the correspondence rules map directly between syntactic structure and conceptual structure, and that both rules of inference and rules of pragmatics are mappings from conceptual structure back into conceptual structure. This is the view assumed in most work on artificial intelligence, when it treats syntax independently at all; it is defended by Fodor, Fodor, and Garrett (1975) and adopted by Chomsky (1975 and later). (1.4) represents the structure of this alternative.

How might one distinguish these two views? One could argue for the autonomous semantic level of (1.3) by showing that there are primitives and/or principles of combination appropriate to the formalization of linguistic inference that are distinct from those appropriate to the communication of visual information to the linguistic system. Conversely, if one could show that linguistic inference is but a special case of more general modality-independent principles that must be attributed even to nonverbal organisms, this would argue for view (1.4), in which semantic structure is subsumed under conceptual structure.

An argument of just this latter sort will be developed in chapters 3–6. Let me summarize the argument in advance, to help the reader see where we are going. We will investigate characteristics common to judgments involving visual information, linguistic information, and combinations of the two. These characteristics must be accounted for in terms of conceptual structure, where the two kinds of information are compatible. We will then show that analogous characteristics arise in judgments of certain fundamental semantic properties of utterances, which are by definition accounted for at the level of semantic structure. Not to treat all these phenomena uniformly would be to miss a crucial generalization about mental computation; hence the semantic and conceptual levels must coincide, as in (1.4).

To sum up the view I will be arguing for, the Conceptual Structure Hypothesis proposes the existence of a single level of mental representation onto which and from which all peripheral information is mapped. This level is characterized by an innate system of conceptual

(1.3)

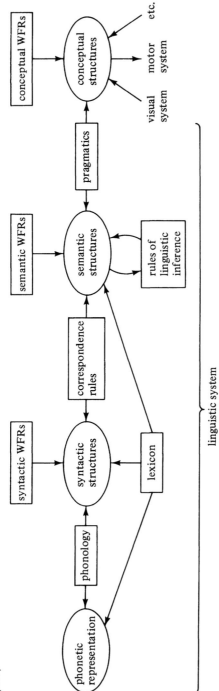

(1.4)

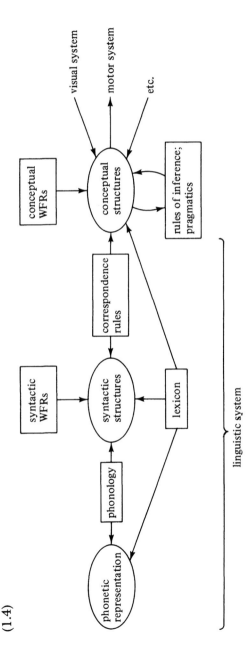

well-formedness rules. Under the organization diagrammed in (1.4), the concerns of semantic theory with the nature of meaning and with the mapping between meaning and syntax translate into the goals of describing the conceptual well-formedness rules and the correspondence rules, respectively. Significantly, the former goal overlaps with the goals of the theory of vision, which is concerned with the nature of visual information (at least some of which is represented in conceptual structure) and how it is derived from retinal stimulation. The theories of the other senses and of action overlap with semantic theory in a similar way. Insofar as the subject matter of these theories overlaps at conceptual structure, they can be used to constrain and enrich each other. In the present study, we will at first primarily be using vision to constrain semantic theory. As we go on, however, we will move increasingly in the other direction, using language to enrich the theory of cognition.

Chapter 2
Sense and Reference

This chapter is concerned with some basic consequences of the Cognitive Constraint—the fundamentals of a semantic theory that addresses the question of how we can talk about what we see. In order to lay the groundwork, we must address a prior question: What indeed do we see? Our way of approaching this question will profoundly color all that follows.

2.1 The Real World and the Projected World

We begin by sharpening one of the basic questions of the last chapter. Rather than ask simply what meanings are like, we divide the question into two parts: What is the information that language conveys? What is this information *about*? The first of these is essentially the traditional philosophical concern with *sense* or *intension*; the second, *reference* or *extension*. Naive introspection yields these answers: the information conveyed consists of ideas—entities in the mind; the information is *about* the real world. A great deal of the philosophical literature on language has been concerned with debunking one or the other of these answers, and with proposing (and debunking) alternatives. The first answer in particular has come under strong and steady attack. In fact, even the first *question* has sometimes been argued to be illegitimate or irrelevant, often in concert with general attacks on the notion of mind as a legitimate subject for empirical or theoretical inquiry.

The view to be taken here, of course, is that it is indeed legitimate to question the nature of the information conveyed, and that the answer of naive introspection is in some sense correct. That is, following the discussion of chapter 1, we will assume that there is a level of human organization that can plausibly be termed *mental*, that this level is causally connected with, but not identical to, states of the nervous system, and that the function of this level can (at least in part) be treated as processing of information. The Cognitive Constraint in effect states that certain aspects of this mental information constitute the information encoded in language.

On the other hand, I will take issue with the naive (and nearly universally accepted) answer that the information language conveys is about the real world. To see why, we must step back from language for a while and consider some issues at the foundations of psychology.

Perhaps the most significant general result of the school of Gestalt psychology (see Wertheimer (1923), Köhler (1929), Koffka (1935)) was its demonstration of the extent to which perception is the result of an interaction between environmental input and active principles in the mind that impose structure on that input.[1] Two trivial and well-known examples appear in (2.1) and (2.2).

(2.1) •   •   (2.2)

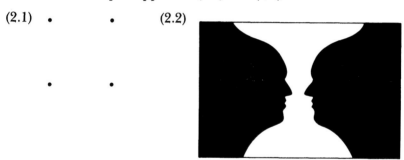

    •   •

The four dots in (2.1) are quite naturally seen as forming a square, although no linear connections are present on the page. Why? And why these particular linear connections rather than, say, an X, which is logically just as possible an organization? Moreover, why is the organization of the four dots in (2.3) into a square so much less apparent, even though they are in exactly the same spatial relations?

(2.3)   1.05   John!

    Why not?   ,,,.,,,

(2.2) is one of the famous ambiguous figures; Wittgenstein's (1953) "duck-rabbit" (2.4) is another, and many of the same arguments apply.

(2.4)

As is well known, (2.2) can be seen as a profile of a vase against a black background or as two profiles of faces against a white background. If fixated, the example usually switches periodically from one interpretation to the other; that is, the environmental input does not change at all, but what is seen does change. Moreover, though the example is a diagram in the plane, in the "vase" interpretation the two black areas are seen as constituting a unified background that extends behind the white area; in the "faces" interpretation the white area is seen as extending behind the two black areas.

These examples, which are probably familiar to most readers, are representative of a vast body of phenomena investigated by the Gestalt theorists. They show that what one sees cannot be solely environmental in origin, since the figures are imbued with organization that is not there in any physical sense, that is by no means logically necessary, and that in the case of the depth in (2.2) is inconsistent with the physical facts. This organization, which involves both segmentation of the environmental input and unification of disparate parts, must be part of the mind's own encoding of the environmental input.

The mental processes that create this organization of the input are both automatic and unconscious. They are susceptible to voluntary control only to the extent that one can, for example, choose to see the "faces" rather than the "vase" in (2.2). But the choice is at best between different organizations, not between organized and unorganized input; and some organizations (e.g., the disparity of lengths in the Müller-Lyer illusion (2.5)) are notoriously difficult or impossible to overcome willfully.

(2.5)

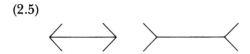

Thus, the world as experienced is unavoidably influenced by the nature of the unconscious processes for organizing environmental input. One cannot perceive the "real world as it is."

What makes this last assertion so contrary to common sense is that the organization of the input is experienced not as part of the act of thinking, but as part of the environment. My perception tells me that the square in (2.1) is not in my head; rather, it is out there on the page. The vase and the faces in (2.2) are out there on the page too, though not both at once; and, disturbingly, they have mutually inconsistent properties. Moreover, as Wittgenstein (1953, 195) observes, "I describe the alternation [between the two ways of seeing it] like a perception; quite as if the object had altered before my eyes." That is, the change in its nature is out there too, not in my head at all.

We are not at liberty to dismiss examples such as these as mere psychologist's tricks and to claim that perception of the ordinary *real* world is quite different. Why should the perceptual process arbitrarily distinguish those inputs that happen to be used by psychologists as examples from those inputs that are "ordinary"? A more reasonable position is that all inputs, in and out of the context of psychological experiments, are organized by the same processes, and that perceptual ambiguities and illusions are cases where what is experienced is noticeably different from what, for some reason, we believe *ought* to be experienced. According to this view, examples that result in out-of-the-ordinary perceptual judgments are an important source of evidence in developing a theory of the mental processes that organize perceptual input, altogether comparable to the linguist's use of unusual sentences in studying grammatical competence. In short, illusions are not wrinkles to be added into the theory after "ordinary experience" is accounted for.

Such a view, however, seems to compel us to claim that potentially vast areas of our experience are due to the mind's contribution, even though the experience is of things "out there in the real world." The only solution to this apparent conflict between theory and common sense is for the theory to include "out there" as part of the information presented to awareness by the unconscious processes organizing environmental input. That is, "out-thereness" is as much a mentally supplied attribute as, say, squareness.

To see that this solution is not just an escape hatch, an unfalsifiable way of defining oneself out of the problem, consider dreams and hallucinations, where "out-thereness" is (temporarily) ascribed to an experience for which there is *no* necessary environmental input. For such an ascription to take place, the mind must be supplying the same feature of "out-thereness" that it does in ordinary perception—although, unlike ordinary perception, this ascription is contradicted rather than confirmed by subsequent experience. The reverse of a hallucination also occurs, for instance when one hears a strange faint sound in the woodwork and after a while wonders if one had been imagining it (it later turns out to have been, say, a cracking roof beam). Here one is prepared to deny "out-thereness" to an experience that did in fact result from environmental input. Thus, it is possible to tease the mentally supplied attribute of "out-thereness" apart from physical externality.

According to this account, then, the reason that it seems counterintuitive to ascribe so much of the organization of experience to the mind is that a part of this organization is the ascription of the organization itself to the world. We are constructed so as normally to be unaware of our own contribution to our experience.

For another kind of evidence, consider the perception of music (Lerdahl and Jackendoff (1982), Jackendoff and Lerdahl (1981)). In order to account for the kinds of intuitions people have about music—from elementary intuitions about phrasing and meter to more subtle intuitions such as those involving the relation between a theme and its variations—one must ascribe to pieces of music an elaborate abstract structure. Intuition tells us, and the standard tradition of musical analysis takes for granted, that the structure inheres in the music itself. But if one starts to look for musical structure out there in the real world, it vanishes. What reaches the ear other than a sequence of pitches of various intensities, attack patterns, and durations? More pointedly, how do we locate something like Beethoven's Fifth Symphony in the real world? One may be tempted to tie such an entity somehow to the written score.[2] But this is clearly unsatisfactory, since there are many unwritten musical traditions in which pieces can still be named and identified. And even in a written tradition, as every musician knows, a large part of what goes into a performance of a piece is not in the score, but resides in the performer's unwritten (and probably unwriteable) understanding of the style. This suggests that the term "Beethoven's Fifth Symphony" refers to an abstract structure that the listener constructs in response to a performance of the sequence of events partially represented by the score, and which he attributes to that sequence of events, out there. Beethoven had this structure in mind, in part unconsciously, and wrote the notes he did in order to evoke this structure in the listener.[3]

Linguistic structure tells the same story, even at the relatively "low" level of phonetic perception. Though one unavoidably hears speech as a sequence of discrete phonetic segments, and, in a language one knows, as a sequence of discrete words, the segmentation is hardly in evidence in the acoustic signal. Moreover, the aspects of the acoustic signal that enable us to discriminate one vowel from another and one consonant from another sound like chirps and whistles, not like speech at all, when heard in isolation. Despite several decades of intensive research (reviewed by Liberman and Studdert-Kennedy (1977)), we are as yet unable to build a speech recognizer for more than the most limited artificial situations. We can build a fairly acceptable speech synthesizer, but only because human listeners are apparently so eager to impose linguistic structure on anything remotely resembling speech that they are unconscionably forgiving of the machine's sins.

What makes the musical and linguistic evidence for the nature of perception more unequivocal than the usual visual evidence is that, while one might conceivably claim that the structure of visual experience ordinarily models something preexisting in the real world, musical and linguistic structure must be thought of ultimately as products of the mind. They do not exist in the absence of human creators. Nonetheless, they are experienced as part of the world "out there"; here it is even clearer than in the visual case that we are simply unaware of how much our own minds contribute to the experience.

If indeed the world as experienced owes so much to mental processes of organization, it is crucial for a psychological theory to distinguish carefully between the source of environmental input and the world as experienced. For convenience, I will call the former the *real world* and the latter the *projected world* (*experienced world* or *phenomenal world* would also be appropriate).[4]

Note well that the projected world does *not* consist of mental images. Experiencing a horse is one thing; experiencing an image of a horse is another. These correspond to different, though probably related, projections of mental constructions. There is much of interest to say about images (see section 8.4 and chapter 11; also Kosslyn

(1980) and references therein); for the moment, though, it is sufficient to observe that while images are surely among the denizens of the projected world, they are far from the only ones. To forestall another possible misunderstanding, I should stress that the projected world is much richer than the "percepts" of traditional psychology: it embraces not only direct perceptual experience, with all its attendant organization, but also a wide variety of abstractions and theoretical constructs, as will be seen. Thus I am not returning to a sensationist view. Nor am I taking a solipsist position: I am not claiming that there is no real world—only that it is not what we see. This should become more apparent in section 2.3.

I should also make clear that this distinction between the real world and the projected world is not new. Something much like it appears at least as early as Kant; Neisser (1967) traces roots of such a "constructivist" view in psychology back to Brentano and James. What I think will be relatively new here is the application of the distinction in a systematic way to the semantics of natural language.

2.2 Truth and Reference: Preliminary Argument

It should now be clear why we must take issue with the naive position that the information conveyed by language is about the real world. We have conscious access only to the projected world—the world as unconsciously organized by the mind; and we can talk about things only insofar as they have achieved mental representation through these processes of organization. Hence *the information conveyed by language must be about the projected world*. We must explain the naive position as a consequence of our being constituted to treat the projected world as reality.

According to this view, the real world plays only an indirect role in language: it serves as one kind of fodder for the organizing processes that give rise to the projected world. If this is the case, we must question the centrality to natural language semantics of the notions of truth and reference as traditionally conceived. Truth is generally regarded as a relationship between a certain subset of sentences (the true ones) and the real world; reference is regarded as a relationship between expressions in a language and things in the real world that these expressions refer to. Having rejected the direct connection of the real world to language, we should not take these notions as starting points for a theory of meaning. Thus an approach such as that of

Davidson (1970), which attempts to explicate natural language semantics in terms of a Tarskian recursive theory of truth, is antithetical to our inquiry.

Nor does it help to relativize the notion of truth to "truth in a model," unless the choice of model is determined through empirical investigation of the character of the projected world. For instance, one cannot, as Lewis (1972, 175) does, found a theory of the model on a cavalier stipulation like "A possible world corresponds to a possible totality of facts, determinate in all respects." As we will see repeatedly in this study, what is to count as a fact is very much a psychological issue; and the notion of "determinate in all respects" is a chimera, an idealization that leads to counterproductive results.[5]

There is a natural objection to the claim that linguistic information most directly concerns the projected world. This claim implies that people could differ in the interpretations they put on the environmental input, and hence it should in principle be impossible to be sure that any two people are talking about the same things. How can language be that subjective and yet still be apparently intelligible? (This objection is essentially Quine's (1960) doctrine of "indeterminacy of radical translation," applied now to each individual.)

The answer is in two parts. First, as Katz (1972, 286–287) points out, one possibility is to claim that the processes by which we construct the projected world are the same in each of us. More specifically, part of one's genetic inheritance as a human being is a set of processes for constructing a projected world, and these processes are either largely independent of environmental input or else dependent on kinds of environmental input that a human being cannot help encountering. Current research in human and animal psychology strongly supports the claim that much of the organizing process is indeed innate; this innateness can account for our apparent ability to understand each other.

On the other hand, there are aspects of the projected world whose construction is underdetermined both by universals of human heredity and by common environment, and here we do find wide interpersonal and/or intercultural differences. For example, people have varying abilities to understand mathematics or music or chess; ethical, political, and religious notions too are open to considerable (though probably constrained) variation. These areas present situations where people in fact cannot convey information to each other, because their construals of experience are incompatible. Hence I can grant without damage the observation that, according to the present theory, language must be subjective. It is, but the fact that we are all human beings, with similar mental structure, guarantees that in a vast range of useful cases our projections are for most purposes compatible. Thus we can reasonably operate under the assumption that we are talking about the same things, as long as we are vigilant about detecting misunderstanding.

2.3 The Metalanguage and Some Examples

In a theory that distinguishes the real from the projected world, it is useful to introduce a metalanguage that clearly differentiates the two. To that end, my practice here will be to designate real-world entities without any special marking, but to surround references to projected-world entities by # #. To make the metalanguage sufficient for our purposes, we also must be able to talk about the mental information, or conceptual structure, that gives rise to the projected world. This information will be designated in capitals. Finally, it is convenient to be able to specially designate linguistic expressions. Ultimately, they are projected entities—sequences of sound to which are attributed a capacity to bear information. How they manage to do so will be discussed in chapter 11. In the meantime, the metalanguage will treat linguistic expressions as outside both the real and the projected world, by the not unsurprising device of enclosing them in quotation marks. Thus we adopt within the theory a metaphysics that embraces four domains: the real world, the projected world, mental information, and linguistic expressions. Among the goals of the theory is to explicate the relationships of these domains to each other.

This procedure may at first seem paradoxical: having just denied the possibility of referring to the real world, I am nonetheless introducing a metalanguage that purports to do so. To be clear about what is going on, however, we must keep in mind that, like most theories, the present theory is stated from the point of view of a hypothetical omniscient observer; it conveniently (and purposely) overlooks the fact that the theorist is by necessity among his own experimental subjects. That is, within the present discourse, both the real world and the projected world have the status of theoretical constructs, which like any other theoretical constructs are useful insofar as they have explanatory value. The theory claims that our experimental subjects can speak only of the projected world—but it can do so only by assuming tacitly that we, as hypothetically omniscient observers, are not so limited. Such methodological separation of ourselves as theorists from ourselves as explicanda of the theory is altogether the norm in psychology. The only difference here, I think, is that when we talk about the theory of reference, the artifice is more patent than when we are dealing, say, with low-level visual perception or with phonology.

To get a feel for the metalanguage and the theoretical claims behind it, let us examine a fairly simple example that distinguishes real-world entities and projected-world #entities#. Consider the theory of light and color. In our present terms, physics (as carried on by our experimental subjects) can be seen as an attempt to develop #theoretical entities# and #relations# whose structure is isomorphic to that of entities and relations in the real world. If physics is right, for instance, the real world contains, among other things, electromagnetic radiation of various wavelengths and energies traveling in various directions; the properties of electromagnetic radiation are isomorphic to the #properties# of the theoretical construct #electromagnetic radiation#.

Psychology, on the other hand (again as carried out by our experimental subjects—we are now inspecting ourselves through a microscope), is concerned with the structure of the projected world. In the projected world, the counterpart of certain (real) radiation is #light# of various #colors#; the counterpart of certain other radiation is #heat#; and much of electromagnetic radiation (e.g., X-rays) has no projected counterpart at all except as a theoretical construct. The structure of #color# can be characterized by the #color solid#, a theoretical construct that formally expresses the internal structure of the mental information that gives rise to #color#. In the metalanguage, this mental information will be designated by the notation COLOR.

Psychology is also concerned with the links between the real world and the projected world. For one thing, it seeks principles that establish the correspondence between real-world phenomena and projected-world #phenomena# (for example, the theories of color perception, color constancy, and so forth). The correspondence is nontrivial, involving complex contextual considerations—it is not simply that a particular wavelength corresponds to a particular #color#.[6] In addition, psychology studies the correlates in the real-world nervous system of the processes of mental organization that give rise to mental representations and to the projected world (for example, the chemical structure of retinal cells, neural maps for the visual system, and so forth).

In the description just given, it is crucial to notice that there is no mention of (real-world) light and color—only #light# and #color#. #Color# is part of the organism's projected response to the pattern of electromagnetic radiation impinging on the visual system. The nervous system brings about a nonisomorphic mapping between the real and the projected phenomena. Thus, in the metalanguage we will say that the pattern of electromagnetic radiation is processed by neural mechanisms to yield among other things a conceptual structure COLOR; COLOR may then be projected into awareness as #color#—or it may remain unconscious (i.e., unnoticed or unattended).

Let us consider some other examples of the metalanguage. Except for one remark about mental images, I may have given the impression that the projected world is experienced as completely outside the body. Now I want to correct this impression and at the same time sharpen what it means to say that the projection is "out there."

Think about the perception of pain. Though pain is sensed as being localized in various parts of the body, the experience of pain is well known to be mediated by the brain. This suggests that, in our metalanguage, we should speak not of pain but of #pain#: #pain# is a projection onto a part of the body, in response to a chain of neural events beginning with excitation of pain receptors. The projective nature of #pain# is especially well revealed by the phenomenon of phantom limbs, in which amputees experience #pain# in body parts they no longer possess. The projected world must thus include #phenomena# within one's own #body#.

Next think about mental images, such as what one experiences when carrying out instructions like "Imagine a square" or "Imagine a major triad." Intuitively, these images are evidently experienced as being "in the mind." But recall what has always been the decisive objection to the existence of mental images (even if most of us have them): there is no room in the head for a little projection screen and a little person to view it. Most recent research on imagery (see Kosslyn (1980) and references there) has tried to bypass this objection by treating mental images solely in terms of processing of mental information. However, this leaves unexplained the fact that mental images are not *experienced* as information processing any more than ordinary perception is. The right approach emerges if we add to the information-processing theories the claim that the experience of mental images, like the experience of ordinary sensation, results from the projection of information being processed by the brain. And just as with ordinary sensation, the projected #mental image# may bear no direct resemblance at all to the real-world phenomena that give rise to it.

Finally, consider the nature of knowledge. Since we do not take truth as a cornerstone of semantic theory, we cannot adopt a conventional treatment of knowledge as justified true belief. Rather, an interesting ambiguity in the problem is revealed: are we speaking of the theory of (real) knowledge, or of the theory of (projected) #knowledge#? These turn out to be quite distinct endeavors. The former is the problem of cognition—how people form mental representations. The second, by contrast, is the question of what it is that people intuitively ascribe to someone when they say that he knows something; here the answer might well be #justified true belief#. The two problems are as different as the physics of electromagnetic radiation and the psychology of #color#. Most of the present study concerns the former problem; we return to the latter in chapter 11.[7]

2.4 The Mind-Body Problem and Gestalten

The relationship between mental information (e.g., COLOR) and the projected world (#color#) is the locus in the present theory of the classic mind-body problem. Mental information is presumably reducible to some configuration of brain states. However, the projected world is made up not of brain states, but of experiences; and no one seems to have any idea what experience is, nor how configurations of brain states are transmuted into it by the mechanism of projection. For example, we find it difficult even to imagine what it would mean to answer the question "Does a computer have experiences?"[8] I suspect that the mind-body problem is one that human beings are congenitally unequipped to be able to solve.

It is possible to sidestep this problem without jeopardizing the entire enterprise by making the reasonable assumption that the mapping between projected mental information and the projected world is an isomorphism. That is, the character of #color#, for example, is to be accounted for directly in terms of the information constituting COLOR. What makes the problem interesting, though, is that much of the *internal* structure of COLOR cannot be independently projected; that is, it is not accessible to consciousness. Hence one cannot determine the structure of #color# by mere introspection; we need an empirical discipline of psychophysics to explicate it.

This situation, which I believe is typical of projected #entities#, provides an account in the present framework of the "gestalt" or "holistic" character of experience—the fact that perceived #wholes# are often greater than or different from the sum of their #parts#. The explanation is that, of the mental information that is projected as the #whole#, only those components that are *independently projectable* can result in perceived #parts#. The presence of the rest may be sensed intuitively through the disparity between the #whole# and the #parts#, but its nature cannot be revealed in any simple way by introspection alone. Such an account of the holistic nature of experience, I believe, removes some of the mystery surrounding the central doctrine of Gestalt psychology as presented in, for example, Wertheimer (1922) and Köhler (1920). We will make use of this characteristic of mental information throughout our analysis in subsequent chapters.

2.5 Reference as Projection

Since it is in the nature of experience not to wear its internal structure on its sleeve, we come around again to the need for a theory of cognition to explicate it. Cognitive theory in this sense is the study of mental information—including both "propositional" information such as Fodor's (1975) "inner code" or Miller and Johnson-Laird's (1976) "conceptual structure," and "nonpropositional" information such as Marr's (1982) "3D model" or the contents of Kosslyn's (1980) "visual buffer."

An especially important part of the theory will be a specification of those expressions of the inner code that are projectable (i.e., that can give rise to projected entities in the world of experience). Both apparent regularities and apparent anomalies in the nature of the projected world should be explicated in terms of the nature of the inner code and in particular by the properties of the projectable expressions. This part of the theory, then, is the link between structure and process descriptions on the one hand and phenomenological description on the other; it is crucial to an account of why the world appears to us as it does.

Turning back to the two questions of semantics raised at the beginning of this chapter, let us see how all the intervening discussion of psychology bears on them. We can now say that the information that language conveys, the *sense* of linguistic expressions, consists of expressions of conceptual structure. What the information is about—the *reference* of linguistic expressions—is not the real world, as in most semantic theories, but the projected world. The *referring expressions* of natural language will be just those expressions that map into projectable expressions of conceptual structure.

What difference does this view of sense and reference make to semantic theory? The difference most crucial to our enterprise here lies in the justification of the ontological presuppositions of natural language—what sorts of entities, in a very broad sense, linguistic expressions can be said to be talking about. Given the traditional assumption that language talks directly about reality, it has always been a problem to motivate the existence of abstract entities like propositions, sets, predicates, numbers, and properties, all of which we talk about as if they were outside us. There have been three main alternatives in treating these: either claiming that they are some sort of incorporeal Platonic entities to which we somehow mysteriously have access; or claiming that natural language doesn't *really* talk about them, because they don't exist, and that semantics must therefore reduce them to concrete terms; or, finally, avoiding the psychological issues altogether. Clearly, none of these is a satisfactory solution for a semantic theory that aspires to psychological reality.

In the present view, though, the ontological presuppositions of natural language are far less dependent on the nature of reality. They are linked to the nature of *projected* reality and thus to the structure that human beings impose on the world. For instance, it is perfectly satisfactory to posit #color# as the reference of color words, even though there is no such thing in the real world; #color# is a consequence of the structure of mind. Similarly, it is difficult if not impossible to find real-world reference for phrases like "the cause of the accident"; one gets immediately embroiled in statistics, counterfactual conditionals, or other side issues. In the present theory, though, causality can be treated as a mentally imposed relationship between two perceived #events#, proceeding from the innate nature of conceptual structure. Part of the discussion about real-world correlates then falls into questions of psychophysics: what range of real-world inputs leads to an attribution of causality?[9] In other cases, the real world plays little if any role at all.

Thus, this view of reference frees us from a false reliance on physics as the ultimate source of ontological insight. At the same time, it places empirical, psychological constraints on ontological claims, so that reference cannot be treated arbitrarily: one's choice of theory should not be a matter just of metaphysical or notational preference.

The next chapter takes up one aspect of the ontological problem in some detail, illustrating how essential the projective view of reference is to the description of semantic generalizations in natural language. In turn, subsequent chapters will build on this ontological basis. Thus the notion of reference as projection stands at the foundation of the theories of semantics and cognition to be developed here.

Part II

COGNITIVE FOUNDATIONS OF SEMANTICS

Chapter 3
Individuation

In this section of the book we will develop some of the fundamental principles of a theory of conceptual structure, and see that these principles are also at the basis of inference in natural language. At the same time we will work out a number of formal and substantive characteristics of conceptual structure, embody them in appropriate notation, and contrast them with more familiar alternatives.

The most elementary type of expression in standard versions of formal logic is usually an *individual constant,* a unitary symbol that is intended to refer to a fixed individual. This chapter uses the Cognitive Constraint and the Grammatical Constraint to investigate the expressions in conceptual structure that play roughly the role assumed by individual constants in logic.

As in chapter 2, we begin with psychology, exploring some of the conditions involved in the individuation of projected-world #things# in the visual field. From this we will see that it is far from innocuous to make the usual assumption that there is a well-defined class of objects to which logical constants can be assigned. Rather, the class of #objects-in-the-world# is determined by complex perceptual and cognitive principles. This overview of #object#-perception will not only ground the arguments of this chapter in well-known psychological phenomena; it will also serve as a foil for later arguments on categorization (chapters 5 and 6) and word meanings (chapters 7 and 8).

After discussing #object#-perception, we will combine visual and linguistic evidence to show that reference in language must go beyond #objects#, to include a wide range of ontological categories such as #places#, #actions#, and #events#, and that the class of referring expressions includes not only NPs but also Ss, VPs, PPs, and AdvPs.

3.1 Individuation of Objects in the Visual Field

One of the most obvious aspects of the projected world is that it is divided up into #things#—#entities# with a certain kind of spatial and temporal integrity. In the simplest case, a #thing# is the figure of a figure-ground opposition in the visual field; by contrast with the figure, the ground is unattended and relatively less vivid. In more complex cases (such as ordinary life), a multitude of #things# are perceived in the visual field, standing or moving in various relations to one another.

In order to support the projection of an #individual thing# into awareness, there must be a corresponding mental representation from which the #thing# can be projected. Let us use the term *conceptual constituent* to mean a unitary piece of mental representation; we will encode conceptual constituents within square brackets. In order to account for the fact that people perceive #things#, we require a class of projectable conceptual constituents with the nominal structure [THING], to which further internal information may be added, corresponding to the character of the #thing# in question. In order to individuate the mental representations of distinct #things#, we add to this a subscript when necessary: $[THING]_i$ is projected into a different #thing# than $[THING]_j$.

It is beyond the scope of this book to provide a thorough account of what the visual system does to produce a mental representation $[THING]_i$ in response to a presented field. However, a number of aspects of this process are important for our concerns here. First, beyond the fact that there is a #thing# being perceived, mental representation does not necessarily include any *projectable* information about what the #thing# is. It might be #something# such that one has never seen anything remotely like #it# before. Or one might be observing #it# under degraded conditions such as dim light, great distance, or tachistoscopic presentation, when observers may well report "There is something there, but I don't know what."

This is not inconsistent with the possibility that the conceptual constituent contains further information that is *not* independently projectable. For example, people can perform same-different tasks to some extent under degraded conditions, where they cannot specify the similarities or differences explicitly. For a more everyday case, consider face recognition. Though one can recognize, distinguish, and compare thousands of faces, one cannot in most cases consciously decompose faces and say specifically what makes them recognizable and different from one another. In present terms, each face is a #thing#, represented mentally as a [THING], but much of the distinctive information within this conceptual constituent is not independently projectable into awareness as a #part of the face#. This does not preclude mental processing based on this information; it means only that the processing will be experienced as "intuitive" rather than "rational."[1]

One of the basic problems of perception treated by the Gestalt tradition was the question of what properties of the visual field lead to the emergence of a figure from the ground. In present terms, this question can be restated as: What external (or real-world) conditions lead to a package of mental information that achieves projectability as a #thing#?

What the Gestalt psychologists found out is that in general one cannot state a set of necessary and sufficient conditions on the external field that lead to the emergence of a #thing#. We have already mentioned dreams and hallucinations as cases where *no* external input is necessary for projection of a #thing#. It is also worth looking at cases where the projection occurs in response to a real visual field, since characteristics appear that are important to our purposes here.

Aside from certain preconditions—that the field be visually rather than auditorily presented, that it have size, brightness, and contrast that facilitate visual detection, and so forth—the conditions on #thing#hood that spring most immediately to mind are spatial and temporal continuity. These conditions, however, are *intensional:* they are attributed to any segment of the field that is perceived as a #thing#, but they are neither necessary nor sufficient conditions on the field itself.

First consider spatial continuity. The four dots seen as a #square# in chapter 2 are not spatially continuous: it is the projected connections between them that make the projection continuous. Similarly, in (3.1) the two shaded regions are unified in the projection into a single #thing#, seen as #extending behind the unshaded rectangle#; spatial continuity is supplied by the observer.

(3.1)

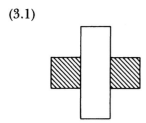

A somewhat different case is that of "apparent motion" (Wertheimer (1912), cited in Neisser (1967)). In the simplest version, two lights flash alternately in a dark surround. Given the proper timing of flashes and not too great a distance between them, the observer experiences #one thing moving back and forth#; the projection supplies motion that unifies the two positions. These cases show that spatial continuity of the field is not necessary for #thing#hood; it is rather #spatial continuity# of the *projection* that is necessary.

Likewise, temporal continuity is a necessary condition for the projection, not for the field. Consider a cartoon in which a dot moves toward the boundary of a rectangle and disappears when it reaches the boundary; then, after an interval, a dot appears on the opposite boundary of the rectangle and moves away. (3.2) represents successive stages in this cartoon.

(3.2)

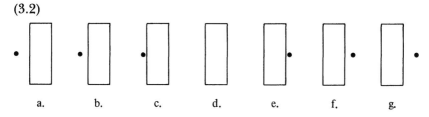

a.	b.	c.	d.	e.	f.	g.

There will be a strong tendency to see #the dot go behind the rectangle and reemerge#. That is, there is a single #thing#, #the dot#, to which one attributes temporal continuity by postulating temporary invisibility. This temporal continuity is not a property of the field, which is just a cartoon that simply happens to lack a dot in frame (d). The temporal continuity is part of the projection.

Nor are spatial and temporal continuity of the field *sufficient* for projection of a #thing#. One natural way of seeing (3.3) is as #a square with a hole in it#, so that the central region is not a #thing# but just that part of the #background# that happens to be #visible through the hole#.

(3.3)

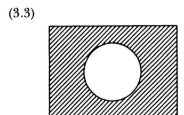

This central region is spatially and temporally continuous, but in this way of seeing (3.3) it does not give rise to the projection of a #thing#.[2] For an even simpler case, notice that unless we make an issue of it, the segment of the line (3.4) between 2 and 4 inches from the left-hand side of the page does not form a #thing#, even though it is of course spatially and temporally continuous.

(3.4)

Suppose that we experiment with fields topologically equivalent to (3.1) and ask whether the two outer regions are unified into a #thing#. (3.5) presents some possibilities.

(3.5)

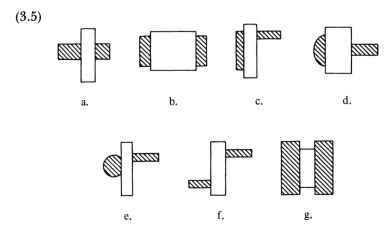

The first point to observe here is that one makes judgments of #thing#hood *creatively*; that is, one can discern #things# in arbitrary new visual configurations. As in the classic arguments for generative syntax, this observation means that the judgments must be based on a set of *rules* rather than on some finite set of templates to which patterns are rigidly matched. (The rules may include templates, but it is the ability to go beyond templates and deal with indefinitely many different inputs that is essential.)

But (3.5) is especially interesting because of the distribution of judgments. As already observed, the two shaded regions in case (a) are quite naturally seen as #a single thing partially occluded by the vertical rectangle#. Case (g) represents the other extreme, where the two outer regions are most naturally seen as #two separate things joined by the center rectangle#. The intermediate cases yield a gradation of judgments between these two extremes, and one is not so sure of them; they progress from fairly strong unification in (b) and (c) to quite weak in (e) and (f). (I can see (d) as a #partially occluded profile of some sort of bolt-shaped object#, but beyond that point in the series it is difficult even to *make* myself see a single #thing#.)

This range of judgments, from "of course yes" through "not sure" of various degrees to "of course no," is a characteristic gradation of *salience* in #thing#-formation. This gradation shows that the rules of #thing#-formation cannot be stated in terms of a simple system of necessary and sufficient conditions, since, in such a system, a single "no" judgment on one of the conditions would have the effect of ruling out the presented field as a #thing# altogether. That is, necessary and sufficient conditions produce categorical rather than graded judgments. In chapters 7 and 8 we discuss rule systems that have the requisite properties for producing graded salience phenomena.

Figures (3.1)–(3.5) illustrate only one set of dimensions involved in judgments of #thing#hood, related to Gestalt principles of good form and good continuation. Nonetheless, the behavior of these aspects of the visual field is typical of a great number of the Gestalt principles. More appear in section 8.1.

In addition, #thing#hood is affected by factors involving the viewer's internal state rather than immediate environmental input. For example, features of the visual signal interacting with the viewer's *intention* or *need* can make certain #things# more salient than they otherwise might be. This aspect of #thing#-formation is prominent in the children's puzzles that ask the reader to find three rabbits and two bears hidden in the forest, or in the Hirschfeld cartoons in the *New York Times,* in which the reader who is in on the joke is to find a stipulated number of instances of the name NINA. These #things# would not emerge at all were it not for the viewer's intention to find them. For a more mundane case, one never notices water fountains until one is thirsty.

Similarly, features of the visual signal interacting with the viewer's *knowledge* may make certain #things# more salient. For instance, someone who has worked with automobile engines will perceive a number of distinct #things# under the hood, where a novice sees only a #mess#. For an auditory case, a speaker of French will hear a sequence of #words# (auditory #units#) in the acoustic signal produced by another speaker of French, where a nonspeaker hears only an #undifferentiated stream#.

To be sure, there likely are levels of visual representation in which intention, need, and knowledge are not implicated. For example, Marr's (1982) theory of vision contains a number of such levels, culminating in what he calls the 2 1/2D sketch. However, as Marr makes quite clear, these levels do not exhaust the mechanisms involved in object recognition; rather, they are as far as one can go with purely visual information. At the level of the 3D model representation, where Marr claims that shapes are identified and categorized, cognitive factors not present in the visual field are deeply implicated.

This discussion of #things# hardly scratches the surface of research on perception. Still, it should be sufficient for making clear how much goes into a psychological treatment of what standard logic treats as the simplest possible expression—a constant denoting an individual. We have seen that complex mental computations are involved, for which the idealization to a set of necessary and sufficient conditions is inadequate.

We have also seen that treating the *extension* of the expression "(visually perceived) thing" as a *real* thing is not very useful in a mentalistic theory; it is necessary to talk about what structure we attribute to the world in *projecting* #things#. In particular, in cases such as (3.1) and (3.2) we attribute spatial and temporal continuity by assuming a partial occlusion of the perceived #thing#, but it doesn't really matter what is *actually* the case. Similarly, in accounting for the judgments about (3.5), it doesn't even really make sense to ask which visual configurations actually *are* things. That is, the notion of truth relative to reality does not enter in any direct way into a description of the ability to make such judgments. Rather, the important questions to ask are: What are the mental representations that project into #things#, and what are the processes that give rise to these representations?[3]

This very general outline of the problems of #thing#-perception lays the groundwork for an investigation of referential expressions in language and their conceptual counterparts.

3.2 Pragmatic Anaphora and Ontological Categories

Suppose that someone points and simultaneously utters (3.6).

(3.6) I bought that yesterday.

What must the hearer do to fully understand the speaker? He must of course understand the words and the syntactic structure, and be able to use the correspondence rules involved in interpreting the sentence; but he also must interpret the word "that." In this utterance "that" is an instance of what has been called (Hankamer and Sag (1976)) *pragmatic anaphora*. In order to interpret the pragmatically controlled pronoun "that" in (3.6), the hearer must pick out the intended referent, a #thing#, in his visual field, perhaps with the aid of the speaker's pointing gesture.

To make clearer what is involved in interpreting pragmatic anaphora, consider an example where no #thing# emerges that can correspond appropriately to the pronoun. Suppose for instance that speaker A utters (3.6) and points to a blurry photograph: "I bought that yesterday—isn't it gorgeous?" Speaker B, unable to make out anything in the picture, doesn't fully understand the utterance and responds, "What are you talking about?" Speaker A replies, "That boat!" B peers at the photograph and, sure enough, suddenly a #boat# is visible in the picture: "Oh, that! How could I miss it?" B has only now understood A's original utterance so that discourse can continue.

The reader is probably familiar with such experiences. It is a case of the interaction between the visual field and nonvisual factors in #thing#-perception, as discussed in the previous section: the visual field does not change, but in response to linguistic suggestion, the #visual field# does change. The relevance of this sort of example to pragmatic anaphora is this: *In order for a pragmatically controlled pronoun to be understood, its intended referent must emerge as a projected #entity# for the hearer.* In turn, for such an #entity# to emerge, *the hearer must have constructed from his visual field a projectable expression at the level of conceptual structure*—that level where visual and linguistic information are compatible. Thus, there is an important connection between #thing#-perception and the use of pragmatic anaphora.

So far, the only #entities# in visual perception that we have dealt with are #things# and possibly #shapes#. By and large these are the kinds of #entities# that have been investigated in research on visual perception. But, as Hankamer and Sag (1976) point out, there are many grammatically different sorts of pragmatic anaphora, for example those illustrated in (3.7).

(3.7) a. Pro-prepositional phrase:
    Your coat is here [*pointing*] and your hat is there [*pointing*].
    He went thataway [*pointing*].

b. "do it/that":
    Can you do that [*pointing*]?
    Can you do this [*demonstrating*]?

c. "that . . . happen":
    That [*pointing*] had better not happen again around here.

d. Pro-manner adverbial:
$$\text{You shuffle cards} \begin{Bmatrix} \text{thus} \\ \text{so} \\ \text{this way} \end{Bmatrix} [\textit{demonstrating}].$$

e. Pro-measure expression:
$$\text{The fish that got away was} \begin{Bmatrix} \text{this} \\ \text{that} \\ \text{yay} \end{Bmatrix} [\textit{demonstrating}] \text{ long.}$$

The syntactic properties of these pragmatic anaphors are revealed by what syntactic substitutions are possible. "Here," "there," and "thataway" substitute for prepositional phrases such as "on the table," "under the sofa," and "toward the OK Corral"; they should be regarded as intransitive prepositions (as argued by Klima (1965), Emonds (1970), and Jackendoff (1977a)). "Do it" or "do that" substitutes for a verb phrase such as "Stuff that ball through that hoop."[4] "That . . . happen" is also a unit, replaceable only by the subject and predicate of some other sentence, as in "John better not kick Billy again around here." ("That" alone can be replaced only by abstract NPs like "that disaster.") "Thus," "so," and "this way" substitute for manner and means adverbs and prepositional phrases such as "slowly," "carefully," "with caution," or "by holding the cards between your fingers and blowing." In (3.7e), "this," "that," and "yay" substitute for degree and measure phrases such as "two feet," "very," "as (long) as my arm." In short, each of these constructions represents a grammatically distinct form of pragmatic anaphora.

The same conditions holding on "that" in (3.6) also hold on the comprehensibility of these pragmatic anaphors. For example, if the hearer is unable to see or figure out what goings-on the speaker is pointing at in (3.7c), he will not fully understand the utterance—he will not have received all the information he is intended to receive.

Given that it is necessary to have an appropriate visually supplied projectable expression in conceptual structure in order to comprehend the pragmatic "that" anaphor in (3.6), a projectable expression must be necessary for all the pragmatic anaphors in (3.7) as well. From the semantic contexts in which these constructions appear, though, we see that the #entities# referred to cannot be #things# or #shapes#. Rather, each corresponds to a different sort of projected #entity#, distinct from #things#. Roughly, "here" and "there" refer to #places#, "thataway" to a #direction#, "do it" to an #action#, "that . . . happen" to an #event#, pro-manner adverbs to #manners#, and pro-measure expressions to #amounts#. Each of these types of projected #entity# represents an organization of the visual field quite different from #things#. (There are contexts—for instance, "What was that?"—that are ambiguous as to type of #entity#, but the contexts in (3.7) are fairly clear.)

To support the projection of this variety of #entities#, conceptual structure must contain, in addition to [THINGS], constituents whose major features are [PLACE], [DIRECTION], [ACTION], [EVENT], [MANNER], and [AMOUNT]. Such constituents may of course contain [THINGS] as part of their internal structure. For example, the [PLACE] expressed by "on the table" contains as a subconstituent the [THING] expressed by "the table," in a fashion to be discussed in the next chapter. But a [PLACE] simply is not the same as a [THING]; it is of distinct conceptual character. To make this clear, contrast the information conveyed by (3.8a) and (3.8b).

(3.8) a. Here is your coat, and there is your hat.
      b. This is your coat and that is your hat.

(3.8a) *locates* the coat and hat, while (3.8b) *identifies* them—two entirely different sorts of information. The conceptual distinctness of

DIRECTION, EVENT, ACTION, MANNER, and AMOUNT can be demonstrated with similar arguments.

The feature [THING] therefore forms an opposition with these other features. Only one can be present as the major feature of a conceptual constituent: intuitively, an #entity# cannot be both a #thing# and a #place#, for example. We will call these features (along with various others such as SOUND and SMELL and TIME) the features identifying the *major ontological categories*; they characterize the distinction among the major classes of #entities# that we act as though the #world# contains.

3.3 Against Reduction of the Ontological Categories

An important aspect of the argument from pragmatic anaphora is that the distinctions among ontological categories must be represented *at the level of conceptual structure:* it is precisely at this level that the visual system can provide information to specify the content of the anaphoric expressions. One might object that all these types of entities should be reduced by the theory of conceptual structure to concurrences of [THINGS] over time (say as a four-dimensional space-time map) and that such concepts as [PLACE] and [EVENT] should play only a derivative role in linguistic semantics. But such a view would assume that there is some privileged role to be accorded to the concept [THING]—for example, that [THING] can be straightforwardly correlated with reality. As shown in section 3.1, this assumption is simply false. Most of the literature of perception is concerned with how we manage the remarkable feat of construing the #world# as full of more or less stable #things#, given constantly shifting patterns of environmental stimulation.

What seems to me a more productive approach is to abandon the goal of reduction and to claim that the ontological categories expressed by the pragmatic anaphors in (3.7) are all present as primitives of conceptual structure. Formally, this means that the conceptual well-formedness rules must allow for conceptual constituents of each type, account for their differing contributions to experience, and provide an algebra of relationships among them, specifying that #a thing can occupy a place#, #an event may have a certain number of things and places as parts#, and so forth. Under this approach, linguistic semantics is not concerned with reducing out events, places, and so forth, from the formal description, but with clarifying their psychological nature and with showing how they are expressed syntactically and lexically.

If any reduction is to take place, it will be in the theory of perception, which now must explain the relations of retinal stimuli not only to #thing#-perception but to #place#-and #event#-perception as well. If this view is correct, one would expect these other aspects of perception to have many of the same gestalt properties as #thing#-perception: dependence on proximity, closure, "good form," and so on. The work I have encountered on perception of #entities# other than #things# and their #properties#[5] does reveal just what we are led to expect. This suggests that there is no fundamental new difficulty for perception in admitting ontological categories other than [THING] into conceptual structure—just more of the old problem of how we manage to perceive anything at all.

The introduction of a nontrivial collection of ontological categories again stresses the importance of the distinction between the real world and the projected world. The existence of a particular ontological category is not a matter of physics or metaphysical speculation or formal parsimony, but an empirical psychological issue, to be determined on the basis of its value in explaining the experience and behavior of humans and other organisms.[6]

3.4 Further Linguistic Evidence

In arguing from the varieties of pragmatic anaphora to the varieties of ontological categories, we have made essential use of the Cognitive Constraint of chapter 1, in that we bring visual evidence to bear on questions of semantics. In addition, we have invoked the Grammatical Constraint, by requiring pragmatic anaphora to be treated as a semantically unified phenomenon. Specifically, the maximally simple NP "that" expresses a minimally specified [THING] in (3.6), and the visual field is the source of the remaining information in the intended message. Similarly, the other expressions of pragmatic anaphora are maximally simple PPs, VPs, etc., and therefore should likewise correspond to minimally specified [ENTITIES] of the semantically proper type. Again, the remainder of the intended message is conveyed through the visual system.

This section will make further use of the Grammatical Constraint. We will see that several grammatical constructions characteristic of reference to #things# find close parallels in constructions that refer to other ontological categories. These grammatical parallels will re-inforce the conclusions of section 3.2: that expressions other than NPs can be used referentially, and that they refer to #entities# other than #things#, having equal ontological status.

First, each of the ontological categories of section 3.2 permits the formation of a *wh*-question. In the case of [THING], [PLACE], [DIRECTION], [MANNER], and [AMOUNT], the *wh*-word is of the same syntactic category as the corresponding pragmatic anaphor; in the case of [ACTION] and [EVENT], the *wh*-word substitutes for the "it" of the compound pragmatic anaphor.

(3.9) a. What did you buy?   [THING]
       b. Where is my coat?   [PLACE]
       c. Where did they go?   [DIRECTION]
       d. What did you do?   [ACTION]
       e. What happened next?   [EVENT]
       f. How did you cook the eggs?   [MANNER]
       g. How long was the fish?   [AMOUNT]

While each of these questions can be answered by a sentence (e.g., "I bought a fish" for (3.9a)), each also has a reduced answer of the appropriate syntactic category. The phrases in (3.10a–g) are reduced answers for (3.9a–g), respectively.

(3.10) a. A fish.
        b. In the bathtub.
        c. Into the bathtub.
        d. Go to the store.
        e. Billy fell out the window. (no reduction of S, of course)
        f. Slowly./With cheese./By putting them in a coffee pot.
        g. Twelve feet (long).

Moreover, if one is feeling laconic, one can answer silently, by producing the fish, pointing to the place or in the direction, performing the action, pointing to the event (or its result), demonstrating the manner, or demonstrating the size.

It is reasonable to assume that the asker of a *wh*-question is seeking to fill in information in a conceptual structure. However, according to our theory of consciousness, one can formulate a *wh*-question only if the gap in one's knowledge is a *projectable* gap. In other words, the answer to a *wh*-question must be a phrase denoting a projectable #entity#—or in the case of the silent answers, a nonlinguistic designation of the projectable #entity#. Thus, each of the constructions in (3.10) must be referring when used as an answer to (3.9).

Another grammatical construction that supports the ontology is the expression of identity and individuation with "same" and "different." (3.11) shows that each ontological category supports a notion of identity.[7]

(3.11) a. Bill picked up the same thing ($\begin{Bmatrix} \text{that} \\ \text{as} \end{Bmatrix}$) Jack did. [THING]

   b. Bill ate at the same place Jack did.   [PLACE]
   c. Bill went the same way Jack went.   [DIRECTION]
   d. Bill did the same thing (as) Jack did.   [ACTION]
   e. The same thing happened today as happened yesterday.
                                                                      [EVENT]
   f. Bill shuffles cards the same way (as) he cooks eggs (—meticulously).   [MANNER]
   g. Bill is as tall as Jack is.   [AMOUNT]

These clearly are grammatically parallel, with the exception of the use of "as . . . as" in (3.11g). However, even this case shows some parallelism. The subordinate clause following "same" in (3.11a–f) is optionally introduced by "as," and both "the same . . . as" and "as . . . as" may be preceded by a class of modifiers such as "just," "almost," "not quite," etc., with parallel semantic effect. Thus "as . . . as" displays considerable syntactic and semantic generalization with the other phrases, despite some syntactic difference. (See Reed (1974) for more discussion of their parallelism.)

In each of the constructions in (3.11a–f), nonidentity between #entities# can be expressed by substituting "a different . . . than" for "the same . . . as." In (3.11g), the corresponding substitution is "-er than" for "as . . . as." Again, the same subordinating conjunction, "than," appears in both cases.

These assertions of identity and nonidentity are not about identity of linguistic expressions. They assert the identity of the #entities# to which the expressions refer. Thus there must be individuable #entities# in the projected world for each of the requisite ontological categories. What the conditions of individuation are, and how clear-cut a result they provide, are empirical issues. Thus, for example, when Davidson (1967b, 1969) finds problems for the ontological status of #actions#, it is partly because he indiscriminately applies the standards of individuation appropriate to #things#. I maintain that the correct approach is to investigate what evidence people take as relevant when they make judgments of identity or nonidentity. The evidence might well differ from one ontological type to another, because of the spatial and temporal characteristics peculiar to each.[8]

Still another characteristic of #things# as the referents of linguistic expressions is that one can quantify over them. But quantification in language is not reserved for expressions for #things#: a paradigm parallel to (3.6–7), (3.9), and (3.11) can be constructed for existential and universal quantification. The parallel is defective only in the amount expressions.

(3.12) a.   Bill picked up $\begin{Bmatrix} \text{something} \\ \text{everything} \end{Bmatrix}$ that Jack picked up.

$\left.\begin{matrix} \text{b.} \\ \text{c.} \end{matrix}\right\}$ Bill $\begin{Bmatrix} \text{has been} \\ \text{went} \end{Bmatrix}$ $\begin{Bmatrix} \text{someplace} \\ \text{somewhere} \\ \text{everyplace} \\ \text{everywhere} \end{Bmatrix}$ that Jack $\begin{Bmatrix} \text{has been.} \\ \text{went.} \end{Bmatrix}$

d.   Bill did $\begin{Bmatrix} \text{something} \\ \text{everything} \end{Bmatrix}$ Jack did.

e. $\begin{Bmatrix} \text{Something} \\ \text{Everything} \end{Bmatrix}$ that happened yesterday also happened today.

f.   Bill can shuffle cards (in) $\begin{Bmatrix} \text{some way(s)} \\ \text{every way} \end{Bmatrix}$ that Jack can.

g.   (no parallel for amounts)

The expressions "nothing" and "anything" generalize over this paradigm too: "noplace/nowhere," "anyplace/anywhere"; "do nothing," "do anything"; "nothing happened," "anything happened"; "in no way," "in any way." In each case, the "any"-words are dependent on the presence of an affective context (such as negation, yes-no question, or generic—see Klima (1964)), and their interpretations vary in precisely the same way as that of "any" in a noun phrase.

In addition, the expressions of individuation "else" and "other" can be added to each of these quantifying expressions, as in "something everything else," "some/every other thing," etc. The semantic parallelism extends across all the ontological categories, following the syntactic parallelism.

These paradigms show, then, that quantification over #places#, #directions#, #actions#, #events#, and #manners# must be countenanced in natural language semantics, and its behavior should parallel that of quantification over #things#.

3.5 Conclusion

This chapter has shown, through a combination of linguistic and nonlinguistic arguments, that the level of conceptual structure must contain a rich range of ontological categories, corresponding to different categories of projected #entities#. Furthermore, corresponding to several noun phrase constructions that are normally taken to depend on the individuation of #things#, there exist constructions of other grammatical categories that argue for the individuation of these other sorts of #entities#.

The reader should be cautioned against concluding that the ontological categories presented in this chapter exhaust the possibilities. These simply happen to be the categories for which linguistic and visual evidence are both present most prominently. For a different sort of case, *"That* sounds like Brahms" motivates a category of #sounds#. Furthermore, if a language other than English were to display different varieties of pragmatic anaphora, this would not lead to an argument that speakers of this language have different conceptual structure—only that this language happens to have proforms for a different selection of ontological categories. The total set of ontological categories must be universal: it constitutes one basic dimension along which humans can organize their experience, and hence it cannot be learned (see chapter 1).

One should not be afraid of metaphysical difficulties in positing this ontological variety. Sections 2.1 and 3.1 have shown some of the formidable problems one must confront in positing #things# alone. If one confronts these problems seriously, the metaphysics of the richer ontology does not appear to present problems of a significantly higher order of magnitude.[9]

Chapter 4
The Syntax of Conceptual Structure

This chapter combines the conclusions of chapter 3 with the Grammatical Constraint to motivate a grammar of conceptual structure that is considerably richer than traditional quantificational logic and at the same time is related to the syntax of natural language in a much more general way.

The syntactic evidence that will be adduced in favor of this account of conceptual structure comes from the so-called X-Bar theory of grammatical categories (Chomsky (1970), Emonds (1976), Jackendoff (1977a)). The main point of this theory for present purposes is that all major lexical categories (noun, verb, adjective, adverb, and preposition)[1] admit of essentially the same range of types of modification. Hence, a theory that makes a sharp distinction in principle between the syntactic properties of, say, nouns and verbs misses crucial generalizations about the nature of language.

We will use the syntactic generalizations among categories as evidence for parallel semantic generalizations. Our concern will be primarily with finding an adequate solution to the problems that standard predicate-argument structure is intended to solve. Section 4.1 lays out the difficulties with the usual approach, and section 4.2 develops a richer alternative. Sections 4.3 and 4.4 deal with further details of the system.

4.1 Problems for Standard First-order Logic

Though virtually no one believes anymore that first-order quantificational logic is an adequate theory of the semantic structure of natural language, its assumptions have nevertheless pervaded work in philosophy, linguistics, and to a lesser extent psychology and artificial intelligence. Too many different enrichments of first-order logic have appeared in the literature for us to discuss them all here, but this section will focus on aspects that are basic to most alternative versions.

First consider the treatment of individual constants. In common practice, individual constants are taken primarily as translations of proper nouns and indexical pronouns. For example, a pragmatic anaphor such as "that" in "I bought that [*pointing*] yesterday" would be translated as an individual constant whose reference is determined pragmatically. However, as shown in chapter 3, the Grammatical Constraint forces us to adopt parallel treatment of all types of pragmatic anaphor: there must be individual constants corresponding to the PPs "here," "there," "thataway"; to the VP "do that"; to the S "that . . . happened"; to the Adverb Phrases "thus," "so"; and to the measure phrases "this," "that," and "yay." In support of the referentiality of these expressions, we have shown that they all alternate with *wh*-questions and with individuating expressions using "same" and "different." Thus, the first-order notion of individual constant must be syntactically enriched.[2]

The notion of variable suffers from the same difficulty. As shown in (3.12), all but one of the syntactic categories in (3.7) permit universal and existential quantification. Hence, variables too must correspond to a range of syntactic constructions richer than NPs alone.

Next recall the discussion in section 1.5 concerning indefinite NPs. In order for the phrase "a glass" to be referential in "Floyd broke a glass," its first-order translation must include a variable bound by an existential quantifier, violating the syntactic integrity of the construction. We have now expanded the class of referential phrases; according to the Grammatical Constraint, this variety of referential phrases must lead to a corresponding proliferation of quantifiers in logical expressions. Consider a simple sentence like (4.1).

(4.1) Floyd broke a glass violently.

This sentence includes five referring expressions, picking out two #things#, an #event#, an #action#, and a #manner#.[3] A possible logical form for (4.1), as closely parallel to standard logical practice as I can make it (though hardly first order), is (4.2). "Floyd" corresponds to a constant, but all the other referential phrases are translated as variables bound by existential quantifiers.

(4.2) $\exists x(\text{Event}(x) \ \& \ x = \exists z(\text{Action}(z) \ \& \ z(\text{Floyd}) \ \& \ z = (\exists w(\text{glass}(w)$
$\& \ \text{break}(w) \ \& \ \exists u(\text{violently}(u) \ \& \ u(z))))))$

Though one could certainly quibble over details, the point is that
(4.2) represents the general degree of complexity that any standard
logical translation must contain: four existential quantifiers, each of
which binds a variable of the appropriate ontological category. All
vestiges of resemblance to natural language syntax have vanished.

   Though we have so far been questioning the adequacy of first-
order constants and variables, similar problems can be found in the
treatment of predicates. Verbs are the quintessential predicates.
Corresponding to each NP that a verb strictly subcategorizes, there is
an argument place in the predicate the verb expresses. Thus an intransitive verb is a one-place predicate, whose single argument corresponds to the subject; a transitive verb is a two-place predicate; a
verb that takes direct and indirect objects (as in "Sue gave Paul a
banana") is a three-place predicate.

   As a first indication that something is amiss, notice that verbs can
strictly subcategorize not only NPs but also APs (4.3a), PPs (4.3b),
AdvPs (4.3c), Ss (4.3d), and possibly VPs (4.3e).[4] (The relevant subcategorized phrases are italicized.)

(4.3) a. We painted the house *red*.
        You make me *very angry*.

      b. Harry put the clothes *in the attic*.
        Sue went *out of the room*.

      c. The job paid *handsomely*.
        Bill dresses *splendidly*.

      d. We forgot that *the sun rises in the east*.
        That *the sun rises in the east* proves that *alligators are mammals*.

      e. Everyone saw the sun *rise in the east*.
        Bill tried to *convince Harry*.

Moreover, the property of being able to govern arguments is not restricted to verbs. Nouns can strictly subcategorize PPs, Ss, and VPs
(4.4), and so can adjectives (4.5).

(4.4) a. the destruction *of the city*
        the author *of the book*
        an argument *with Bill*

   b. the proof that *the sun rises in the east*
      the idea that *alligators are mammals*

   c. an attempt to *convince Harry*
      the good fortune to *be invited to the party*

(4.5) a. afraid *of monsters*
         full *of ideas*
         angry *at Sam*

      b. proud that *he is a frog*
         surprised that *the sun rises in the east*

      c. welcome to *come in*
         lucky to *have an alligator*

The lowly preposition turns out to have an especially rich syntax. Prepositions may occur "intransitively" (i.e., subcategorizing no following phrases) (4.6a), and they may subcategorize NPs (4.6b), APs (4.6c), PPs (4.6d), or Ss (4.6e).[5]

(4.6) a. downstairs
         thereafter
         outside

      b. in *the park*
         on *the steps*

      c. (they regard him) as *stupid*
         (Bill went) from *happy* to *sad* (in three seconds flat)

      d. out *of the room*
         from *inside the closet*

      e. before *Max left*
         until *alligators are proved to be mammals*

Since in predicate logic it is predicates that govern arguments, not only verbs but nouns, adjectives, and prepositions as well must be translated into predicates. The usual approach is to treat "is a man," for example, as a simple one-place predicate M, so that "John is a man" translates into M(JOHN). Then "author" becomes a two-place predicate $A(x,y)$—"x is the author of y"; "red" is a one-place predicate "is red"; "afraid" is a two-place predicate "is afraid of" (and thus just like the verb "fear"); "outside" is a one-place predicate "is outside"; and "on" is a two-place predicate "is on."[6]

Notice that all of these logical translations include the verb "be" as an essential part. "Man" alone has no logical translation; only "is a man" does. Moreover, "is" has no separate logical status in these constructions. It might as well be regarded as a mere grammatical artifact, bearing no relation to the "be" usually translated as equality in "The morning star is the evening star."

Because of this treatment of common nouns, a common noun that is *not* preceded by "be" in a sentence requires a more complex translation into logical form. For example, "Bill kicked a man" translates into $\exists x(M(x)$ & $K(B,x))$. The existential quantifier is present to express the referentiality of "a man"; but in addition a syntactically unmotivated logical connective must be introduced to unite the two predicates "kick" and "is a man."

Such a move is more than inconvenient. It leads to real descriptive inadequacies, most notably in the treatment of prepositions. Consider (4.7), in which various prepositions have been translated into two-place predicates. (For the sake of clarity, the putative logical translations in examples to follow omit the quantification necessary to express referentiality of the NPs and PPs; a correct first-order translation would of course have to include them.)

(4.7) a. The book lies on the table.
   LIE (BOOK) & ON (BOOK, TABLE)

   b. Sam put the book on the table.
   PUT (SAM, BOOK) & ON (BOOK, TABLE)

   c. John headed toward the burning building.
   HEAD (JOHN) & TOWARD (JOHN, BURNING BUILDING)

   d. Sue ran around the lake.
   RUN (SUE) & AROUND (SUE, LAKE)

   e. The sign points into the room.
   POINT (SIGN) & INTO (SIGN, ROOM)

The most direct English translation of the logical form in (4.7a) is "The book is lying and it is on the table." Not only is this uncomfortable, but it is also unclear whether it is indeed synonymous with "The book is lying on the table," as it ought to be. By parallelism, (4.7b–e) should be equivalent to "Sam put the book and it was on the table," "John headed and he was toward the burning building," "Sue ran and she was around the lake," and "The sign points and it is into the room." Each of these is clearly inadequate as a logical translation, either because the first clause, based on the verb, is alone incomprehensible, or because the second clause, based on the preposition, is incomprehensible or means the wrong thing. In fact, the translations of (4.7c–e) suffer from both defects.

One might try to relieve this inadequacy in various ways. One might say that "put," for example, is a three-place predicate, taking a sentence as its third argument. Then the translation of (4.7b), "Sam put the book on the table," would be (4.8).

(4.8) PUT (SAM, BOOK, ON (BOOK, TABLE))

This is to be read something like "Sam put the book to be on the table," parallel to "Sam caused the book to be on the table." This is a better solution for (4.7b), but it suffers from two problems. First, it presents a purely syntactic problem of accounting for when "be" appears and when it does not; if this problem is taken seriously and studied systematically, it proves surprisingly intractable. (See Wasow (1977), Borkin (1973), Baker (1979).) Second, this solution still does not help for (4.7c–e), where the contribution of the preposition simply cannot be specified by a dyadic predicate. John is not toward the burning building, Sue is not around the lake, and the sign is not into the room.

Another solution, proposed by Thomason and Stalnaker (1973) and Miller and Johnson-Laird (1976), is to treat "lie on," "put on," "head toward," etc., as complex predicates, derived compositionally from the verb and the preposition. The preposition is to be thought of as an operator that adds one more argument place to the verb. So, for example, (4.7a) becomes something like (4.9a) or (4.9b).

(4.9) a. [ON (LIE)] (BOOK, TABLE)
      b. ON (LIE (BOOK), TABLE)

These solutions do not make the mistake of equating running around with running plus being around, or pointing toward with pointing plus being toward. But notice how each violates the Grammatical Constraint in an entirely new way. In (4.9a), the preposition, which in syntactic structure forms a constituent with its object, now instead forms a constituent with the verb in logical form. There do exist morphemes in languages of the world that form a constituent with the verb and have the semantic effect of adding an argument—for example, causative affixes; but it seems quite implausible to treat prepositions as semantically parallel with them. In (4.9b), the preposition becomes the outermost operator of the logical form, rather than being embedded under the verb. In either case, what is not expressed is that "put" is fundamentally a three-place predicate and "head" is a two-place predicate: "Sam put the book" and "John headed" are nonsense in isolation.

Perhaps the most serious objection to all these solutions is that they run counter to the evidence from sections 3.2 and 3.4 that prepositional phrases can be used referentially. Consider the translation of "John ran thataway [*pointing*]" under the four solutions we have considered:

(4.10) a. RAN (JOHN) & THATAWAY (JOHN) (like (4.7))
        b. RAN (JOHN, THATAWAY (JOHN)) (like (4.8))
        c. [THATAWAY (RAN)](JOHN) (like (4.9a))
        d. THATAWAY (RAN (JOHN)) (like (4.9b))

In each of these, the translation of "thataway" is a function with open argument places—not a logical constant, as its referential use requires under the assumptions of first-order logic. How can something be both an open function and a constant? Rather than explore more convoluted alternatives, let us reconsider.[7]

4.2 A Better Syntax-Semantics Mapping

The underlying problem with first-order logic is that it does not have enough categories to go around. To express the syntactic constructions explored above, it has only predicates and terms that fill argument places of predicates. Our attempt to treat prepositions in this framework has shown that they apparently can play both roles at once, leading to a contradiction within the first-order framework.

In an effort to find a better account, let us review the properties of the syntactic categories of language, following the general outlines of X-Bar theory (Chomsky (1970), Emonds (1976), Jackendoff (1977a)). A primary distinction is customarily made between the *lexical categories* (or parts of speech)— e.g., Noun (N), Verb (V), Adjective (A), and Preposition (P)—and the *phrasal categories*—e.g., Noun Phrase (NP), Verb Phrase (VP), Adjective Phrase (AP), Prepositional Phrase (PP), and Sentence (S). Each phrasal category contains a *head*—a member of one of the lexical categories—plus a variety of possible *modifiers*, which are typically other phrasal categories. Corresponding to each lexical category there is a *major phrasal category*, that phrasal category which maximizes the possible modifiers of the lexical category. The major phrasal category corresponding to N is NP; that corresponding to V is S.

To make this less abstract, (4.11b–e) illustrate typical tree structures for the four major phrasal categories S, NP, AP, and PP, giving a range of possible modifiers. In each of these, the major phrasal category dominates a constituent belonging to a double-primed phrasal category (or X″); this in turn dominates a constituent belonging to a single-primed phrasal category (X′), which itself dominates the corresponding lexical category. This sequence of nodes from top to bottom of the tree, illustrated for the general case in (4.11a), constitutes the structural skeleton of the major phrasal category, to which various modifiers are attached at various levels. (The specific details of the structures in (4.11) follow Jackendoff (1977a); other possibilities have been proposed, but the general topology of the trees is widely accepted.)

(4.11) a. major phrasal category

$$X''$$

$$X'$$

X (lexical category—head of construction)

(4.11) b.

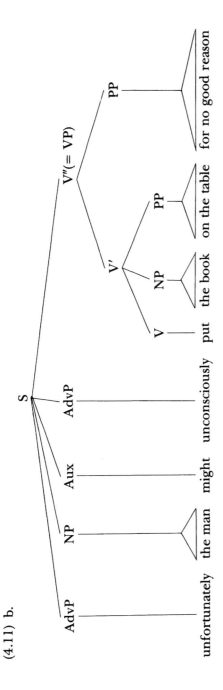

c.

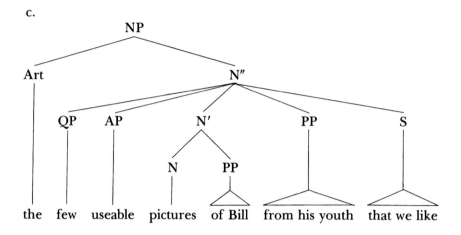

d.

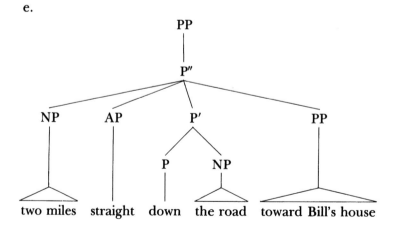

e.

The phrases that a lexical item *strictly subcategorizes* are all major phrasal categories. They appear in two positions: as daughters of the single-primed phrasal category (e.g., direct and indirect objects) and as daughters of the major phrasal category (e.g., subjects of Ss and of NPs such as "*the enemy*'s destruction of the city"). We return to modifiers other than strictly subcategorized phrases in section 4.3.

This outline of the principles of phrase structure is sufficient for us to state a quite simple relationship between syntax and conceptual structure. First, every major phrasal constituent in the syntax of a sentence corresponds to a conceptual constituent that belongs to one of the major ontological categories. If a major phrasal constituent is used *referentially*, it corresponds to a *projectable* instance of a major ontological category. In other words, all major phrasal categories play the role assigned to NPs alone in first-order logic.

Second, the lexical head X of a major phrasal constituent corresponds to a function in conceptual structure—a chunk of the inner code with zero or more argument places that must be filled in order to form a complete conceptual constituent. The argument places are filled by the readings of the major phrasal constituents strictly subcategorized by X. (The maximum number of argument places is three or possibly four.)

For a concrete example, consider "The man put the book on the table." The head of the S is the verb "put," which strictly subcategorizes a subject NP, a direct object NP, and a PP. "Put" expresses a semantic function that maps three arguments into an [EVENT]. The arguments, corresponding to the readings of the subject, the object, and the PP, are two [THING]s and a [PLACE] or [PATH]. Thus a first approximation to the conceptual structure of this sentence is (4.12).

$$(4.12) \quad \begin{bmatrix} \text{EVENT} \\ \text{PUT} \left(\begin{bmatrix} \text{THING} \\ \text{THE MAN} \end{bmatrix}, \begin{bmatrix} \text{THING} \\ \text{THE BOOK} \end{bmatrix}, \begin{bmatrix} \text{PLACE} \\ \text{ON THE TABLE} \end{bmatrix} \right) \end{bmatrix}$$

Now consider the internal structure of the three arguments. Since the lexical items "man" and "book" strictly subcategorize nothing, they are to be treated as zero-place functions (i.e., constants) that map into the major ontological category [THING]. Thus the first two arguments have no internal functional structure. On the other hand, "on," the head of the PP, strictly subcategorizes an NP. Hence it expresses a one-place function that maps a [THING], the reading of the NP, into a [PLACE], the reading of the PP. The third argument of (4.12) therefore has the internal functional structure (4.13a), giving (4.13b) as the complete functional structure for the sentence. The embedding in this structure duplicates the syntactic embedding in the sentence.[8]

(4.13) a. $\begin{bmatrix} \text{PLACE} \\ \text{ON } (\begin{bmatrix} \text{THING} \\ \text{THE TABLE} \end{bmatrix}) \end{bmatrix}$

   b. $\begin{bmatrix} \text{EVENT} \\ \text{PUT } (\begin{bmatrix} \text{THING} \\ \text{THE MAN} \end{bmatrix}, \begin{bmatrix} \text{THING} \\ \text{THE BOOK} \end{bmatrix}, \\ \qquad\qquad \begin{bmatrix} \text{PLACE} \\ \text{ON } (\begin{bmatrix} \text{THING} \\ \text{THE TABLE} \end{bmatrix}) \end{bmatrix}) \end{bmatrix}$

Which major ontological category is expressed by a particular major phrasal constituent depends on the semantics of the head. Some verbs, like "put," map into EVENTs. Others, the so-called *stative* verbs such as "seem," "know," "believe," and "be," map into STATES— things that are the case rather than things that happen. Nouns like "table" and "house" map into THINGs, but "destruction" maps into an EVENT and "mile" maps into an AMOUNT. Adjectives typically map into PROPERTIES; prepositions into PLACEs and PATHs.

Since the relationship between syntactic and ontological categories is not one-to-one, we need not claim that the correspondence observed in English is universal. For example, consider languages that lack the syntactic category adjective. In such a language, a [PROPERTY] might be expressed by a noun phrase, as in Warlpiri, or by a prepositional phrase, like "out of shape" in English. Alternatively, the [STATE] of something having a [PROPERTY] might be expressed by an intransitive verb, as in Navajo. Thus variation among languages in their repertoire of syntactic categories does not damage the theory. What must be universal is (i) the distinction between lexical categories and major phrasal categories, and (ii) a system of subcategorization in which lexical categories subcategorize major phrasal categories. (I am grateful to Kenneth Hale for help on this paragraph; see also section 9.5.)

Notice how this theory of conceptual structure overcomes a number of the difficulties with first-order logic pointed out in the previous section. Instead of constants and variables, we have conceptual constituents of various ontological categories. Instead of predicates that map into propositions when their argument places are filled, we have functions that map into major ontological categories when their argument places are filled. In short, we use the same formal device, function-argument structure, but with a much richer range of function and argument types. This enables us to represent "The man put the book on the table," for example, without sacrificing expressive accuracy, without inverting the functional dependence of syntactic elements, and without introducing syntactically unmotivated connectives such as conjunction. Furthermore, we can treat in a perfectly general fashion the relation between strict subcategorization in syntax and argument places in conceptual structure.

One result of this is that a sentence like "The book is on the table" is to be regarded as a two-place relation between a [THING] and a [PLACE], mediated by the verb "be."[9] The preposition "on" is no longer a two-place predicate but a one-place function mapping a reference object, a [THING], into a [PLACE]. Analogously, then, the indexical phrase "here" in "The book is here" is a zero-place function (a functional constant) that maps into a [PLACE]; the value of the constant is determined pragmatically, as discussed in section 3.2. This is exactly parallel to the indexical pronoun "that," a zero-place function that maps into a [THING] in sentences like "I bought that." Thus we avoid the paradoxical result that "here" is both a constant and a one-place predicate.

This theory does not yet determine which phrases in a sentence are referential, the information expressed by the existential quantifiers in first-order logic. Toward that end, observe that, in natural language, referentiality is the unmarked case, not a condition that requires an overt marker such as a quantifier. By contrast, the *non*referential use of a phrase in a sentence can generally be traced to the presence somewhere in the sentence of an explicit lexical or grammatical marker. Such markers include future tense, modal functions such as "possible," predicative verbs such as "be" and "become," and verbs of propositional attitude. Each of these elements affects referential status in a characteristic fashion (see sections 5.4 and 6.1, chapter 11, Jackendoff (1972, chapter 7), and Jackendoff (1975b). This distribution of referential phrases in natural language can be expressed in preliminary form as the following principle:

Referentiality Principle
Unless there is a linguistic marking to the contrary, all phrases that express conceptual constituents are referential.

According to the Referentiality Principle, "The man put the book on the table" refers to an #event#, three #things#, and a #place# — the projections of the five conceptual constituents in (4.13b). This eliminates the need for those existential quantifiers and bound variables in first-order logic that serve the purpose of directly representing referentiality. This does not exclude the possibility of quantifier-like operators in conceptual structure, but they can be limited to genuine cases of quantification like "all" and "every." (See the end of the next section for further remarks.)

4.3 Conceptual Relations Other Than Function-Argument

So far we have considered only modifiers that are strictly subcategorized by the head of the phrase and that are treated semantically as a functional argument to the head. A number of other kinds of modifiers deserve mention, none of which is strictly subcategorized by the head. I will only try to characterize them very roughly.

Restrictive modifiers add further conditions on the character or identity of the possible referents of the expression. (4.14) presents some examples, with the restrictive modifiers in italics.

(4.14) a. In NPs:
      i.   the *red* hat
      ii. the man *who came to dinner*
      iii. a dog *from Australia*
      iv. *Sarah's* pajamas
   b. In Ss:
      i.   Jack *quickly* dropped the diamonds.
      ii. Heather bopped Bradley on the head *with a cucumber*.
      iii. Nicholas made everyone happy *by eating his lunch*.

    c. In APs:
        i. *quietly* obnoxious
        ii. yellow *with age*
        iii. tired *from overwork*
    d. In PPs:
        i. *straight* down the street
        ii. *high* on the hill
        iii. up the hill *toward the river*

Jackendoff (1977a) argues that most restrictive modifiers in English are represented syntactically as daughters of the appropriate double-primed phrasal category. One exception is the possessive NP (4.14a.iv), a daughter of the major phrasal category NP.

These modifiers have received varied treatment within first-order logic. The nominal modifiers (4.14a) are generally treated as predicates conjoined to the predicate standing for the head noun, for instance, "the x such that x is a hat and x is red," "the x such that x is a man and x came to dinner," etc. The advantage of this representation is the ease of existential generalization: one can get directly from "There is a red hat here" to "There is something red here" by the inference rule $p \mathrel{\&} q \rightarrow p$. One disadvantage is, as usual, that this representation is so distant from the syntax. Another is that, by cutting the interpretation of the adjective loose from that of the head noun, this representation cannot account for the interpretation of *syncategorematic* adjectives such as "good" and "big," whose precise interpretation depends on the identity of the head (goodness in a knife is different from goodness in a nurse, and a big mouse is smaller than a small elephant).

Different treatments of manner adverbs (4.14b.i) have been proposed by Davidson (1967a), Parsons (1972), and Thomason and Stalnaker (1973). Fodor (1972) points out some difficulties in Davidson's approach; each of them has difficulties dealing with the others' examples. Only Davidson's analysis brings out the semantic and syntactic parallelism between the adverb-verb relation and the adjective-noun relation—an important consideration for the Grammatical Constraint (one would, for example, want similar treatment of "recover quickly" and "quick recovery"). As for most of the other examples of restrictive modification in (4.14), I am unaware of any semantic treatment in print.

For present purposes, it is sufficient to furnish a provisional notation to express the relationship of restrictive modification uniformly across categories. The crucial properties of this notation are (1) that the modifier itself forms a conceptual constituent, (2) that the modifier forms a part of the conceptual constituent expressed by the major phrasal category that contains it, and (3) that the modifier is not a functional argument. (4.15) illustrates the notation with representations of some of the examples in (4.14).

(4.15) a. $\begin{bmatrix} \text{THING} \\ \text{HAT} \\ \begin{bmatrix} \text{PROPERTY} \\ \text{RED} \end{bmatrix} \end{bmatrix}$ (4.14a.i)

b. $\begin{bmatrix} \text{EVENT} \\ \text{DROP} ([\text{JACK}], [\text{DIAMONDS}]) \\ \begin{bmatrix} \text{MANNER} \\ \text{QUICKLY} \end{bmatrix} \end{bmatrix}$ (4.14b.i)

c. $\begin{bmatrix} \text{PROPERTY} \\ \text{OBNOXIOUS} \\ \begin{bmatrix} \text{MANNER} \\ \text{QUIETLY} \end{bmatrix} \end{bmatrix}$ (4.14c.i)

d. $\begin{bmatrix} \text{PATH} \\ \text{DOWN} \left(\begin{bmatrix} \text{THING} \\ \text{STREET} \end{bmatrix} \right) \\ \begin{bmatrix} \text{PROPERTY} \\ \text{STRAIGHT} \end{bmatrix} \end{bmatrix}$ (4.14d.i)

This representation is still crude, in that it does not account for syncategorematicity. For such cases, the modifier must be connected with some internal part of what we have so far treated as an undecomposable head. For example, the reading of "big" must affect a feature of stereotypical size (see chapter 8); the reading of "good" must affect a feature of stereotypical function (see Katz (1966, 288–317)). For a different and worse case (pointed out to me by R. Oehrle), the reading of "missing" in "There is a missing sparkplug" must affect some feature of identifiability.

For the simple, nonsyncategorematic cases such as "red," it is necessary to provide an inference rule that derives the desired existential generalization. Taking C to be the ontological category of the conceptual constituent in question, and X and Y to be collections of internal constituents, we may state the rule as (4.16).

(4.16)

$$\begin{bmatrix} C \\ X \\ Y \end{bmatrix} \rightarrow \left\{ \begin{bmatrix} C \\ X \end{bmatrix} \\ \begin{bmatrix} C \\ Y \end{bmatrix} \right\}$$

This rule says that if (4.15a) is a conceptual constituent, one may derive (4.17a) ("a hat") and (4.17b) ("something red"). Similarly, if (4.15b) is a conceptual constituent, one may derive (4.17c) ("Jack dropped the diamonds") and (4.17d) ("something happened quickly").

(4.17) a. $\begin{bmatrix} \text{THING} \\ \text{HAT} \end{bmatrix}$

b. $\begin{bmatrix} \text{THING} \\ \begin{bmatrix} \text{PROPERTY} \\ \text{RED} \end{bmatrix} \end{bmatrix}$

c. $\begin{bmatrix} \text{EVENT} \\ \text{DROP} ([\text{JACK}], [\text{DIAMONDS}]) \end{bmatrix}$

d. $\begin{bmatrix} \text{EVENT} \\ \begin{bmatrix} \text{MANNER} \\ \text{QUICKLY} \end{bmatrix} \end{bmatrix}$

I will only briefly mention three other kinds of modifiers: nonrestrictive modifiers, measuring or bounding modifiers, and logical modifiers. *Nonrestrictive modifiers* are best exemplified by appositive relative clauses in NPs (4.18a), but they also occur as appositives in other major phrasal categories and as sentential adverbials.

(4.18) a. In NPs:
Bill, *who is missing a tooth,* is going to the dentist.
Poor Max lost his marbles.

b. In Ss:
John hit the nail with a hammer, *which surprised no one.*
(EVENT antecedent)
John hit the nail with a pliers, *which I would never do.*
(ACTION antecedent)

John hit the nail, $\left\{ \begin{array}{l} \textit{fortunately.} \\ \textit{of course.} \\ \textit{I think.} \end{array} \right\}$

c. In APs:
Martha is proud of her height, *which you'll never be.*

d. In PPs:
We went from Aspen to Denver, *which seems like a long way,* in less than four weeks.

There are several well-known differences, both syntactic and semantic, between these and restrictive modifiers (see Jackendoff (1977a, sections 4.1, 7.2, 7.3, and 7.9)). For present purposes it is sufficient to note that they do not contribute to the identification of a referent, but instead comment on a referent already identified by the rest of the major phrasal category.

Measuring or *bounding modifiers* set specifications on the interpretation of the feature BOUNDED (see chapter 3, note 9). They occur in all the major phrasal categories.

(4.19) a. In NPs:
three tamales
a number of objections
six inches of rope

b. In Ss:

They walked around the tree $\begin{Bmatrix} \textit{a little bit.} \\ \textit{three times.} \\ \textit{for nine minutes.} \end{Bmatrix}$

c. In APs:
nine feet tall
a little bit tired

d. In PPs:
eight miles down the road
far into the night
along the road *a little ways*

Again, I do not want to make any strong proposals about the conceptual structure of these modifiers. I simply want to point out that this type of modification is semantically distinct from the other types observed so far.

Finally, *logical modifiers* include not only the familiar definite article, NP quantifiers, and sentential negation, but also the quantifiers within all the different ontological categories, as illustrated in (3.12).

Moreover, the logical modifiers must include, in addition to the standard universal and existential quantifiers of logic, such distinctions as those among the so-called universal quantifiers "all," "every," "each," and "any" (Vendler (1967)), between stressed and unstressed "some," and between the negative "few" and nonnegative "a few" (Klima (1964)). The semantic treatment of *wh*-morphemes ("who," "which," "why," etc.) also belongs in the theory of logical modification, since, as is well known (Klima (1964), Jackendoff (1972, chapter 7), Chomsky (1977)), these morphemes share much of their behavior with quantifiers and negation.

While I will offer no general theory of quantification here (and this is a serious gap in my critique of first-order logic), we see that the range of constructions that an adequate theory must account for is considerably larger than usually considered. Moreover, the interaction of definite descriptions with discourse phenomena (see, for example, Webber (1978)) and the interaction of quantification with verb meanings (see section 10.3) make it harder to conceive of a relatively self-contained theory of quantification than is often assumed.

Some facets of traditional quantification theory have been treated in the present framework. The Referentiality Principle eliminates the need for a whole class of quantified constructions. Chapters 5 and 6 deal with the nonreferentiality of predicate NPs; chapter 11 provides a solution to the referential puzzles of belief-contexts. A number of other scope phenomena are discussed in Jackendoff (1972, chapter 7), some of which interact intimately with the theory of bounding and multiplicity (see chapter 3, note 9). Thus a general form of approach to the problems addressed by traditional quantification should be evident, even if a full account is as yet lacking.

The point of listing all these different sorts of modification is to see that there are at least five different ways of embedding a conceptual constituent within another, only two of which—functional argument and perhaps some aspects of quantification—are adequately expressed in first-order logic. The conclusion therefore is that conceptual structure must be richer than first-order logic not only in the class of major ontological categories and functional types, but also in its principles of combination.

4.4 Compositionality

In chapter 1 we distinguished between strong and weak versions of the compositionality of syntax vis-à-vis semantic interpretation. The strongest version is that every syntactic constituent in a sentence must correspond to an independent and identifiable contiguous piece of semantic structure. The weakest version is that each part of the sentence must somehow contribute to the whole, but not necessarily as a discrete piece; the contributions of various constituents may be freely interwoven.

We have arrived at a hypothesis intermediate between these two, though closer to the strong version: every major phrasal constituent in a sentence corresponds to a conceptual constituent in the semantic structure of the sentence.[10] However, with one exception, there are no conceptual constituents corresponding to single- and double-primed categories. The exception is ACTION, which corresponds to VP (V″). We have not yet considered how ACTION constituents are derived; we will return to this problem in section 9.4.

Given the Grammatical Constraint, one might well ask why there should be intermediate single- and double-primed phrase categories that have no independent interpretation. My conjecture is that they help make up for the lack of differentiation in syntactic dependency compared to the variety of semantic dependencies. While there are at least five ways for semantic constituents to be embedded, syntax has only a single dependency relation, that of node X being a daughter of (dominated by) node Y.

In support of this conjecture, observe that syntax tends to group modifiers of different types under different intermediate nodes. For instance, in English, functional arguments other than subjects are under single-prime nodes; restrictive modifiers are mostly dominated by double-prime nodes; and nonrestrictive modifiers are mostly dominated by major phrasal nodes. These tendencies are not absolute even in English, and they apparently differ somewhat from language to language (see Jackendoff (1977a, sections 4.1, 10.2)). However, insofar as one can trust teleological arguments, it appears plausible that the function of the intermediate phrasal nodes is to provide enough syntactic distinctions for expressing the variety of subordination relations in semantics, rather than to express a wider variety of independent conceptual constituents.

Chapter 5
Categorization

An essential aspect of cognition is the ability to categorize: to judge that a particular thing is or is not an instance of a particular category. A categorization judgment is expressed most simply in English by a predicative sentence such as "*a* is a dog" and represented in first-order logic by an atomic sentence such as "D*a*." This chapter will develop the basic elements of conceptual structure necessary to represent categorization.

We should note at the outset that categorization judgments need not involve the use of language: they are fundamental to any sort of discrimination task performed by dogs or rats or babies. In order to reliably press one lever when presented with a square and another when presented with a circle, an animal must make a judgment about the proper categorization of the newly presented stimulus. It must also distinguish experimental stimuli from food, other animals, the bars of the cage, and so forth. More generally, the ability to categorize is indispensable in using previous experience to guide the interpretation of new experience: without categorization, memory is virtually useless.[1] Thus an account of the organism's ability to categorize transcends linguistic theory. It is central to all of cognitive psychology.

5.1 Preliminary Formalization

The usual logical metalanguages explicate atomic sentences in terms of the conditions under which they are true:

(5.1)

$$\text{"D}a\text{" is true iff} \left\{ \begin{array}{l} \text{a. D}a \quad \text{(Tarski)} \\ \text{b. the extension of "}a\text{" is a member} \\ \quad \text{of the extension of "D"} \quad \text{(set-theoretic} \\ \quad \text{semantics)} \\ \text{c. what "}a\text{" maps into in some model} \\ \quad \text{is a member of the set that "D" maps} \\ \quad \text{into} \quad \text{(model-theoretic semantics)} \\ \text{d. among the semantic markers of "}a\text{" is} \\ \quad \text{the marker [+D]} \quad \text{(Katz)}^2 \end{array} \right\}$$

These treatments all make an assumption that we rejected in chapter 2: a fixed, preestablished connection of truth between sentences and the real world.[3] By contrast, we are concerned with how the organism makes the judgment, or with what is involved in *grasping* an atomic sentence. We thus take the theory of categorization to concern not whether a particular categorization is true, but what information and processing must be ascribed to an organism to account for its categorization judgments.

Since there can be no judgment without representation, categorization cannot be treated simply as the organism's comparison of some component of reality "*a*" to a preexisting category of dogs. Rather, the comparison must be made between the internal representations of *a* and of the category of dogs. Moreover, categorization can involve input through any combination of sensory media—vision, language, smell, and so forth. Thus the mechanism of categorization must be assigned to the level of conceptual structure, where all these types of information are available. In short, *a categorization judgment is the outcome of the juxtaposition of two conceptual structures.*

We will refer to the representation of the thing being categorized as a [TOKEN] concept and that of the category as a [TYPE] concept. The [TOKEN], corresponding to the constant of a first-order logic atomic sentence, is a concept of the sort discussed in chapter 3: a mental construct of potentially elaborate internal structure, which can be projected into awareness as a unified #entity#. Chapter 3 showed that [TOKENS] exist across a wide range of major ontological categories; we may thus speak of [THING TOKENS], [PLACE TOKENS], [EVENT TOKENS], and so forth.

A [TYPE] concept is the information that the organism creates and stores when it learns a category. Since #entities# of different ontological categories can be categorized, [TYPES] likewise divide into [THING TYPES], [PLACE TYPES], [EVENT TYPES], etc.

A categorization judgment might be represented formally in two ways. The first resembles first-order logical notation, in that the [TYPE] concept is treated as a one-place predicate whose argument is a [TOKEN]. This gives a representation like (5.2) for "*a* is a dog."

(5.2) $\begin{bmatrix} \text{THING TYPE} \\ \text{DOG} \end{bmatrix} \left(\begin{bmatrix} \text{THING TOKEN} \\ a \end{bmatrix} \right)$

Alternatively, the [TOKEN] and the [TYPE] may both be variable-free structures that are compared by a two-place function. Such a formalization resembles the set-theoretic notation "$a \in D$," with the two-place function playing the role of the relation "$\in$":

(5.3) IS AN INSTANCE OF $\left(\begin{bmatrix} \text{THING TOKEN} \\ a \end{bmatrix} \right.$,

$\left. \begin{bmatrix} \text{THING TYPE} \\ \text{DOG} \end{bmatrix} \right)$

The theory of syntax-semantics correspondence developed in chapter 4 provides preliminary evidence in favor of the latter formalization. In that theory, NPs correspond to variable-free conceptual constituents, and verbs correspond to functions whose argument places are filled by strictly subcategorized syntactic categories. The typical categorization sentence "*a* is a dog" contains two NPs connected by the verb "be." Thus (5.3) corresponds in the proper way: the subject and predicate NPs correspond to the two arguments, and the verb "be" translates into the function IS AN INSTANCE OF (x, y). By contrast, (5.2) is a version of the theory of common nouns as predicates, which section 4.1 rejected.

However, (5.3) does not specify what the two-place function comparing the two relata maps into. In predicate logic or set theory, the answer would be a truth value; the categorization would be either true or false. But truth values are not part of our metalanguage. Rather, according to the correspondence principles of chapter 4, the function must map into a conceptual constituent belonging to a major ontological category.

The proper category would appear to be [STATE TOKEN]. Just in case a [STATE TOKEN] with internal structure (5.3) turns out to be projectable, the organism experiences it as #a state that obtains in the world#—in other words, it makes a positive categorization judgment. Thus "(5.4) is projectable" is our metalanguage's counterpart of the expression "'Da' is true" in the metalanguage of logic.

(5.4)
$$\begin{bmatrix} \text{STATE TOKEN} \\ \text{IS AN INSTANCE OF } (\begin{bmatrix} \text{THING TOKEN} \\ a \end{bmatrix}, \\ \begin{bmatrix} \text{THING TYPE} \\ \text{DOG} \end{bmatrix}) \end{bmatrix}$$

Notice that in this formalism it is just as easy to categorize [TOKENS] of other major ontological categories. For example, (5.5) asserts that a is a case of Max sleeping.

(5.5)
$$\begin{bmatrix} \text{STATE TOKEN} \\ \text{IS AN INSTANCE OF } (\begin{bmatrix} \text{EVENT TOKEN} \\ a \end{bmatrix}, \\ \begin{bmatrix} \text{EVENT TYPE} \\ \text{SLEEP } (\begin{bmatrix} \text{THING TOKEN} \\ \text{MAX} \end{bmatrix})) \end{bmatrix})$$

In addition to the function IS AN INSTANCE OF, we need an operator that I will call *INSTANCE OF,* which maps a [TYPE] constituent into a feature of a [TOKEN] constituent. This feature encodes the presupposed category membership(s) of the [TOKEN]. For example, (5.6) is a [TOKEN] that has previously been judged to be an instance of [TYPE DOG].

(5.6)
$$\begin{bmatrix} \text{THING TOKEN} \\ \text{INSTANCE OF } (\begin{bmatrix} \text{THING TYPE} \\ \text{DOG} \end{bmatrix}) \end{bmatrix}$$

The kinship of the operator INSTANCE OF and the function IS AN INSTANCE OF is intuitively obvious. Formally, the operator could be treated as an abstraction operator that binds the first argument of the function, e.g., λx(IS AN INSTANCE OF $(x,$ [TYPE])). Since for the moment nothing hangs on the exact formalization, though, I leave it in the simple form shown in (5.6).

The relation between the categorization judgment (5.4) and the presupposed categorization (5.6) can be expressed by inference rule (5.7), a mapping from one class of conceptual structures into another.

(5.7) $\begin{bmatrix} \text{STATE TOKEN} \\ \text{IS AN INSTANCE OF } ([\,\text{TOKEN}\,]_i, [\,\text{TYPE}\,]_j) \end{bmatrix}$ ↔

$\qquad\qquad\qquad\qquad \begin{bmatrix} \text{TOKEN} \\ \text{INSTANCE OF } ([\,\text{TYPE}\,]_j) \end{bmatrix}_i$

Using this inference rule, an organism that has made a categorization judgment about [TOKEN]$_i$ can incorporate the information about [TYPE]$_j$ into [TOKEN]$_i$ itself; or, using the rule in reverse, it can extract explicit categorization information from within [TOKEN]$_i$ into the form of a categorization judgment.

A converse operator, which I will call *EXEMPLIFIED BY*, maps a [TOKEN] into a feature of a [TYPE] that it is an instance of. This operator is used for incorporating examples of a [TYPE] into the information listed in the [TYPE] concept itself, should one wish to do so. (5.8) shows the effect of incorporating the information that *a* is a dog into [TYPE DOG].

(5.8) $\begin{bmatrix} \text{THING TYPE} \\ \text{DOG} \\ \text{EXEMPLIFIED BY } (\begin{bmatrix} \text{THING TOKEN} \\ a \end{bmatrix}) \end{bmatrix}$

Parallel to (5.7), we can state an inference rule (5.9) that relates the operator EXEMPLIFIED BY to categorization judgments.

(5.9) $\begin{bmatrix} \text{STATE TOKEN} \\ \text{IS AN INSTANCE OF } ([\,\text{TOKEN}\,]_i, [\,\text{TYPE}\,]_j) \end{bmatrix}$ ↔

$\qquad\qquad\qquad\qquad \begin{bmatrix} \text{TYPE} \\ \text{EXEMPLIFIED BY } ([\,\text{TOKEN}\,]_i) \end{bmatrix}_j$

An interesting hypothesis emerges from this formalization of categorization judgments. In the first-order logic and set-theoretic notations, tokens and categories are treated syntactically as entirely distinct: constants vs. predicates and elements vs. sets. In the present formalization, though, [TOKENS] and [TYPES] are less differentiated: they are both variable-free conceptual constituents, marked in similar fashion for major ontological category.

Let us push this formal similarity further. We will claim that, aside from the distinction expressed by the TOKEN/TYPE feature opposition, the internal structures of [TOKEN] and [TYPE] concepts are organized by exactly the same principles; in other words, the conceptual well-formedness rules are not bifurcated into rules specific to [TOKENS] and rules specific to [TYPES]. As a consequence, many if not all of the formal relations and processes that apply to [TOKENS] will also apply to [TYPES]. From this claim we will develop in chapter 6 an important and unexpected consequence about the nature of logical inference.

The next two sections will provide some evidence for the formal similarity of [TOKENS] and [TYPES], on cognitive and grammatical grounds, respectively.

5.2 The Creativity of Categorization

5.2.1 [TYPES] Contain Rules
First note that one can in general identify novel #things# as #instances of a known type#, such as #another chrysanthemum# or #another piano concerto#. This means that the internal structure of a [TYPE] cannot consist merely of a list of all the [TOKENS] one has encountered that instantiate it. A [TYPE] may of course list some prominent examples, as provided for in our theory with the operator EXEMPLIFIED BY. But the categorization process must also include a set of principles that may be used creatively to categorize arbitrary new [TOKENS].

Moreover, one can create new [TYPE] concepts at will. One of the simplest ways to do this is to construct, for an arbitrary [TOKEN]$_i$, a [TYPE] of THINGS LIKE [TOKEN]$_i$, where likeness can be determined along any arbitrary class of dimensions. For each of the indefinitely many [TOKENS] that one can construct in response to environmental stimulation, there are any number of such [TYPES]. These in turn can be used to categorize arbitrary [TOKENS].

The creativity of [TYPE]-formation shows that a [TOKEN] concept cannot consist merely of a list of all the [TYPES] it is an instance of, since there may be indefinitely many of these.[4] Some [TYPE]-inclusions may be explicitly encoded within the [TOKEN], by use of the operator INSTANCE OF—but by no means all.

Now consider the function IS AN INSTANCE OF ([TOKEN], [TYPE]). Since a [TOKEN] is not a list of [TYPES], the function cannot simply examine the [TOKEN] to see if the [TYPE] is included in it. Conversely, since a [TYPE] is not a list of [TOKENS], the function cannot simply examine the [TYPE] to see if the [TOKEN] is included. Such lookup functions, which relate categorization judgments to internal lists in the [TOKEN] and [TYPE], are present in the theory as inference rules (5.7) and (5.9). However, because of the creativity of categorization and of [TOKEN] and [TYPE] formation, they alone are not enough. The function IS AN INSTANCE OF must examine the internal structures of both relata for compatibility.

The discussion so far already provides two arguments for the claim that the internal organization of [TOKENS] and [TYPES] is the same. First, such parallel organization would facilitate the operation of the function IS AN INSTANCE OF, which must make a comparison of the internal structures of a [TOKEN] and a [TYPE]. Second, the easiest formal way to derive a $[TYPE]_j$ of THINGS LIKE $[TOKEN]_i$ would be to copy internal information from $[TOKEN]_i$ into $[TYPE]_j$ intact. This is only possible if a [TYPE] can be organized along the same lines as a [TOKEN].

We also have reason to reject Fodor's (1975) theory that all possible [TYPES] are innately given as unanalyzed monads: a [TYPE] without internal structure cannot be compared with novel [TOKENS] to yield categorization judgments. Moreover, Fodor's theory entails that there is only a finite number of [TYPES], since there is only a finite space in the brain for storing them all. This consequence Fodor seems willing to live with. But if one can generate new [TYPES] at will on the basis of given [TOKENS], then either the set of [TYPES] must be infinite, contra Fodor, or else the set of [TOKENS] must be finite and innate, a totally implausible conclusion. Section 7.5 will discuss Fodor's arguments for his theory, along with alternatives; for the moment we note that it is impossible to maintain such a theory in the face of the creativity of categorization.

5.2.2 The Character of Rules Within [TYPES]

We conclude therefore that [TYPE] concepts contain as part of their internal structure a set of principles, rules, or conditions that make creative categorization possible. These principles are not generally projectable; that is, they are not accessible to introspection. In this respect they parallel the characteristics of [TOKEN]-formation discussed in section 3.1. However, the unconscious character of rules for [TYPES] has been more widely remarked, and it is worth giving some representative quotations to illustrate the scope of the phenomenon.

> What does it mean to know what a game is? What does it mean, to know it and not be able to say it? . . . Compare *knowing* and *saying:*
> how many feet high Mont Blanc is—
> how the word "game" is used—
> how a clarinet sounds.
> If you are surprised that one can know something and not be able to say it, you are perhaps thinking of a case like the first. Certainly not of one like the third.
>
> (Wittgenstein (1953, 35–36))

> Everyone has perceived such traits as suppressed anger in a face, gaiety in a movement, or peaceful harmony in a picture. Often these perceptions seem very direct. We do not first notice the tightness of the jaw and then infer the anger; more often it is the other way around. Such reactions are not so rare that cognitive psychology can afford to ignore them. According to many developmental psychologists, they are the rule rather than the exception in children.
>
> (Neisser (1967, 96))

> Although the expert diagnostician, taxonomist and cotton-classer can indicate their clues and formulate their maxims, they know many more things than they can tell, knowing them only in practice, as instrumental particulars, and not explicitly, as objects. The knowledge of such particulars is therefore ineffable, and the pondering of a judgment in terms of such particulars is an ineffable process of thought. This applies equally to connoisseurship as the art of knowing and to skills as the art of doing, wherefore both can be taught only by aid of practical example and never solely by precept.
>
> (Polanyi (1958, 88))

> Obviously, every speaker of a language has mastered and internalized a generative grammar that expresses his knowledge of his language [i.e., the category [SENTENCE OF LANGUAGE L]—RJ]. This is not to say that he is aware of the rules of the grammar or even that he can become aware of them, or that his statements about his intuitive knowledge of the language are necessarily accurate.
>
> (Chomsky (1965, 8))[5]

What are the unconscious principles encoded in a [TYPE] concept like? Recalling that (5.4) is the conceptual equivalent of an atomic sentence "Da" of logic, we might be tempted to think of these rules as necessary and sufficient conditions, like Tarski's. But this cannot be the case: as we will see, categorization judgments follow the same yes/no/not-sure distribution that we encountered with #things# in section 3.1. Since necessary and sufficient conditions cannot produce such a distribution, we have a preliminary argument against them. Here we will examine only two simple cases, leaving elaboration of the argument for chapter 7.

Consider an operant conditioning experiment in which an animal is trained to signal discrimination between two types of stimuli. In learning the task, the animal has had to construct two [TYPE] concepts. If it does not respond at all, it has not perceived an #instance of either type#; if it responds in one way or the other, the presented stimulus has been perceived as an #instance of one type and not the other#. Suppose, however, that the animal is trained on two different colors or pitches and tested on an intermediate one; or suppose that it is trained on red squares and blue circles and then presented with a red circle. In various situations of this sort, the animal may be unsure, and rightly so—we would be, too. (Pavlov apparently claimed he could induce neurosis in his animals if he set the tasks up right.) Moreover, it misses the point to ask which [TYPE] the novel stimulus is *truly* an instance of: these experiments are designed to explore the animal's capabilities for forming [TYPES], not to find out how good the animal is at ascertaining the truth. The latter goal hardly makes sense.

Similarly, Labov (1973) presented human subjects with pictures of containers that differed in the ratio of width to height, asking them to label the pictures "vase," "cup," or "bowl."

(5.10)

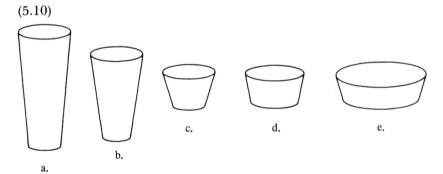

At certain ratios such as (5.10a,c,e), the responses were relatively uniform; but at intermediate ratios such as (5.10b,d), two different responses were equally probable. At these ratios, the choice is highly sensitive to context effects such as the exact form of the question or the immediately preceding examples. Such a graded response pattern shows that the boundaries of "vase," "cup," and "bowl" are not precisely defined, as they would be if the [TYPES] were necessary and sufficient conditions. And again, the *truth* of the categorization judgment in these intermediate cases is not at issue: (5.10b) is what it is, and if one person chooses to call it "a vase" and another "a cup," is either of them *wrong?*

We thus can identify four important characteristics both in non-verbal categorization tasks such as discrimination and in verbal categorization tasks such as labeling: (1) judgments are made creatively and hence must be governed by a set of rules; (2) the rules are generally unconscious; (3) the judgments are distributed in a yes/no/not-sure pattern and hence cannot be formalized by necessary and sufficient conditions; (4) it is odd to talk about the truth of the judgments in the borderline cases. The interchangeability of these two sorts of tasks is pointed out in studies such as Rosch and Mervis (1975) and Rosch et al. (1976). Their similarity is a central argument for the position that categorization sentences are evaluated at the level of conceptual structure, where inputs can be compared independent of modality.

Moreover, these four characteristics of categorization are qualitatively entirely parallel to the characteristics of #thing#-perception discussed in section 3.1. (In particular, compare paradigm (5.10) to (3.5) of section 3.1.) In other words, we seem to be dealing with systems whose formal properties lead to the same sort of judgmental results. Although many different theories of the organization of [TOKENS] and [TYPES] might be made consistent with this generalization, it is in fact a *consequence* of the theory we are proposing here: if [TOKENS] and [TYPES] have the same principles of internal organization, then individuation and categorization judgments cannot help but have similar qualitative characteristics.

5.2.3 Acquisition of [TYPES] through Ostensive Definition

Since in general the rules encoded in a [TYPE] are not available to consciousness, they cannot be explicitly taught. Rather, as Polanyi points out in the passage just quoted, a good proportion of [TYPE] teaching is necessarily limited to the presentation of examples, leaving the student to figure out the principles. That is, much [TYPE] learning (and *all* of it in nonverbal organisms) takes place at best through the examination of a number of #things# stipulated to be #instances# or #noninstances# of the type in question. Wittgenstein

(1953) exercises himself a great deal over how such learning could possibly take place at all, in the face of underdetermination of the rules by any given amount of evidence. The trouble is that it does indeed occur.[6]

In order to account for [TYPE] acquisition on the basis of such ostensive definition, we must presuppose an active, unconscious mental process that can construct [TYPES] from the information in the [TOKENS] given as examples and nonexamples. I am inclined to consider the theory of this process to be about the most fundamental problem of cognitive psychology. At the very least it is responsible for all generalization of experience into a form usable as a guide to future action. In a grander guise, it is the unconscious force behind creativity in science and art, the "ripening" of unattended ideas that eventually spring into awareness fully formed.

Miller and Johnson-Laird (1976, 215) discuss this process basically in despair: ". . . we do not know how perceptual paradigms develop from perception of a finite number of exemplars. Conditions affecting the rate and accuracy of inductive learning have been studied in psychological experiments, but the process itself remains a mystery."

In the present formalism, the problem can be stated as follows. On the basis of stipulated examples, inference rule (5.9) can be invoked repeatedly to construct a [TYPE] concept that consists of a list of the presented [TOKENS], like (5.11).

$$(5.11) \quad \begin{bmatrix} \text{TYPE} \\ \text{EXEMPLIFIED BY } [\text{TOKEN}]_i \\ \text{EXEMPLIFIED BY } [\text{TOKEN}]_j \\ \text{EXEMPLIFIED BY } [\text{TOKEN}]_k \\ \vdots \end{bmatrix}$$

For creative categorization, though, the information within the [TOKENS] must be extracted and generalized into a [TOKEN]-independent set of principles. The problem of learning from ostensive definition can thus be restated in terms of asking what happens to the [TOKEN] information in the extraction process.[7]

It would obviously be a formal advantage for the acquisition process if the information extracted from [TOKENS] and the resulting information in [TYPES] were of essentially the same organization— especially since once the principles are constructed, they will be turned around and compared with information in new [TOKENS].

In fact, in all the attempts I have seen to characterize aspects of perceptual learning (e.g., Winston (1970), Rosch and Mervis (1975), Miller and Johnson-Laird (1976)), such a relationship of [TOKEN] and [TYPE] information is taken for granted. In general, [TYPE] information may be less highly specified in some respects and more highly specified in others (see chapter 8), but the two kinds of information are easily interchangeable.[8]

5.3 Linguistic Treatment of [TOKENS] and [TYPES]

We turn now to evidence from the Grammatical Constraint that [TOKENS] and [TYPES] have parallel internal structure. The fundamental fact here is that [TOKENS] and [TYPES] of a given *ontological* category are expressed by the same *syntactic* category, and may have the same range of internal syntactic structure. For instance, both [THING TOKENS] and [THING TYPES] are expressed by NPs, not by nouns and verbs respectively, as predicate logic might lead one to expect.

To elaborate this argument, notice the semantic effect of different choices for the NP after "be" in (5.12).

(5.12) a. Clark Kent is a reporter.
       b. Clark Kent is Superman.
       c. Clark Kent is the man drinking a martini.

(5.12a) expresses a categorization judgment of the form (5.13a). (5.12b), however, expresses the identity of two [TOKENS], so its semantic structure (5.13b) involves a different relationship between the two relata, which I will call *IS TOKEN-IDENTICAL TO*.

(5.13) a.
$$\begin{bmatrix} \text{STATE TOKEN} \\ \text{IS AN INSTANCE OF (} \begin{bmatrix} \text{THING TOKEN} \\ \text{CLARK KENT} \end{bmatrix}, \\ \\ \begin{bmatrix} \text{THING TYPE} \\ \text{REPORTER} \end{bmatrix}) \end{bmatrix}$$

b. $\left[\begin{array}{l} \text{STATE TOKEN} \\ \text{IS TOKEN-IDENTICAL TO } \left(\begin{bmatrix} \text{THING TOKEN} \\ \text{CLARK KENT} \end{bmatrix} , \right. \end{array}\right.$

$$\left. \begin{bmatrix} \text{THING TOKEN} \\ \text{SUPERMAN} \end{bmatrix} \right) \Bigg]$$

(5.12c) is ambiguous between these two readings.[9] On the token-identity reading, the definite article serves as a demonstrative—"that one over there, the man drinking a martini." On the categorization reading, the definite article expresses uniqueness of the categorized [TOKEN] within its [TYPE]: "Here's how you can tell which is Clark Kent: he will be the (only) man drinking a martini." In general, an indefinite NP in predicate position leads to a [TYPE] reading like (5.13a); a proper noun leads to a [TOKEN] reading like (5.13b); a definite NP may lead to either, but various modifiers such as demonstratives and "only" may restrict the choice. (Note that the modifiers that explicitly distinguish the two readings are mutually incompatible: "that only man drinking a martini" is unacceptable.)

The possibility of both [TOKEN] and [TYPE] readings in (5.12) is a property of this particular syntactic position and this choice of verb. In other positions, such as the subject of "walk in" or the object of "buy," all NPs express [TOKENS], regardless of definiteness.[10]

(5.14) a. $\begin{Bmatrix} \text{A reporter} \\ \text{The man drinking a martini} \\ \text{Clark Kent} \end{Bmatrix}$ walked in.

b. Max bought $\begin{Bmatrix} \text{a dog.} \\ \text{the dog in the store.} \\ \text{Snoopy.} \end{Bmatrix}$

In other words, it is the verb "be" that is responsible for the choice of readings for the NPs in (5.12).[11]

Now consider the two functions IS TOKEN-IDENTICAL TO and IS AN INSTANCE OF. In set-theoretic semantics, these would be entirely unrelated: the former is "=" and the latter "∈". Similarly, in predicate logic, token-identity is expressed by "=" and categorization by predicate-argument structure. These analyses seem to suggest that the verb "be" has two unrelated readings; it is just coincidence that a single morphological form expresses both token-identity and categorization.

In the present theory, though, these two functions are not so different. IS AN INSTANCE OF must compare the structure of its first argument with that of a [TYPE] in the second argument. IS TOKEN-IDENTICAL TO must compare the structure of the first argument with that of a [TOKEN] in the second argument—which may include [TYPE]-information embedded under the operator INSTANCE OF. Since there is no reason to believe that the two functions make any different use of the [TYPE] information in the second argument, IS TOKEN-IDENTICAL TO must do all the work of IS AN INSTANCE OF, and more.

Suppose, as we have been claiming, that [TOKEN] and [TYPE] structures are not internally distinguished. Then it is possible for there to be a function one of whose argument places is indifferently a [TOKEN] or a [TYPE]. Such a function need not be a disjunction of unrelated functions, as it would have to be in predicate logic or set-theoretic semantics; it can simply be insensitive to the feature opposition TOKEN/TYPE. In this case, it can be claimed that IS TOKEN-IDENTICAL TO and IS AN INSTANCE OF are not only related, but in fact the *very same function*. That is, the verb "be" surrounded by two NPs has only a single reading, which we may call BE (x, y), capable of comparing either two [TOKENS] or a [TOKEN] and a [TYPE]. This is just the sort of explanatory advantage that the Grammatical Constraint leads us to seek.[12]

If "be" were an isolated example, we might be able to live with the position that it expresses two distinct functions, one for [TOKENS] and one for [TYPES]. However, a variety of verbs display similar behavior, and under this hypothesis all of them would have to be lexically split. Here are three cases.

(5.15) Clark {looks like / resembles} {a. President Roosevelt. / b. a famous politician. / c. a turtle.}

(5.16) Max {is looking for / is seeking} {a. Charlie. / b. a friend of mine. / c. an honest politician.}

(5.17) This suit fits {a. Clark. / b. a seven-year-old boy.}

In the (a) cases, the second NP clearly expresses a [TOKEN]. In the (c) cases, though, it expresses a [TYPE], and the (b) cases are ambiguous. In the [TYPE] reading, there is no particular turtle that Max resembles, Max would be satisfied with any old honest politician, and the suit is seven-year-old-boy size.[13]

But do we want to say that comparing Clark on the basis of [TOKEN] criteria is essentially a different process from comparing him on [TYPE] criteria? Or that Max's quest is different if [TOKEN] rather than [TYPE] features are his criteria for success? Or that one is making an essentially different assertion about the size of the suit in the two cases? My intuition is that these are not distinct senses, and that a lexical split in these verbs would serve no purpose other than formal necessity. It would be far better to explain the morphological unity of these verbs by claiming that they express a single function, and that only the TOKEN/TYPE feature of the second argument varies. Under the theory that [TOKENS] and [TYPES] are structurally compatible conceptual constituents, this is the most natural account. By contrast, it is not an account especially congenial to the predicate logic or set-theoretic notations for categorization. Thus these verbs provide further confirmation for the unification of [TOKEN] and [TYPE] structure and for the conceptual unity of the verb "be." (This argument will be extended in section 6.1.)

5.4 The Nonprojectability of [TYPES]

The reader may have noticed my careful avoidance of the issue of reference in the previous section. The time has now come to ask the fateful question: What is the reference of an NP that expresses a [TYPE]?

According to the view of reference developed in chapter 2, the reference of a linguistic expression must be an #entity# projected from the conceptual structure the phrase expresses. Considerable effort was spent in chapter 3 to demonstrate that [TOKENS] of many major ontological categories are projectable into visual experience, and hence that many more linguistic expressions refer than are usually assumed to. This section, by contrast, will claim that [TYPES] as such have *no* projection, and hence that phrases expressing [TYPES] are nonreferring.

Let us see what such a claim would mean. It does not deny the existence of [TYPES]; the conceptual processing involved in making categorization judgments must go on whether or not [TYPES] have projections. The claim is simply that [TYPES] do not correspond directly to experience. We can't point to a #type# but only to #instances of a type#, which is why one must learn [TYPES] indirectly, on the basis of ostensive definition.

Without being projected, [TYPES] can still contribute vitally to the character of experience. For example, when we see #something# as #a dog# ("Lo! A dog!"), we are seeing #it# as #an instance of a type#, and this is a different experience from seeing #it# as #Rover# (i.e., simply as a #token#) or as #a brown physical object# (i.e., #instance of a different type#). We can even use pragmatic anaphora to signal that a #token# is to be seen in the role of #instance of a type#, as in (5.18).

(5.18) Those [*pointing to a single Cadillac*] are expensive.

But is one seeing a #type# under these conditions? I don't think so. The #token# has not disappeared, as for instance #the faces# do when one is seeing #the vase# in (2.2). At most the character of the #token# changes as different categorizations are attended to. One experiences the [TYPE] only through the character of its projected #instance#.

Many previous semantic theories have been hampered by regarding a categorization judgment as the grasping of something true about the real world. This inevitably leads one to search for something in the real world that the categorization judgment is about: a category to which things may belong.

But theories of reference for category terms have been notably unsuccessful. Among the more popular have been (1) a stereotypical instance; (2) a mental image of a stereotypical instance; (3) the good old Platonic essence (e.g., of "dogness"); (4) the extension of the predicate (e.g., the set of all dogs). Stereotypes have well-known problems. For example, does the stereotypical animal have any particular number of legs? If so, how can it be representative of animals with a different number? If not, how can it be representative of animals at all, since surely every instance does have a particular number of legs? (See Fodor, Bever, and Garrett's (1974, 152–162) summary of these arguments. We return to stereotypes in chapter 8.) The Platonic essential animal suffers from the same problems, not to mention the difficulty many of us have with the idea of Platonic essences out there somewhere, just waiting to be grasped.

Thus, most theorists seem to have settled on the notion of *extension* as the proper explication of categories; it looks nice and objective.

But in fact it too leads to serious trouble. Putnam (1975) constructs an argument that senses and extensions cannot be related in the way they are supposed to be. According to the usual assumptions, the language user grasps the senses of the words he uses, and the sense of a word determines its reference (i.e., its extension). However, Putnam argues in detail that what one knows cannot in general determine the extension of the word.[14] For instance, the things that one judges to be gold may or may not really be gold, and it may be that only an expert can tell, or maybe only an expert two centuries from now or on another planet. Thus the sense of the word "gold"—that is, the knowledge on which one supposedly bases judgments—does not determine the extension.

Putnam concludes from this that one does not know what "gold" really means. But where else is there to put word meanings but in people's minds?[15] One must either deny that there are such things as word meanings or else (like Katz (1980)) treat meanings as Platonic entities that we humans grasp only imperfectly. Such tactics, however, totally remove semantics from the domain of psychology; it is not the semanticist's business anymore to ask how people internalize language. Inasmuch as our central concern here is human linguistic and cognitive ability, we must find a different way out of Putnam's argument. I vote for giving up the assumption that reference equals real-world extension.

Chapter 2 argued that, in the case of [TOKENS], the theory should substitute projected-world extension for real-world extension. In this way, sense still determines reference—almost trivially so, since projected-world #entities# are mental constructs isomorphic to a subset of conceptual structures. But consider a parallel substitution (e.g., the set of all #dogs#) for the extension of [TYPE] concepts. One cannot experience the set of all #dogs# as one experiences an individual #dog#, especially when we include not only all past and future #dogs# but all *possible* #dogs#, whatever *they* are. In fact, it is not even clear that the notion of the set of all #dogs# is coherent. Such an attempt to provide an extension for [TYPE] concepts seems to account for little besides the theorist's desire to provide extension equally for [TOKENS] and [TYPES]: it does not correspond to anything in experience, and it does no computational work.

In the absence of a viable candidate for the projection of [TYPE] concepts, then, we may conclude that [TYPES] have no projection.

Turning back to issues of language, this means that "a dog" in "That is a dog" is a nonreferring expression, since it expresses a [TYPE]. It therefore contrasts with the same NP used in "A dog bit me," which expresses a [TOKEN] and so refers to a particular #dog#. As observed in the previous section, the difference is due to the semantic structure of the verb "be," which specifies that its second NP, if indefinite (or under various other conditions), expresses a [TYPE]. This property of "be" is what gives the NP after it the special characteristics of a predicate nominal; a similar marking is present in all verbs such as "become" and "resemble" that condition the predicate nominal construction.

This conclusion prompts a revision to the Referentiality Principle of section 4.2, which did not distinguish between [TOKEN] and [TYPE] constituents. An appropriate restatement for the moment is as follows:

Referentiality Principle II
Unless there is a linguistic marking to the contrary, all phrases that express [TOKEN] constituents are referential; phrases that express [TYPE] constituents are nonreferential.

The evident analogy between designation by pointing and designation by use of clearly referential expressions like "Clark Kent" fuels an illusion that the purpose of language is to describe the world. Such a view, however, leaves mysterious the function of nonreferential expressions such as predicate nominals—unless one posits notions like extension or Platonic essence for them to refer to. If, on the other hand, one takes the view that the purpose of language is to make one's internal structures projectable to others as #sounds#—i.e., to express thought—then there is nothing at all puzzling about nonreferential expressions. It is just that some internal structures correspond directly to experience and some do not, a conclusion that should come as no surprise in any contemporary theory of mind.

Chapter 6
Semantic Structure Is Conceptual Structure

Chapter 1 made a distinction in principle between two levels of mental representation: conceptual structure, the level at which linguistic and nonlinguistic information are mutually compatible, and semantic structure, the level at which semantic properties of sentences such as synonymy, anomaly, presupposition, and inference can be formally captured. In subsequent chapters I have not been especially careful to preserve the distinction, tending to use the term *conceptual structure* when talking about nonlinguistic matters and *semantic structure* when discussing the relation to language.

The time has come to make good on my unscrupulousness. This chapter will argue that once enough machinery has been developed to meet the needs of conceptual structure, the semantic properties of sentences can be formalized with little further ado. It would therefore miss an important generalization to insist that there is a separate semantic level of mental representation, with its own special characteristics, whose purpose is only to account for logical inference and the like. We will conclude that the terms *semantic structure* and *conceptual structure* denote the same level of representation.

6.1 Generic Categorization Sentences

Consider the three sentence types in (6.1).

(6.1) a. A dog is a reptile.   (Generic categorization)
      b. Clark Kent is Superman. (Token-identity)
      c. Max is a dog.   (Ordinary categorization)

(6.1a) differs semantically from the others in that it is a *generic* sentence; it makes an assertion not about a particular individual but about dogs in general. Its usual first-order logic translation (6.2a) involves a universal quantifier and a conditional, obviously quite far removed from natural language syntax. The set-theoretic notation (6.2b) looks more promising, in that it divides into three parts that correspond to the subject, verb, and predicate NP of (6.1a).

(6.2) a. $\forall x(\mathrm{D}x \to \mathrm{R}x)$
     b. $\mathrm{D} \subseteq \mathrm{R}$

However, since we have abandoned set-theoretic notation for ordinary categorization sentences, generality requires us to abandon it here as well.

Within the theory developed in chapter 5, (6.1a) appears to express a judgment on the relationship of two [TYPE] concepts. Tentatively calling the relationship *IS INCLUDED IN*, we can formulate (6.3) as the appropriate conceptual structure.[1]

$$(6.3)\ \begin{bmatrix} \text{STATE} \\ \text{IS INCLUDED IN } (\begin{bmatrix} \text{THING TYPE} \\ \text{DOG} \end{bmatrix}, \begin{bmatrix} \text{THING TYPE} \\ \text{REPTILE} \end{bmatrix}) \end{bmatrix}$$

I wish to show, however, that IS INCLUDED IN is identical to the function BE that is responsible for token-identity and ordinary categorization judgments. If so, the only thing that makes (6.1a) a generic rather than an ordinary categorization sentence is that its subject expresses a [TYPE] rather than a [TOKEN]—not that a different relation holds between the two NPs. The evidence for this claim will parallel the evidence given in sections 5.2–3 for the conceptual unity of IS TOKEN-IDENTICAL TO and IS AN INSTANCE OF.

First notice that there are no formal considerations standing in the way of collapsing IS INCLUDED IN and BE, as there would be if [TOKEN] and [TYPE] structure were as distinct as the constants and predicates of first-order logic. Since BE must in any event make use of [TYPE] structure embedded inside the [TOKEN] in the first argument, nothing prevents it from reading such information out of a [TYPE] as the outermost constituent. Moreover, since [TOKEN] and [TYPE] information are in large part formally compatible, it would be a loss of generality not to allow BE to apply to [TYPES] in the first argument.

So far, this shows only the formal feasibility of treating IS INCLUDED IN as a special case of BE. Grammatical and lexical structure give positive arguments for doing so. The evidence centers around the fact that the same verb "be" occurs in all the sentences of (6.1). In set-theoretic notation it must express "⊆", "=", and "∈", respectively; in predicate logic it expresses "→", "=", and predicate-argument structure. By contrast, the present theory assigns "be" an invariant translation in the context between two NPs. Thus, if one asks why the linguistic facts are the way they are, only the present theory offers an explanation.

What are the grammatical criteria for translating the subject of (6.1a) into a [TYPE] rather than a [TOKEN] constituent? Recall that in ordinary categorization sentences, the predicate NP is read as a [TYPE] because of a lexical property of the verb "be." The analysis of (6.1a), however, is somewhat more complex. A combination of factors, including definiteness of the NP, choice of verb, and tense or aspect, combine to lead to the possibility of a generic [TYPE] reading in English. Let us survey these factors very roughly.

Consider definiteness first, holding the verb "be" and the tense constant. If the subject is indefinite, as in (6.1a), there is a generic reading. If the subject is definite, as in "The man is an idiot," there is only a [TOKEN] reading—unless the noun labels a species of animal or is read facetiously as one. For example, (6.4a) is ambiguous between categorization of a specific tiger and generic categorization of tigers; (6.4b) is similarly ambiguous, the generic reading having tongue-in-cheek overtones from treating "the linguist" as a species.

(6.4) a. The tiger is a frightening beast.
      b. The linguist is a connoisseur of Chinese food.

Next consider conditions on the verb. If the verb is stative (expresses a [STATE]), all the NPs that express arguments of the verb must satisfy the definiteness conditions for a [TYPE]. Thus (6.5a) is generic, since all the NPs are indefinite, but (6.5b) is specific.

(6.5) a. A cowboy has a gun.
      b. A cowboy has the gun (that you're looking for).

If the verb expresses an [EVENT], it must appear in simple present rather than present progressive. Thus (6.6a) is generic, (6.6b) specific.

(6.6) a. A beaver builds a dam.
      b. A beaver is building a dam.

Whatever the peculiarities of these conditions (along with others I have not bothered to mention), the point is that the [TYPE] interpretation this time is not the product of a special lexical marking on the verb, as it is in the case of the predicate NP. Rather, any verb can be used with a generically interpreted subject NP, provided a rather elaborate set of syntactic and semantic conditions is satisfied.

What this means is that the semantic treatment of generic categorization sentences must be sufficiently general to apply equally to all kinds of generic sentences. If we choose a solution in which "be" expresses a different function in generic sentences, we must accept the consequence that every verb does so. Conversely, if our solution permits all other verbs to retain their semantic structure in generic sentences, there is no reason to single out "be" for special treatment. The best possible explanation of the linguistic facts is to claim that the reading of "be" remains constant, the interior information in the reading of the subject remains constant, and only the TOKEN/TYPE feature of the subject varies in the specific-generic alternation.

Before considering another kind of evidence for the identity of BE and IS INCLUDED IN, let us mention some interesting formal consequences. Section 5.1 proposed the operator INSTANCE OF to incorporate explicit categorization information into a [TOKEN] and stated inference rule (5.7) to relate incorporated [TYPES] to categorization judgments.

$$(5.7) \quad \begin{bmatrix} \text{STATE TOKEN} \\ \text{IS AN INSTANCE OF } ([\text{TOKEN}]_i, [\text{TYPE}]_j) \end{bmatrix} \leftrightarrow$$
$$\begin{bmatrix} \text{TOKEN} \\ \text{INSTANCE OF } ([\text{TYPE}]_j) \end{bmatrix}_i$$

Generalizing categorization to [TYPE] inclusion makes possible a simple extension of INSTANCE OF, to explicitly incorporate a superordinate [TYPE] into a [TYPE] concept, as in (6.7).

$$(6.7) \quad \begin{bmatrix} \text{THING TYPE} \\ \text{DOG} \\ \text{INSTANCE OF } (\begin{bmatrix} \text{THING TYPE} \\ \text{ANIMAL} \end{bmatrix}) \end{bmatrix}$$

The inference rule that yields (6.7) from a generic categorization sentence is simply a generalization of (5.7):

(6.8) $\begin{bmatrix} \text{STATE} \\ \text{BE} \left([\,\text{X}\,]_i, \, [\,\text{TYPE}\,]_j \right) \end{bmatrix} \leftrightarrow \begin{bmatrix} \text{X} \\ \text{INSTANCE OF} \left([\,\text{TYPE}\,]_j \right) \end{bmatrix}_i$

Thus we have simplified both the formal syntax of INSTANCE OF—omitting the specification that it must be inserted into a [TOKEN]—and the inference rule relating this operator to BE. These two simplifications together give the system the capacity to incorporate categorization information explicitly into either [TOKENS] or [TYPES].

Similarly, the operator EXEMPLIFIED BY and its associated inference rule (5.9) can be generalized to express both exemplification and subcategorization of [TYPES]. For example, [TYPE DOG] may include the sort of information given in (6.9).

(6.9) $\begin{bmatrix} \text{THING TYPE} \\ \text{DOG} \\ \text{EXEMPLIFIED BY} \left(\begin{bmatrix} \text{THING TOKEN} \\ \text{SNOOPY} \end{bmatrix} \right) \\ \text{EXEMPLIFIED BY} \left(\begin{bmatrix} \text{THING TYPE} \\ \text{POODLE} \end{bmatrix} \right) \end{bmatrix}$

The generalized inference rule is (6.10).

(6.10) $\begin{bmatrix} \text{STATE} \\ \text{BE} \left([\,\text{X}\,]_i, \, [\,\text{TYPE}\,]_j \right) \end{bmatrix} \leftrightarrow \begin{bmatrix} \text{TYPE} \\ \text{EXEMPLIFIED BY} \left([\,\text{X}\,]_i \right) \end{bmatrix}_j$

As a further illustration of the flexibility of [TOKEN] and [TYPE] structure, consider inference rule (6.11).

(6.11) $\begin{bmatrix} \text{X} \\ \text{INSTANCE OF} \left(\begin{bmatrix} \text{TYPE} \\ \text{Y} \end{bmatrix}_j \right) \end{bmatrix}_i \leftrightarrow \begin{bmatrix} \text{X} \\ \text{Y} \end{bmatrix}_i$

Deriving from left to right, (6.11) incorporates into either a [TOKEN] or a [TYPE] certain features of a [TYPE] of which it is an instance. Thus, for example, (6.12a) leads to (6.12b), and (6.13a) to (6.13b).

(6.12) a. $\begin{bmatrix} \text{THING TYPE} \\ \text{SPANIEL} \\ \text{INSTANCE OF} \left(\begin{bmatrix} \text{THING TYPE} \\ \text{DOG} \\ \text{INSTANCE OF} \left(\begin{bmatrix} \text{THING TYPE} \\ \text{ANIMAL} \end{bmatrix} \right) \end{bmatrix} \right) \end{bmatrix}$

b. $\begin{bmatrix} \text{THING TYPE} \\ \text{SPANIEL} \\ \text{INSTANCE OF } \left(\begin{bmatrix} \text{THING TYPE} \\ \text{ANIMAL} \end{bmatrix} \right) \end{bmatrix}$

(6.13) a. $\begin{bmatrix} \text{THING TOKEN} \\ \text{SOCRATES} \\ \text{INSTANCE OF } \left(\begin{bmatrix} \text{THING TYPE} \\ \text{MAN} \\ \begin{bmatrix} \text{PROPERTY} \\ \text{MORTAL} \end{bmatrix} \end{bmatrix} \right) \end{bmatrix}$

b. $\begin{bmatrix} \text{THING TOKEN} \\ \text{SOCRATES} \\ \begin{bmatrix} \text{PROPERTY} \\ \text{MORTAL} \end{bmatrix} \end{bmatrix}$

The parallelism of these derivations to standard syllogisms should be obvious.

Deriving from right to left, (6.11) is a way of abstracting features of a [TOKEN] or a [TYPE] to form a new [TYPE]. This is the rule alluded to in section 5.2 that derives from an arbitrary $[\text{TOKEN}]_i$ a [TYPE] of THINGS LIKE i. Thus (6.11) can be seen basically as a way of recombining features to create new or more highly specific concepts.

In sum, the unification of [TOKEN] and [TYPE] information results in a theory remarkably general in its treatment of categorization, exemplification, and relationships among categories.

6.2 The Creativity of Generic Categorization

This section will show that generic and ordinary categorization have not only parallel formal properties but similar qualitative characteristics as well, as should be expected if they are essentially the same process.

There are two strategies for arriving at a generic categorization judgment. One, which might as well be called the *deductive* strategy, is to derive it by inference rules from previously stored generic categorizaton judgments. For instance, one might derive a dissenting judgment to "A dog is a reptile" from the conceptual equivalents of "A dog is a mammal" and "A mammal is not a reptile." This sort of strategy is modeled in theories like Fodor's (1975) meaning postulate theory or Collins and Quillian's (1969) theory of semantic networks: meaning postulates or links in the network represent (among other things) prestored generic categorization judgments between closely related concepts, and principles for traveling through the network represent rules of inference. These theories claim that all possible relations between concepts are either explicit in the network or derivable through chains of inference or association. (More discussion of these theories appears in section 7.5.)

While this sort of derivation of generic categorization judgments doubtless goes on, and can be modeled in the present theory by inference rules like (6.11), it cannot be all there is. It presupposes that every [TYPE] is linked to at least one other by a meaning postulate or an associative link, that is, that there is already at least one prestored generic categorization judgment from which others can be derived. However, it provides no way to establish the initial links. Fodor's solution to this difficulty is to claim that all the [TYPES] and links are innately given; the artificial intelligence tradition usually sidesteps the problem by restricting discourse to a microworld where all links can be stipulated.[2] However, as we saw in section 5.2, it is possible to construct new [TYPES]—in principle, at least one for every new [TOKEN]—and the links of these [TYPES] to the deductive network cannot in general be innately given. Hence there must be another source of generic categorization judgments besides deductive derivation from prestored information.

The alternative strategy for deriving a generic categorization judgment is, of course, to use whatever principles one uses in evaluating ordinary verbal and nonverbal categorization. In the present theory this alternative is freely available, since, with the exception of one feature, conceptual structure is the same for generic and ordinary categorization. As stressed in section 5.2, the creativity of categorization and category acquisition shows that this process cannot be any simple sort of lookup, but must instead be based on comparing the internal structures of the two relata.

This second strategy for arriving at generic categorization judgments might well be called the *inductive* strategy, since it represents a creative extrapolation from experience. What is significant in the present theory is that induction is not an isolated mystery, but is instead directly linked to the big mystery of ordinary categorization.

If [TYPE]-inclusion can be established by the same process that tests whether a [TOKEN] is an instance of a [TYPE], we should find the same overall pattern of judgments that appeared in ordinary categorization. The issue is complicated by the fact that people will whenever possible claim that a judgment is deductive, hence "objective," citing the premises from which it follows. However, the deductive method allows only two answers—yes or no—while inductive generic categorization, like ordinary categorization, should produce a three-way distribution of judgments into yes, no, and not sure. Since graded not sure judgments cannot be produced deductively, it is these that will reveal the characteristics of inductive generic categorization.

With this in mind, let us examine some cases for which people give either not sure or widely differing judgments.

(6.14) a. A piano is a percussion instrument.
        b. An australopithecine was a human.
        c. Washoe (the chimp)'s sign system is a language.
        d. An abortion is a murder.

In these cases, we have essentially all the relevant factual information, but we are at a point where intuition about the right-hand relatum is unclear. Instances of the left-hand [TYPE] are certainly not *typical* instances of the right-hand [TYPE], but they are also not distinct enough from the right-hand [TYPE] that we are sure we want to call them something else.

But even in these cases we are liable to contaminate the evidence. When something important is at stake, like lives, money, or even reputations, people get very emotional about the truth or falsity of such sentences. In fact, though, these sentences are not objectively true or false in the real world. Rather, they are analogous to the dubious #things# in section 3.1 and the dubious cup-bowl judgments in section 5.2. A piano is what it is, and maybe it's useful to call it a percussion instrument and maybe it's not. It is not a question of fact but of the user's needs. Though it may be of some importance to be able to say whether the sentences in (6.14) are true or false, the issue of their truth ultimately makes no sense in absolute terms.[3]

In sum, generic categorization judgments in the inductive mode share the general characteristics of ordinary categorization observed in section 5.2. They can be made creatively, comparing novel concepts at will; they have a distribution that includes not sure as well as yes and no; in those cases where a not sure judgment is not a consequence of inadequate factual knowledge, what is true of the world is not at issue.

I am inclined to suspect that not only is the purely deductive solution to generic categorization sentences insufficient, but in many situations it is little more than a surrogate for intuitive thinking, an attempt to consciously simulate the effects of the unconscious inductive solution. When we try to provide a definition for a word we all know (as opposed to a newly coined term), we test the definition by appeal to linguistic intuitions or to intuitions about instances of the categories in question. In other words, the intuitive judgment is the ultimate test—when one can make it.[4]

There has been a strong tendency in semantics to idealize away from situations where a judgment cannot be reached deductively and intuition does not provide a clear yes or no. When their existence is acknowledged, such situations are often treated as an inadequacy of factual knowledge (as in Putnam's (1975) treatment of "gold" mentioned in section 5.4)—or even as reason to throw up one's hands at the possibility of doing formal semantics (many have read Wittgenstein (1953) this way, for example). The appeal of such an idealization is that it treats relations among concepts as somehow immune from the vagaries of ordinary categorization (even if the real world isn't well-behaved, at least our thoughts should be!). I have tried to show here, though, that the idealization is inappropriate, in that it severs generic categorization from ordinary categorization. A more adequate approach is to seek a theory that both unifies the two processes and explains the possibility of uncertain judgments in either case.

6.3 Some Semantic Properties

We have argued that the treatment of generic categorization sentences (GCSs) must be unified with that of ordinary categorization, which in turn can be based on information derived through either linguistic or nonlinguistic modes. By definition, conceptual structure is the level at which such intermodal processing takes place. Hence GCSs must be evaluated at the level of conceptual structure.

This section will show that the information necessary to judge GCSs is also sufficient to make a variety of other linguistic judgments that have normally been called *semantic properties* of utterances. Since

GCSs are evaluated at the level of conceptual structure, these other semantic properties must be as well.

I do not want to claim here that *all* semantic properties of utterances can be reduced to properties of GCSs, but only that the information involved in GCS judgments plays a necessary role in a representative sample of the properties discussed by Katz (1972, 4–6). Since these examples are typical of those on which many theories of word meanings are based (see chapter 7), we will have shown that the ability to deal with GCSs bites off a substantial chunk of the traditional domain of semantic theory.[5]

First, judgments of *superordination* and *subordination* are directly related to judgments about GCSs. For example, the judgment that "bird" and "chicken" form a superordinate-subordinate pair depends on the same information as the judgment that "A chicken is a bird" is true. In fact, the [TYPE]-inclusion judgment (6.3) directly expresses superordination-subordination relations, as do the incorporated operators INSTANCE OF and EXEMPLIFIED BY when applied to [TYPES] as in (6.7) and (6.9).

Second, a judgment that two terms are *synonymous* depends on the same information as the judgment that the terms are mutually subordinate. For example, "A cellar is a basement" and "A basement is a cellar" are together sufficient to establish the synonymy of "cellar" and "basement."

Third, the crucial relationship of *entailment* between sentences depends in an interesting number of cases on the same information as a judgment about a GCS. For example, the judgment that "Max is a chicken" entails "Max is a bird" rests on the premise "A chicken is a bird," which is a GCS. Other cases of entailment cannot be reduced to GCSs, but can nonetheless be formalized in terms of conceptual structure. For example, the entailment from "Max laughed loudly" to "Max laughed" is a consequence of inference rule (4.16), which concerns the extractability of restrictive modifiers in conceptual constituents.

Fourth, the relationship of *inconsistency* between sentences is similar to entailment. For example, the inconsistency of "Max is a chicken" and "Max is a whale" rests on the same information as the judgment that "A chicken is a whale" and "A whale is a chicken" are both false. Again, as with entailment, not all cases can be reduced to GCSs, but other independently motivated rules of inference over [STATES], [ACTIONS], and [EVENTS] in conceptual structure deal with a wide range of further cases (see Jackendoff (1976) for some representative examples).

Fifth, the phenomenon of *semantic redundancy* depends on the same information as a related judgment about GCSs. For instance, the redundancy of "female aunt" depends on the truth of "An aunt is a female." Sixth, the *anomaly* of NPs such as "female uncle" and "silent paint" depends on the same information as the judgment that "An uncle is a female" and "Paint is silent" are nontrue.[6] Seventh, *semantic similarity*—the similarity between such words as "aunt," "cow," "nun," and "actress"—is based on the information that enables one to judge that there is a single y to which all these words are subordinate—in this case, that "x is female" is true with each of these words substituted for x.

6.4 The Nonautonomy of Semantics

We have shown, then, that a significant number of semantic properties of utterances require the same information one needs to evaluate GCSs at the level of conceptual structure. As observed in section 1.4, the defining characteristic of the level of *semantic* structure is that it is responsible for a formal account of semantic properties of utterances. Hence semantic and conceptual structure collapse into a unified level, and syntactic form is mapped by the correspondence rules directly into conceptual structure, without an intermediate level that accounts for purely linguistic inference. (This is the theory diagrammed in (1.4) of section 1.7.)

If this is the case, the distinction between "semantic" rules of linguistic inference and "pragmatic" rules of linguistic interaction with general knowledge is less marked than is often supposed. In a theory with an autonomous semantic level, the two kinds of rules involve different levels of mental representation. Here, however, they both are rules for the manipulation of conceptual structures; they deal with the same primitives and principles of combination. If there is a distinction between semantic and pragmatic rules, then, it lies only in the formal manipulations the rules perform on conceptual structure. For example, the principles involved in judging a sentence *true* potentially involve extralinguistic information as well as information within the sentence itself; hence "true" is a pragmatic notion. On the other hand, a judgment that a sentence is *analytic* involves only information conveyed by the sentence itself plus rules of (semantic) inference; hence "analytic" is a semantic notion. In either case, though, the information conveyed by the sentence is a conceptual structure.

Thus, although a terminological distinction between "semantic" and "pragmatic" notions undoubtedly remains useful, it is an open question whether it is a bifurcation of particular theoretical interest. Philosophers have generally assumed that it is: that there is a system of semantic rules that feeds but is not fed by rules of pragmatics. But there has been little explicit defense of the assumption.[7]

I tend to side with the artificial intelligence tradition in not worrying about whether a particular property is semantic or pragmatic. Chapter 8 will present some basis for making the distinction if one cares to, but evidence in chapter 10 will suggest that it is a mistake to place much theoretical weight on it. Certainly that has been the thrust of all the evidence presented so far.

Part III

WORD MEANINGS

Chapter 7
Problems of Lexical Analysis

7.1 Summary of Arguments in Previous Chapters

An important part of a theory of the information conveyed by language is, obviously, a theory of word meanings—the information conveyed by lexical items. The previous chapters have developed a number of criteria for a theory of word meanings and have used them in passing to criticize various proposals in the literature. The present chapter and the next will consolidate these arguments with other well-known evidence about the nature of word meanings, then present a more satisfactory theory. Briefly, we will see that standard decompositional theories of word meaning, formulated in terms of necessary and sufficient conditions, fail for several reasons. However, retreat to a nondecompositional theory, formulated in terms of prototypes, associative networks, or meaning postulates, is not a defensible alternative. The theory developed in chapter 8 will in fact be decompositional, but with a nonstandard notion of decomposition that meets the usual objections to necessary and sufficient conditions and that squares with the character of other perceptual and cognitive phenomena.

Let us begin by reviewing the relevant arguments from chapters 3–6. We have maintained unrelentingly that word meanings must be treated as internalized mental representations. This rules out in advance an extensional theory of meaning, which identifies the meaning of "dog" with the set of all dogs (or with the set of all dogs in all possible worlds). It also rules out a Platonic theory such as Katz's (1980), where word meanings are abstract objects existing independently of minds.

We may reject as well a theory like Putnam's (1975) doctrine of the "division of linguistic labor," in which only experts are said to possess the meanings of words. Rather, we take it that some people have more highly specified meanings for some words than other people; and it is a sociological fact that people often accept an expert's authority when faced with uncertain intuitions.[1]

More specifically, chapter 6 argued that word meanings are expressions of conceptual structure. That is, there is not a form of mental representation devoted to a strictly semantic level of word meanings, distinct from the level at which linguistic and nonlinguistic information are compatible. This means that if, as is often claimed, a distinction exists between dictionary and encyclopedic lexical information, it is not a distinction of level; these kinds of information are cut from the same cloth. (See sections 7.3–4 for more comment.)

Chapter 4 argued that the meaning of a lexical item of any major syntactic category (noun, verb, adjective, adverb, preposition) is a function of zero or more arguments that maps into a conceptual constituent of one of the major ontological categories. Its arguments are also conceptual constituents, and are filled by the readings of the major phrasal categories that the lexical item strictly subcategorizes. If the lexical item strictly subcategorizes no other phrases (e.g., "dog," "red," "afterward"), its reading is of course a constant, that is, a complete conceptual constituent.

This uniformity of conceptual structure across lexical categories rules out theories in which, say, nouns and verbs are treated in radically different fashion. Because of its inconsistent treatment of the relation between subcategorization and argument places, we cited predicate logic in chapter 4 as one such theory. For another example, a theory of verb meanings such as Simmons's (1973), based entirely on case frames (the roles of strictly subcategorized phrases), accords no content to lexical items that do not strictly subcategorize anything. Such a theory must be supplemented by a different theory for nouns such as "dog" and verbs such as "rain" and is therefore unacceptable. Schank's (1973) Conceptual Dependency Analysis likewise makes extensive claims about verb meanings but offers no analysis at all for nouns, suggesting that it too is susceptible to this objection.

The arguments of chapter 5 established two crucial properties of word meanings. First, from the creativity of categorization and [TYPE] acquisition, we argued that word meanings must have internal structure that can be compared with the structure of other [TO-

KENS] and [TYPES]. Second, from the distribution of categorization judgments into yes/no/not-sure, we argued that the internal structure cannot be a set of necessary and sufficient conditions. Both of these arguments were buttressed by evidence from chapter 3 that perceptually derived [TOKEN] concepts also possess these characteristics. If cognition needs concepts with such properties to deal with perception, we should have no qualms in positing them for word meanings as well.

Because of the property of creativity, we rejected theories in which word meanings are treated as unanalyzed monads whose relationships are established through a network of meaning postulates or associative links. We return to these theories in section 7.5.

Because of the distribution of judgments, we rejected theories in which word meanings are treated as sets of necessary and sufficient conditions on category membership—which is to say, most semantic marker theories. Our argument in chapter 5 was rather cursory, so as not to obscure the main lines of discussion there. Sections 7.2–4 will present a more detailed review of the defects of such theories.

In the course of our discussion, the need for notions like typicality and normality will crop up repeatedly. On most such occasions I will immediately change the subject, deferring more serious treatment of these notions to chapter 8.

It may be useful to mention three issues I will not be concerned with here. First, it is irrelevant whether the lexical entry of a word contains the word's meaning or only a pointer to the index of the word's meaning. For us, the issue is simply what structure the meaning has. Second, some theorists (e.g., Katz and Fodor (1963)) treat polysemous words as having multiple readings attached to a single lexical entry; others (e.g., Weinreich (1966)) argue that such words have multiple lexical entries, one for each reading. The choice between these possibilities is a major concern of Miller (1978). Again, we will be interested only in the information content of the readings, not in exactly how they are stored. For example, it will be important to us to be able to say that the verbs in "John broke the glass" and "The glass broke" are formally related in conceptual structure, and that the two "bank"s in "the river bank" and "the Bank of England" are not. But we will not care whether either "broke" or "bank" is listed in the lexicon once or twice.

Finally, we will not be concerned with deciding what format for storing lexical information facilitates real-time lexical lookup and processing. This appears to be one of the major issues dividing theories of semantic memory (see Smith (1978)). We will subordinate this issue to others because one can represent more or less the same information in either of the two most popular formats, internal features or external network links (see section 7.5). As it is the information itself and not its ease of access that concerns us, we leave the choice of format open, insofar as it affects only questions of processing.

This is not to say that any of these three questions is uninteresting. It is just that for present purposes it is useful to abstract away from them in pursuit of different goals. The proposals to be made here can be incorporated into a theory with readings internal or external to lexical entries, with single or multiple entries for polysemous words, and with predominantly concept-internal or concept-external information structure. I leave the choice to the reader.

7.2 Exhaustive Decomposition into Primitives

Among the theories of word meaning that have been (or can be) cast in mentalistic terms, by far the most numerous and most detailed are based on the following premise:

(7.1) The meaning of a word can be exhaustively decomposed into a finite set of conditions that are collectively necessary and sufficient to determine the reference of the word.

Many make the following assumption as well:

(7.2) The satisfaction conditions are stated in terms of a finite set of semantic/conceptual primitives.

Most philosophical treatments of meaning, particularly those based on Tarskian truth-conditions, assume (7.1), at least relative to some model. Katz's (1966, 1972) fairly explicit theory of decomposition assumes and defends (7.1) and appears to accept (7.2). Generative semantics (e.g., Lakoff 1971)) depends crucially on (7.1) and (7.2), as do Schank's (1973, 1975) theory of Conceptual Dependency Structure and Norman and Rumelhart's (1975) theory of structural networks. The analyses of Miller and Johnson-Laird's (1976) procedural semantics presume both, though these authors express reservations here and there in their discussion. I shudder to admit that even I have been guilty of these assumptions, for example in the verb analyses in Jackendoff (1976).

A theory of necessary and sufficient conditions built from primitives nicely satisfies the common-sense intuition that words have definite and precise meanings. This probably accounts for the theory's great popularity and antiquity, and for the fact that it has so frequently been offered without seeming to need a defense. However, as Putnam (1975, 192–193) cautions,

The amazing thing about the theory of meaning is how long the subject has been in the grip of philosophical misconceptions, and how strong these misconceptions are. Meaning has been identified with a necessary and sufficient condition by philosopher after philosopher.... On the other side, it is amazing how weak the grip of the facts has been.

Fodor, Garrett, Walker, and Parkes (1980) advocate an extreme suspicion of (7.1)–(7.2), on the grounds that the number of convincing exhaustive decompositions in the literature is vanishingly small. To be sure, the partial decompositions offered by nearly everyone are far from uninteresting; but sooner or later, one always seems to encounter a stubborn unanalyzed residue. In the analysis of color terms such as "red," for instance, this happens almost immediately. Surely a decomposition of "red" must include the stipulation that it is a color, in order to account for the simplest inferences and oppositions the word takes part in. But once the marker COLOR is removed from the reading of "red," what is left to decompose further? How can one make sense of redness minus coloration?

An area of the lexicon for which success at decomposition has often been claimed is the class of verbs. In particular, the extraction of components such as causation, change, and action from the readings of verbs has led to substantial insight. However, decomposition is rarely if ever complete. Consider the analysis of "kill" as CAUSE TO BECOME NOT ALIVE, a mainstay of decomposition theory ever since McCawley (1968) used it to motivate generative semantics. CAUSE, BECOME, and NOT are likely primitives, but one is not so sure about ALIVE. Moreover, little descriptive inadequacies ooze around the edges of the decomposition. A rock's being not alive does not qualify it as dead. One can die slowly or horribly, but it is odd to talk of becoming dead slowly or horribly. As Jerry A. Fodor (1970) points out, one can cause someone to die on Tuesday by shooting him on Monday, but one cannot kill someone on Tuesday by shooting him on Monday. These differences are glossed over by the proposed analysis.

If we move to the slightly more complex word "assassinate," the problems are more severe (as observed by Chomsky (1972, 143)). Among the differences between "kill" and "assassinate" are that the object of "assassinate" must be a prominent figure and that the subject must be credited with political motives (for example, it is somewhat odd to speak of John Lennon's murder as an assassination). How such restrictions as these can be decomposed into primitives has never to my knowledge been addressed. Thus the decomposition of verbs, though providing richer structure than the decomposition of "red," ultimately founders on the same difficulty: the appearance of an unanalyzed residue.

The original Katz-Fodor (1963) theory of word meanings dealt with the semantic residue of decomposition by claiming that there are two parts to a word meaning: a collection of *semantic markers* and a *distinguisher*. The semantic markers were to constitute the formal part of the meaning, that is, the part that plays a role in determining semantic properties of utterances. The distinguisher was to be an unsystematic part that played no role in formal semantics; it was here that Katz and Fodor disposed of the semantic residue.

However, Bolinger (1965) demonstrates that the notion of distinguisher is suspect, by constructing phrases that are disambiguated or anomalous on the basis of material that Katz and Fodor had assigned to distinguishers. For instance, for the most salient sense of "bachelor," Katz and Fodor proposed the semantic markers HUMAN and MALE, and the distinguisher NEVER MARRIED. From the anomaly of "the bachelor's legitimate daughter," though, we see that information about the nature of marriage and the legality of offspring can play a role in the semantic properties of "bachelor," and hence that NEVER MARRIED must be broken down into semantic markers. Through numerous examples like this, Bolinger shows that inference and anomaly can turn on the most obscure aspects of a word's meaning; hence the distinguisher must be virtually void of content, and exhaustive decomposition is to be expected.[2]

McCawley (1978) makes an important proposal that addresses one problem of decomposition. He points out that the adjective "pale" can be applied felicitously to all primary color names except "red." "Pale red" is a little odd, he claims, because there is a lexical item "pink" that covers the same semantic territory. However, there still are uses for "pale red" in fringe cases, for example to designate shades between pink and red, or perhaps to designate a translucent red. McCawley suggests that "pink" indeed has the semantic decomposition "pale red," but that there is a Gricean sort of principle to the effect that the use of the syntactically complex expression in place of the lexical item designates a noncentral instance of the category in question. Since there is no lexical item for "pale green," the principle does not apply, but most applications of "pale red" are displaced by "pink."

McCawley then applies this principle in the case of "kill," noting that one uses "cause to die" most felicitously when there is a relatively indirect relation between the agent and the patient's death; "kill" displaces "cause to die" in the most central cases. On the other hand, since there is no lexical item that decomposes as "cause to laugh," this phrase covers both central and noncentral cases.

While McCawley's proposal gives an interesting account of the disparity between lexical items and putative periphrastic constructions, it does not eliminate the residue of "red" over "color," the political primitives in "assassinate," or the legal kinship primitives in "bachelor." Thus it does not resolve all the problems of exhaustive decomposition. Moreover, it makes crucial use of the notion "central instance of a concept." We now turn to the problems this notion raises for a theory of necessary and sufficient conditions.

7.3 Fuzziness

The objection to necessary and sufficient conditions that played a major role in chapters 3 and 5 is that they predict secure yes or no judgments for categorization. If some object meets all the conditions, it is judged an instance of the category; if it fails to meet one or more, it is judged a nonmember, and that's that. But for many if not most categories this is not the case. Rather, as Putnam (1975, 133) observes,

. . . words in a natural language are not generally "yes-no": there are things of which the description "tree" is clearly true and things of which the description "tree" is clearly false, to be sure, but there are a host of borderline cases. Worse, the line between the clear cases and the borderline cases is itself fuzzy.

We saw this in the case of vases, cups, and bowls in section 5.2, for example.

Three responses to this problem have emerged in the literature. One is Searle's (1958) idea of a collection of criterial attributes, some large enough number of which is sufficient for category membership. Strictly speaking, this does not account for fuzziness without further refinement, for it still predicts a yes answer if "enough" criteria are met and a no otherwise. If a scale could be defined on "enough," though, one could presumably elicit a gradation of judgments. Even so, Searle's proposal still does not account for gradations of judgment that involve variation in only one criterial attribute, such as the height-width ratio in the cup-bowl paradigm and hue in color judgment. Thus this suggestion alone is insufficient. (We will take up a more detailed version of it in section 8.3.)

Another response is to use the notion of "fuzzy set"—a set whose membership is defined not categorically, but in terms of degree or probability of membership. For instance, one might think of a typical bird such as a robin as 100% bird, but a penguin as perhaps only 71% bird and a bat as 45% bird. According to this view, the gradation of judgments is a consequence of the gradation of degree of membership, with values in the neighborhood of 50% resulting in the most difficult judgments. (The mathematics of fuzzy sets is developed in Zadeh (1965); the notion was popularized in linguistics by Lakoff (1972).)

One difficulty with this view (pointed out to me by John Macnamara) is that a penguin is not 71% bird and 29% something else, it just *is* a bird. It may not be a typical bird, but it is still no less a bird than a robin or a sparrow is. One might respond by trying to interpret the percentages in terms of degree of confidence of judgment. But this makes the second objection only more patent: the theory provides no account of where the percentages might have come from. To derive the one-dimensional degree of membership, one needs a theory of the internal structure of the concepts in question—which is what we are trying to develop in the first place. Fuzzy set theory at best gives only a crude way to describe observations about category judgments; it does not even purport to address the mechanism behind them.[3]

Both Searle's proposal and fuzzy set theory have abandoned necessary and sufficient conditions in favor of a less rigid sort of condition, an approach that appears to me to be on the right track. A third possible response appears in Katz (1977): to make a distinction between "dictionary" and "encyclopedia" information associated with a lexical item, and to claim that factors leading to graded judgments are of the latter sort and hence not the responsibility of semantics. Such a move attempts by definition to preserve necessary and sufficient conditions as the semantic structures of lexical items.

However, Katz's position entails that the distinctions among color names must be nonsemantic, since hue information is graded. This means that in this theory (7.3a) is contradictory (false by virtue of its semantic structure) but (7.3b) is not; rather, (7.3b) is only false by virtue of encyclopedia information.

(7.3) a. Green things are not colored.
      b. Green things are blue.

To say that semantic theory, thus narrowly understood, should be responsible for (7.3a) but not for (7.3b) strikes me as an arbitrary bifurcation of the data whose only purpose is to save the theory.[4]

It is perhaps instructive to follow this point a little further. Katz (1974; 1975, section 4) devotes some effort to a reply to Tarski's (1956a) and Quine's (1953) observations that analyticity (truth by virtue of semantic structure) seems to be subject to unclear judgments. Quine concludes from such observations that the analytic-synthetic distinction is incoherent. Katz apparently accepts the validity of Quine's conclusion, granted the premises, for he attacks only the premises, namely, that there are unclear judgments of analyticity. It seems not to occur to either him or Quine that "analytic" is just like almost every other word. Unclear cases of doors and tigers do not make the distinction between doors and nondoors or between tigers and nontigers incoherent; why then should such cases be grounds for rejecting the analytic-synthetic distinction?[5]

Thus an apparently important philosophical dispute has arisen pointlessly, out of a failure to recognize the ubiquity of fuzziness in word meanings. The moral is that fuzziness must not be treated as a defect in language; nor is a theory of language defective that countenances it. Rather, as emphasized in previous chapters, fuzziness is an inescapable characteristic of the concepts that language expresses. To attempt to define it out of semantics is only evasion.

7.4 Family Resemblances

The gradation of height-width ratio in cups and bowls and the gradation of hues in color judgments both represent one sort of problem for necessary and sufficient conditions: the existence of graded attributes along which it is impossible to draw sharp boundaries. A different sort of problem arises with attributes that are subject to discrete exceptions. If it is a necessary part of being human to have two legs or high intelligence, then are one-legged people and imbeciles not human? If having stripes is criterial for tigers, are albino tigers tigers? And so forth. One response to this difficulty is to allow conditions that incorporate the notion of normality (a *normal* tiger has stripes, etc.). However, this solution rests on an adequate treatment of "normal," and many apparently agree with Katz (1975, 99) that a definition involving normality is little better than no definition at all. Nonetheless, there is appeal in this idea, and we will come back to it in section 8.3.

Those who reject the use of normality in definitions must adopt the tactic that only exceptionless conditions can be part of a word's meaning; if we haven't yet found the necessary conditions, we just have to look harder. Putnam (1975), for instance, places his faith in science to determine the extension of natural kind terms like "water" and "gold"; similarly, one might try to explicate "human" and "tiger" in terms of conditions on DNA. But there are two serious objections. First, what we are interested in is the prescientific, intuitive, and probably unconscious theory which people carry around in their heads, and which may lead to the questions that motivate scientific inquiry. People had a meaning for "tiger" long before DNA was dreamed of. (Katz (1974) makes this objection.) Second, even from Putnam's point of view, such a faith in science is only sensible when dealing with words for which there might conceivably be a scientific theory. How could there be (and why would anyone be tempted to seek) a science explicating what is necessary for something to be an instance of "pebble" or "puddle" or "giggle" or "snort" or "cute"? But a theory of word meanings must encompass these words too.

What of the alternative that it is the semanticist rather than the natural scientist to whom the responsibility for necessary and sufficient conditions is to be entrusted? Wittgenstein (1953, 31–32) dashes these hopes in a passage that it is almost a cliché to quote:

66. Consider for example the proceedings that we call "games". I mean board-games, card-games, ball-games, Olympic games, and so on. What is common to them all?—Don't say: "There must be something common, or they would not be called 'games' "—but *look and see*

whether there is anything common to all.—For if you look at them you will not see something that is common to *all,* but similarities, relationships, and a whole series of them at that. To repeat: don't think, but look! . . . Are they all "amusing"? Compare chess with noughts and crosses. Or is there always winning and losing, or competition between players? Think of patience. In ball games there is winning and losing, but when a child throws his ball at the wall and catches it again, this feature has disappeared. [This example is better in the original German, where the term is "Ballspiel."—RJ] Look at the parts played by skill and luck; and at the difference between skill in chess and skill in tennis. Think now of games like ring-a-ring-a-roses; here is the element of amusement, but how many other characteristic features have disappeared! And we can go through the many, many other groups of games in the same way; we can see how similarities crop up and disappear.

And the result of this examination is: we see a complicated network of similarities overlapping and criss-crossing: sometimes overall similarities, sometimes similarity of detail.

67. I can think of no better expression to characterize these similarities than "family resemblances"; for the various resemblances between members of a family: build, features, colour of eyes, gait, temperament, etc. etc. overlap and criss-cross in the same way.—And I shall say: 'games' form a family.

In short, necessary and sufficient conditions (even graded ones) are inadequate to characterize the word "game"; and it is clear from the context of the passage that Wittgenstein considers this not an isolated counterexample but a typical instance of how words are understood.

Wittgenstein's point has been widely appreciated for noun meanings, but in general, faith in decomposition for verbs has remained unshaken. However, section 8.6 will show that the verb "see" has this "family resemblance" character, suggesting that necessary and sufficient conditions are inadequate for any interesting part of the lexicon.

There have been various reactions to Wittgenstein's argument. In the last section we encountered Searle's (1958) suggestion that the totality of conditions in a definition need not be fulfilled—only a sufficiently large number of them. In the case of the single graded conditions under discussion there, this suggestion was inappropriate, but it does apply nicely to the family resemblance problem. Again, we defer discussion to section 8.3.

A related suggestion appears in the work of Smith, Shoben, and Rips (1974), who place on each condition a degree of "definingness." Conditions of lesser degree are permitted to have exceptions, and in cases of doubt, the more highly defining conditions are to be relied upon. However, Smith, Shoben, and Rips assume there is a central core of most essential conditions that serve as a "dictionary" definition. Since this is just what Wittgenstein denies, they have not really solved the problem.

The same difficulty appears in Katz's (1977) attempt to separate out dictionary definitions of necessary and sufficient conditions from an encyclopedia entry that is subject to exceptions. Though he cites Labov in this connection, Katz surprisingly does not mention Wittgenstein (see note 4).

Finally, Rosch and Mervis (1975) and Mervis and Pani (1980) develop a theory of categories in which family resemblance phenomena play an essential part. They show experimentally how artificial categories of objects can be learned whose defining conditions are subject to exceptions. Those instances that satisfy all or most defining conditions are perceived as more central instances and are more easily learned and remembered. This confirms Wittgenstein's argument and extends it beyond word meanings to perceptual concepts.[6]

All of these responses again enrich the narrow theory of necessary and sufficient conditions into something more flexible. Katz (1966, 72–73), on the other hand, attempts to defend it against Wittgenstein's objection. His argument consists essentially of two points. The first is that Wittgenstein has not *proven* that there are no necessary and sufficient conditions for "game"; he has merely been unable to find any. Moreover, there *are* necessary and sufficient conditions for words like "brother" ("male sibling") and "highball" ("drink of diluted spirits served with ice in a tall glass"), and Wittgenstein has not given any principled distinction between these cases and "game." Without such a distinction, Katz says, Wittgenstein has no case.

But clearly it is not up to Wittgenstein to prove that necessary and sufficient conditions never work; it is up to Katz to prove that they *always* work. As Fodor, Garrett, Walker, and Parkes (1980) observe, practically all the plausible examples of necessary and sufficient conditions come from jargon vocabularies ("ketch," "highball"), kinship vocabularies ("grandmother," "bachelor"), and axiomatized systems ("triangle"). Thus Wittgenstein appears closer to the truth than Katz.

Katz's second point is that if "game" turns out not to have necessary and sufficient conditions, we can treat it as an ambiguous lexical item, picking apart the family resemblances into different senses, each of which is a bundle of necessary and sufficient conditions. Even if this move succeeds technically, though, it evades an important issue: is "game" really ambiguous? Katz's proposal treats the varieties of games as being as distinct as a river bank and the Bank of England, which hardly seems correct. Of course, it is not logically necessary that all these diverse activities should be called games, as witness the difference between German "Spiel" of Wittgenstein's original and "game" of the translation; but it does not by any stretch of the imagination seem to be mere coincidence either. The degree to which the collection of activities called "games" is *not* fortuitous is captured by Wittgenstein's notion of family resemblances among them. It is not captured by splitting "game" into a number of separate lexical readings. Thus Katz has failed really to address Wittgenstein's point. (Our discussion of the verb "see" in section 8.6 will reinforce this argument.)

In closing this discussion, I should emphasize that all the objections raised in this section and the past two apply equally to any of the decomposition theories that assume (7.1) and (7.2). I have singled out Katz's work for discussion only because no one else to my knowledge has explicitly defended necessary and sufficient conditions rather than simply assuming them.

To sum up, it appears that at least three sorts of conditions are needed to adequately specify word meanings. First, we cannot do without *necessary* conditions: e.g., "red" must contain the necessary condition COLOR and "tiger" must contain at least THING. Second, we need graded conditions to designate hue in color concepts and the height-width ratio of cups, for example. These conditions specify a focal or central value for a continuously variable attribute; the most secure positive judgments are for those examples that lie relatively close to the focal value of the attribute in question. I will call such conditions *centrality* conditions. Third, we need conditions that are typical but subject to exceptions—for instance, the element of competition in games or a tiger's stripedness. Bundles of such *typicality* conditions lead to the family resemblance phenomena pointed out by Wittgenstein. Words can differ widely in which kinds of conditions are most prominent. Kinship terms, for example, are among the purest cases involving necessary conditions; in color names, centrality conditions play the most crucial role.

As an illustration of the difference between centrality and typicality conditions, contrast redness as such with the redness of apples. The former is a continuously graded notion; as examples get farther from focal red, they are judged to be worse instances of red. There is no "exceptional red" that is close to focal green. On the other hand, since there are yellow and green apples, the redness of apples is a typicality condition. The exceptions are discrete; there is no gradation from red apples through orange apples to yellow and green, with green being the least typical case. Rather, the typicality conditions for apple color specify a number of focal values, with red being most typical or highest valued. (I am indebted to Richard McGinn for this example.)

We cannot go further into centrality and typicality conditions without talking about how multiple conditions interact. I defer this to the next chapter, finishing this one with a discussion of the other most popular candidate for the theory of word meanings: meaning postulates or semantic networks.

7.5 Network/Meaning Postulate Theories

As remarked earlier, this type of theory has arisen in two largely independent lines of research. In the theory of semantic memory and in artificial intelligence (see Collins and Quillian (1969), Simmons (1973), Kintsch (1974), and Scragg (1976)), the representation of lexical information is called an *associative network* or a *semantic net*. In the philosophical tradition, Fodor, following Carnap (1956) and Bar-Hillel (1967), has claimed that lexical information is to be stated in the form of *meaning postulates* (Fodor (1975); Fodor, Fodor, and Garrett (1975); Fodor, Garrett, Walker, and Parkes (1980)). What is common to both is that they treat lexical entries as semantically unanalyzed monads; semantic information about lexical items is stored externally in terms of network links or meaning postulates such as those in (7.4).

(7.4) a. ISA (DOG, ANIMAL)
       b. RED$(x) \rightarrow$ COLORED(x)
       c. KILL$(x,y) \rightarrow$ CAUSE$(x,$ DIE$(y))$

By passing through the network according to various general principles of inference, one can derive a great variety of less immediate connections between concepts.[7]

In sections 5.2 and 6.2 we argued that this cannot be all there is to semantics or cognition, for the productivity of such a system is limited to the finite number of concepts represented as nodes in the network. It cannot account for the production of new [TOKEN] or [TYPE] concepts, nor can it account for creativity in categorizing these new concepts. Accordingly, it must be supplemented with mechanisms for constructing new nodes and links.

Thus supplemented, network theory turns out to be a notational variant of semantic marker theory, at least for purposes of representing lexical information. (It may have different consequences for processing.) As an initial illustration of this point, the inference rules developed in chapter 6 give us means for converting freely between entry-internal and entry-external information formats:

$$(7.5) \quad \begin{bmatrix} \text{TOKEN/TYPE} \\ \text{X} \\ \text{Y} \end{bmatrix}_i \xleftrightarrow{(6.11)} \begin{bmatrix} \text{TOKEN/TYPE} \\ \text{X} \\ \text{INSTANCE OF } \left(\begin{bmatrix} \text{TYPE} \\ \text{Y} \end{bmatrix}_j \right) \end{bmatrix}_i$$

$$\xleftrightarrow{(6.8)} \begin{bmatrix} \text{STATE} \\ \text{BE } \left(\begin{bmatrix} \text{TOKEN/TYPE} \\ \text{X} \end{bmatrix}_i, \begin{bmatrix} \text{TYPE} \\ \text{Y} \end{bmatrix}_j \right) \end{bmatrix}$$

The left-hand expression in (7.5) represents the information Y as an internal semantic marker of concept i. By rule (6.11), Y can be incorporated in a [TYPE] listed within concept i; by rule (6.8), [TYPE]$_j$ can be externalized into an explicit categorization judgment, in effect a meaning postulate for concept i. The derivation can also go the other way, converting a meaning postulate into an internal semantic marker. Judicious use of abstraction operators can help to convert more complex meaning postulates into semantic marker format.

As might be expected of a notational variant, network/meaning postulate theory inherits the defects of semantic marker theory, in only slightly disguised form. First consider the difficulty of exhaustive decomposition. Fodor takes it to be a virtue of his theory that exhaustive decomposition is unnecessary. For example, he claims that "red" needs only the meaning postulate (7.4b); since both "red" and "colored" are primitive, there is no question of an unanalyzed residue in the former. The problems involved in treating "kill" as "cause to die" are handled similarly.

But the resulting theory of "red" is informationally equivalent to a semantic marker theory that gives COLORED as the only marker of "red." It fails to explain how we decide that some #things# are red and some are not. Saying that there is a primitive RED merely evades the issue. Likewise, recall Bolinger's argument against distinguishers:

virtually any obscure aspect of lexical information can be the basis for an inference or an anomaly. In a meaning postulate theory, this means that one is forced to add endless meaning postulates until the inferential properties of the items in question are exhausted; these parallel precisely the semantic markers that must be added in the decomposition theory. Thus nothing is gained in terms of ability to represent lexical information.

The fuzziness and family resemblance problems are not resolved by network/meaning postulate theory either. Fodor (1975, 62) notices that there may be objects such that we cannot be sure whether to call them "chair" or not. He accounts for this by attributing the fuzziness of "chair" not to the connection between the word and the corresponding concept, but to the concept [CHAIR] itself. So far this is exactly the approach adopted here—but it leaves unaddressed how to characterize the fuzziness of the concept, the issue that should be of concern. In chapters 5 and 6 we argued that object categorization and linguistic inference depend on the same kind of information and produce the same range of judgments. Thus, whatever theory Fodor presupposes to account for the uncertain *categorization* of #objects# as #chairs#, it will also account for *inferences* involving the word "chair," fuzziness and all, rendering an independent component of meaning postulates for "chair" superfluous. By failing to recognize the unity of linguistic and nonlinguistic information, Fodor has satisfied himself with too easy an answer. (This seems particularly odd in view of the fact that the main burden of his book is that semantic theory is to be concerned with the "language of thought.")

Any of the refinements of semantic marker theory could of course be incorporated into a network/meaning postulate theory—for example, by allowing a degree of confidence, membership, typicality, etc., as part of a network link or meaning postulate. Alternatively, one could externalize centrality and typicality conditions by distinguishing "necessary," "centrality," and "typicality" links. "Cup," for example, could have a centrality link to a concept "height-width ratio equals 1"; "tiger" could have a typicality link to the concept "striped." Such possibilities crop up in the semantic memory literature from time to time. But patently the same information is being encoded; one must ask exactly the same questions to develop an item's network links as to develop its semantic markers.

What are Fodor's arguments in favor of meaning postulate theory? Besides the hopelessness of stating exhaustive necessary and sufficient conditions, which, as we have seen, he only postpones, his main argument is based on real-time processing. Although I have so far eschewed such arguments, this one can't be avoided.

Fodor says that there would be evidence for semantic marker theory if it turned out that semantically complex words take more processing time than semantically simple words. For instance, if "kill" has the same semantic structure as "cause to die," then one might expect "kill" to take more time to process than "die," because it contains an extra semantic unit. Similarly, it is well known that sentences containing overt negation are significantly more difficult to process than corresponding positive sentences; if "bachelor" contains the negative semantic marker "not married," one might expect it to cause commensurate difficulties. In an elaborate and careful series of experiments, Fodor, Fodor, and Garrett (1975) show that there are no such semantic complexity effects on processing time; they also cite experiments of Kintsch (1974) to this effect. This result, they claim, is predicted by meaning postulate theory, in which each word is of the same semantic complexity, namely, primitive.

I want to undermine this argument indirectly by showing that one should not expect such semantic complexity effects. Consider motor concepts. A skilled musician can look at a passage of printed music, see it as an A-major scale in such-and-such an octave, and rip it off as one gesture. At the level of awareness there is a simplex unit #A-major scale# that is read and executed; but (as Alan Prince pointed out to me) at some level this unit must have enough internal structure to get all the right instructions to the fingers. Any musician can attest that one of the tricks to playing fast is to make larger and larger passages form simplex units from the point of view of awareness—to "chunk" the input and output. This suggests that processing speed is linked not so much to the gross measure of information processed as to the number of highest-level units that must be treated serially. Otherwise chunking wouldn't help.

There is no reason to suppose that semantic processing works differently from motor and visual processing. That is, it is probably mistaken to expect word processing time to reflect word-internal semantic complexity. Rather, a word should be regarded as an encoding of a chunk of semantic information; it is the retrieval of such high-level chunks that should be expected to limit processing speed—exactly the result of Fodor's and Kintsch's experiments.

This takes care of the "kill"-"die" argument, but the argument from negation requires further discussion. The argument is that there are four possible sources of negation in English: explicit negatives such as "not," morphological negatives such as the prefixes "un-" and "in-," implicit negatives such as "deny," and words involving "purely definitional negation" such as "bachelor." The first three of these classes have syntactic effects on the rest of the sentence; for example, they permit the use of the quantifier "any" within their scope, which cannot appear in positive declarative nongeneric clauses (see Klima (1964)):

(7.6) a. *They found any.   (no negative)
       b. They did not find any.   (explicit negative)
       c. It is impossible to find any. (morphological negative)
       d. They deny that they found any. (implicit negative)

By contrast, the purely definitional negatives do not have such syntactic effects. Fodor, Fodor, and Garrett (1975) find that explicit negatives are most difficult to process, morphological and implicit negatives slightly easier, and purely definitional negatives significantly easier, in fact indistinguishable from nonnegative words. They argue that therefore one wants a theory in which the purely definitional negatives contain no negation. This requirement is satisfied by the meaning postulate theory, in which definitional negatives are primitive.

However, this leaves us in the position of having no account of why implicit negatives like "deny" take longer to process, since these too must be semantically primitive in Fodor's theory. The real generalization, it seems to me, is that increased processing time is a function of the magnitude of potential interaction between the negative word and the rest of the sentence. As Klima (1964) shows, explicit negatives have the most drastic effects on the syntactic and semantic composition of the rest of the sentence; morphological and implicit negatives take part in only some of these interactions; and, as noted, purely definitional negatives take part in none. Thus, this hypothesis for the source of processing difficulty, unlike Fodor's, yields the correct gradation of difficulty. Moreover, it is consistent with either a semantic marker or a meaning postulate theory. The problem in this theory, which must be solved in any event for an adequate grammar, is to explain how the different types of negation produce different interactions with the rest of the sentence.[8]

To sum up: we have shown that network/meaning postulate theory is a notational variant of semantic marker theory with respect to the representation of lexical information. All the problems of semantic marker theory arise analogously in network/meaning postulate theory, and at least one set of alleged real-time processing arguments for the latter actually fails to decide between the two, or even perhaps favors the former.

Thus, while I agree with Fodor and his associates on the inadequacy of necessary and sufficient conditions, they have given no valid reason for abandoning the notion of lexical decomposition in semantic theory. We will therefore continue to assume that lexical items do have semantic decompositions, though not into necessary and sufficient conditions. As will be seen, the assumption of decomposition is essential to all the analyses that follow.

Chapter 8
Preference Rule Systems

8.1 Wertheimer's Principles of Grouping

To work out a more comprehensive account of word meanings, we invoke the Cognitive Constraint again. Since among the possible words must be those for perceptual concepts, the theory of word meanings must be at least expressive enough to encompass the kinds of conditions such concepts require. This chapter will begin by investigating one such set of conditions, in order to place a lower bound on the complexity of the theory of word meanings.

Wertheimer (1923) investigates the perceptual principles organizing collections of shapes into larger units. Consider the configurations in (8.1).

(8.1) a.   b.
     ○○○ ○○   ○○ ○○○

(8.1a) is most naturally seen as three circles to the left of two other circles; (8.1b) as two circles to the left of three.[1] One can force oneself to see other organizations, but these are the most salient and arise most spontaneously. The principle behind this grouping evidently involves relative distance: the circles that are closer together tend to form a visual group.

This perceptual principle of *proximity* is a graded condition. Its effect can be enhanced by exaggerating the disparity of distances, as in (8.2a), and it can be weakened by reducing the disparity, as in (8.2b). Among other things, this gradation of strength means that it is harder in (8.2a) than in (8.1a) to make oneself see groupings other than 2–3, and easier in (8.2b). If the circles are equally spaced, as in (8.2c), no particular grouping judgment is favored by the presented configuration.

(8.2) a.   b.   c.

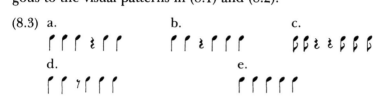

Wertheimer observes that a parallel principle affects temporal groupings. For example, the rhythms in (8.3) have groupings analogous to the visual patterns in (8.1) and (8.2).

(8.3) a.   b.   c.

d.   e.

The effect of temporal grouping is independent of sensory modality, for the rhythms in (8.3) can be presented as beats on a drum, as flashing lights, or as gentle touches of a finger on the back of your neck.

Given appropriate preconditions, the principle of proximity is sufficient to bring about a grouping judgment. However, it is not necessary. Suppose we take (8.2c), to which the principle of proximity fails to apply, and change the sizes of some of the circles, as in (8.4a,b). Salient grouping judgments emerge immediately.

(8.4) a.   b.

Similar effects can be produced by changing the shape or color instead of the size of the elements in (8.2c). The operative principle is one of *similarity:* elements that are more similar in internal structure tend to be grouped together. This principle too is graded. (8.5a), with greater relative differences, enhances the grouping judgment; (8.5b), with smaller relative disparity, weakens it.

(8.5) a.   b.

Again, Wertheimer shows that this principle applies to temporal groupings as well. For instance, in (8.6) the equally spaced notes group by likeness of pitch. The strongest effect appears with distantly spaced groups of like pitch (8.6b); weaker effects occur with less marked disparities (8.6c,d).

(8.6)   a.   b.   c.   d.

Like the principle of proximity, then, the principle of similarity is a graded condition that is not necessary to induce grouping judgments, but that under certain conditions is sufficient.

The principles of proximity and similarity are a commonplace of elementary psychology texts, but most often only as principles of static visual patterning. Their intermodal character is widely overlooked, even by writers as astute as Hochberg (1974), who, surprisingly, suggests attributing these principles of organization to the character of motor programs for eye movements in the visual system. We can see already that he is wrong on two counts: the principles are not exclusively visual; nor can they be motor in origin, since there are no motor processes involved in auditory perception.

It would seem in fact that these principles are best articulated in terms of a level of mental representation that is capable of generalizing both across sensory modalities and across spatial and temporal organizations. In the present theory this is the level of conceptual structure, which we have defined in terms of the first of these desiderata. We will see in section 9.2 that it satisfies the second as well.[2]

In addition to intermodality, Wertheimer discusses another aspect of these principles that is usually overlooked: the way they interact with one another. Consider fields in which both principles apply. In (8.7a) proximity and similarity reinforce each other, since the two small circles are close together and the three large circles are close together. The resulting grouping intuition is quite strong. In (8.7b), though, one of the small circles is near the large circles, so the principles of proximity and similarity conflict. The resulting intuition is ambiguous: one can see the middle circle as part of either the left-hand or the right-hand group, and it may even switch spontaneously, like the vase-faces or the duck-rabbit of chapter 2. As the middle circle is moved even further to the right, as in (8.7c), proximity exerts a still stronger effect and succeeds in overriding the principle of similarity. Intuition now clearly includes it in the right-hand group, though one may still sense the conflict. Alternatively, the effect of similarity in (8.7b) can be weakened by enlarging the small circles, as in (8.7d). Again proximity comes to dominate, though perhaps less decisively.

(8.7) a. ○○ ○○○   b. ○○ ○○○

      c. ○○ ○○○   d. ○○ ○○○

Parallel musical examples appear in (8.8).

(8.8)   a.   b.   c.   d.

Thus the principles of proximity and similarity are both graded conditions, neither of which is necessary and neither of which is sufficient to bring about a grouping judgment. The judgment that emerges depends on the relative strengths with which the two principles apply. If neither applies, as in (8.2c) or (8.3e), intuition is vague. If only one applies, it imposes a grouping judgment. If both apply, they can either reinforce each other, resulting in stronger judgments, or conflict, resulting in weak or ambiguous judgments. In a conflicting situation, if one applies with sufficiently greater strength than the other, it may override the other to impose an unambiguous, though still conflicted or tense, judgment.

8.2 Rules for Musical Grouping

These illustrations have treated only two of many of the principles of organization motivated by Wertheimer, all of which interact in similar fashion. Jackendoff and Lerdahl (1981), Lerdahl and Jackendoff (1982, chapter 3) develop detailed principles of grouping for music; I would like to summarize the results here, to show something of the full complexity of the situation. The visual case is if anything richer.

Grouping in music is the imposition by the listener of a hierarchical segmentation on a sequence of pitch-events (notes or chords). For example, (8.9) shows, by means of slurs beneath the musical notation, the intuitively most natural grouping for the opening phrase of Mozart's Symphony No. 40.

(8.9)

According to this structure, the first three notes form a group, the fourth through sixth notes form a group, and the seventh through tenth notes form a group. In turn, the first two small groups form a group, which combines with the third small group. The resulting group, the first half of the phrase, combines with the identically structured second half to form a still larger group, which itself is combined with other groups, not shown, into larger-scale groupings.

This structure is intuitively evident to the listener, although he probably cannot articulate it without prompting. How evident it is can be ascertained by comparing it with a putative grouping in which, say, the first four notes form a group, the next four form a group, and so on—an organization that bears no resemblance to anyone's intuitions. One of the problems for a theory of musical cognition is to explain how one imposes this structure on the presented musical signal.

The first task of the theory of grouping is to express the fact that there is grouping structure at all rather than some different organization—say, one that associates the first and the last event, the second and the penultimate event, and so forth, in a nesting sort of structure. The essential nature of grouping structure is expressed in a set of *grouping well-formedness rules,* which define necessary conditions on grouping structure. To summarize, a group must be constituted out of a sequence of contiguous events; a piece must be exhaustively segmented into groups; although a group may be completely embedded in another group, it may not overlap a boundary of a group that contains it.

However, the grouping well-formedness rules seriously underdetermine the assignment of structures to pieces; there are many exhaustive hierarchical segmentations possible in (8.9), only one of which conforms to musical intuition. It turns out to be impossible to refine the well-formedness rules to define the correct structure for the general case. Rather, Lerdahl and I were forced to resort to principles called *grouping preference rules,* with characteristics like those of Wertheimer's principles discussed in the previous section. We chose the term "preference rule" because these rules establish not inflexible decisions about structure, but relative preferences among a number of logically possible analyses. Our hypothesis is that one imposes on a musical surface a projected #structure# that represents the highest degree of overall preference, when all applicable preference rules are taken into account. Such a structure is judged the most highly preferred, or most coherent, or most salient, or most stable. In the case of structural ambiguity, more than one possible structure attains sufficient salience to be projectable.

The preference rules for grouping divide into two types: those that are *local* in application, attending only to a single small part of the structure at a time; and those that are *global*, attending to more than one area at once.

One local rule is an elaborated and more explicit form of the principle of proximity. It searches the musical surface for breaks in the musical flow, and says that breaks are preferably to be heard as grouping boundaries. The rule has two cases. The first looks for relatively large spaces between the end of one note and the beginning of the next; it is thus sensitive to the presence of rests (silences). The other case looks for relatively large intervals of time between onsets of successive notes, and is thus sensitive to the presence of long notes.

Another local rule is a more complete version of the principle of similarity, spelling out the dimensions of similarity to which musical grouping is sensitive. Like the proximity rule, it searches for distinctive transitions at which grouping boundaries may be set. It has cases sensitive to relatively large changes in pitch (as in (8.6)), to changes in dynamics, and to changes in prevailing articulation (slurs vs. detached notes, for instance). One might add further cases to deal with change in timbre or instrumentation. Each case in both these rules operates independently of the others, all of them interacting in reinforcement or conflict, as laid out in the previous section.

A third local rule is concerned not with the details of the musical surface, but with the details of the imposed structure. In principle, one could place a group boundary between every successive pair of notes in a piece; but such segmentation would be overly fussy. This rule states a strong preference against extremely short groups, particularly those consisting only of a single note. It expresses the intuition that very small-scale grouping in music is marginal except when supported by very sharp articulation of boundaries—such as when there is very strong evidence from proximity and similarity.

The global preference rules impart to grouping structure its holistic character, whereby the structure of the whole is potentially different from the structures assigned to its parts in isolation. Such differences will appear just at those points where global and local evidence are in conflict, and the global evidence is more powerful. Global evidence can also be used to reduce local ambiguity, in situations where local evidence does not produce a decisive preference.

One of the global rules says to prefer a grouping structure in which subdivided groups contain two parts of roughly equal length (it says nothing, though, about the further division of the parts). This rule thus attempts to impose a degree of symmetry on grouping structure. Like the last of the local rules, it is an abstract normative condition on structure, without regard to content. On the other hand, being only a preference rule, it may be overridden if the content of the musical surface, through the influence of other preference rules, militates otherwise.

Another rule of global effect seeks to form a grouping structure in which the constituent groups are parallel in internal structure. Parallelism in music embraces such factors as motivic and rhythmic similarity, similarity of harmonic structure, similarity of internal grouping, and so forth. An extremely powerful factor in musical cognition, it can lead to placement of boundaries where there is no local evidence, to suppression of boundaries in the face of local evidence, and especially to the establishment of large-scale sectionalization of a piece, which local cues can in no way determine. Presumably, the more parallelism one can detect, the more internally coherent a piece becomes, and the less independent information must be processed and retained in hearing or remembering a piece.

Still another rule relates preferences in grouping structure to other aspects of musical structure called time-span reduction and prolongational reduction. These are independent hierarchical structures, also regulated by sets of preference rules, that express melodic and harmonic aspects of musical cognition that need not concern us here; various principles link choice of grouping structure with possible choices in these two domains. The preference rule in question says that one should prefer a grouping structure that results in more highly preferred time-span and prolongational reductions. In effect, the grouping is not free to do as it pleases: all aspects of the musical structure must form a coherent whole.

All of these preference rules demonstrably play a role in the structuring of music. Even if some apply more frequently and with greater effect than others, the "less important" rules often decide crucial cases. Thus the concept of a musical group, though intuitively quite simple, is revealed as a complex interweaving of well-formedness conditions and preference rules.

8.3 Application to Word Meanings

I have gone into musical grouping in such detail because of its importance in understanding what goes into a word meaning. First of all, assuming that this theory is a roughly correct account of the cognitive principles governing the experience of grouping in music, it is almost trivially obvious that the whole system of grouping well-formedness rules and preference rules must be contained in the sense of the word "(musical) group," for it is these rules that are responsible for deciding whether a particular collection of pitch-events in a musical stream is identified as a #group# or not.[3] The complexity of this system thus sets a lower bound on the potential complexity of word meanings. Many words are doubtless more complex, though few if any have been explored in this depth.

Beyond the particulars of the analysis, it is not hard to see that the rules of grouping have all the properties we have come to expect in a word meaning. [GROUP] is far from an unanalyzed monad, nor is it an exhibition of a sample set of exemplars or templates; it is a set of *rules* that attend to various aspects of the represented field. Some of the relevant details are perceptual—for example, the relative pitches of adjacent notes. Some, however, are purely structural (i.e., intensional), such as the preference rule that desires symmetry and the well-formedness condition that prevents groups from overlapping.

Although some of the rules are necessary conditions, there is no subset of the rules that is both necessary and sufficient. Moreover, an advocate of necessary and sufficient conditions could not simply eliminate the preference rules from the meaning of the word: that would predict that people would identify as groups all kinds of configurations that are patently absurd. The necessary conditions alone are far too unselective.

For certain situations (such as (8.3a)), satisfaction of the necessary conditions plus one preference rule is sufficient to create a judgment. In fact, for nearly every preference rule there is a possible configuration in which it alone is criterial. This characteristic of the rule system enables us to discard Searle's (1958) proposal, cited in section 7.4, that "enough" criterial features must be met to make a positive judgment: since "enough" varies from configuration to configuration, and can be as little as the necessary conditions plus one, it is not very useful to simply count positive rule applications. Rather, as shown by

Wertheimer, we must employ a measure that balances strength of confirmatory rule applications against strength of disconfirmatory rule applications. We will return to this problem shortly.

Grouping judgments follow the same yes/no/not-sure distribution that we found in #token#-identification and categorization judgments in chapters 3–6. For instance, in (8.3a) and (8.9) the first three notes clearly form a group; in (8.6a) and (8.8a) they clearly do not; and in (8.3e), (8.6d), and (8.8b) one is not sure. This paradigm is partly the result of rule applications of graded strength, like the centrality conditions presented in section 7.4. But in addition the preference rule system gives groups a family resemblance character. There are groups bounded by pauses, groups bounded by pitch discontinuities, groups constituted for reasons of symmetry, and so forth. Many groups share a number of these characteristics, but no particular subset of them is "central" or criterial. Thus each preference rule acts as a typicality condition, in the sense of section 7.4—it applies only some of the time. Yet one does not want to say that "group" is an ambiguous term that should be divided into different notions corresponding to the different preference rules (as we saw Katz advocating for "game" in section 7.4); it is a musically and cognitively unified notion.

Some groups are identified as such by nearly all the preference rules, acting in mutual reinforcement. Pieces of music with this kind of grouping are generally very square and straightforward—children's songs, simple folk songs, marches, dances, and the like. They are easily comprehended and may be regarded as stereotypical. The interesting thing is that stereotypes are nowhere directly described in the theory; rather, they arise as an emergent phenomenon from the maximal reinforcement of the preference rules. This is the same way that stereotypes appear in Rosch and Mervis's (1975) treatment of family resemblance phenomena.[4] In short, the principles of musical grouping behave just as a word meaning should.

Musical grouping illustrates a point that is not evident in previous literature: the way the nonnecessary conditions for concept satisfaction—the typicality conditions—form an interactive system that operates according to the principles of reinforcement and conflict pointed out by Wertheimer. To be sure, the interaction of rules has been observed in many individual phenomena, but it has not been stated as a general characteristic of rule systems in cognition. In section 8.7 we will show how general this interactive property is; one example will suffice here. Recall Labov's (1973) graded condition on height-width ratio in cups, bowls, and vases, discussed in chapters 5 and 7. Labov also observes that having a single handle is a typicality condition on cups but not on vases or bowls. As a result, examples with a wider range of height-width ratios will be judged cups if they have handles than if they do not. For example, (8.10b,d), without handles, are vague between cups and non-cups; but (8.11b,d), with the same height-width ratios but handles, are more likely cups. On the other hand, having a handle cannot make more extreme cases such as (8.11a,e) into cups; the influence of the height-width ratio is sufficiently strong to override the handle condition.

(8.10)

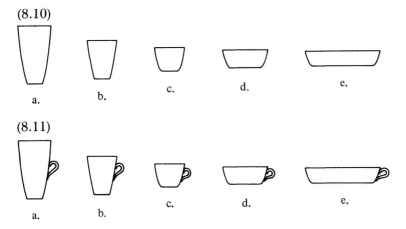

The difficulty in making such a system of interactive principles into a fully predictive theory lies in what happens when rules conflict. Do they balance, giving an ambiguous or unclear judgment, or does one override the other? One's immediate reaction is to try to quantify strength of rule application, and thereby obtain a numerical measure to predict judgments. Such a measure would have to incorporate two factors: the inherent strength (or importance, or criteriality) of each rule, multiplied by the strength of the application of each rule in the particular situation at hand. Both are necessary to derive the sort of balancing effects that occur in (8.7), (8.8), and (8.11). Measures like this appear, for example, in Tenney and Polansky's (1980) computer program for certain aspects of musical grouping and, in effect, in Winston's (1970) program for certain aspects of visual pattern recognition. The measure of *cue validity* discussed by Rosch and Mervis (1975) and Smith and Medin (1981) is also of this nature.

On the other hand, constructing such a measure presumes that one can meaningfully assign numerical values of strength to all rule applications. Return to the theory of grouping. While it is fairly straightforward to measure empirically the relative effect of local rules, it is harder to balance the strength of local rules against the strength of global effects that implicate many points in the structure—and harder yet to compare the strength of two global preferences that converge at one point and diverge elsewhere. Especially problematic is the effect of intercomponential interactions, where the choice of grouping structure indirectly affects the relative stability of the two reductional structures, which in turn reflect back on the stability of the grouping structure. How is one to tease these factors apart and assign them numerical values? For example, how similar do two passages have to be to count as parallel, and to what extent can a far-fetched parallelism override local grouping cues? Much depends on the style of the composition and sometimes even on the particulars of the piece itself. Through judicious manipulation, a composer can create contexts that make radically different passages count as parallel (consider Beethoven's Diabelli Variations, for instance).

For reasons like this, the quantification of rule strength is more complex than is generally supposed. In general, nothing will be satisfactory short of a global measure of stability over all components of the musical structure of an entire piece. To compute such a measure over all plausible analyses appears to lead, for a piece of any complexity at all, to the computational explosion so dreaded in computer simulation. (And the computations required for *composing* music would likely be exponentially worse!)

There is evidence that this computational complexity is psychologically real. Much of the interest in "art" music comes from its exploitation of conflict among preference rules to increase tension and ambiguity. Characteristically, multiple interpretations at a local level are resolved by global considerations, themselves often kept ambiguous by conflict among preference rules. It is these complexities that make such music in all its richness inaccessible to unsophisticated listeners. By contrast, most folk music and "popular" music is characterized by strong reinforcement of preference rules at all levels, so that the most salient structure is computable largely on the basis of local considerations and is never open to doubt. This means that increased musical sophistication may be partially attributed to increased capacity for entertaining multiple large-scale structures simultaneously, hence to a more effective ability to resolve conflicts between local and global factors. Thus, music that is considered more "difficult" does in fact put greater demands on the listener's computational capacity, as the notion of a global stability measure seems to predict.

While the problem of balancing local vs. global rules is not the only obstacle to a completely formalizable theory of preference rule interaction (Smith and Medin (1981) mention some, and another will crop up in section 8.7), it is perhaps the most serious. It appears time and again in the discussion of "bottom-up" vs. "top-down" processing in perception and cognition. Clearly, global or top-down constraints are involved in many domains. For example, in language, one's pragmatic expectations about what the message will be can affect what phonetic segments one perceives. Similarly, "priming" effects in categorization—such as the fact that one will tend to see the duck-rabbit (example (2.4)) as a duck more readily if it is surrounded by unambiguous ducks, or if it has been preceded by presentation of ducks or by the word "duck"—are examples of the global rule of parallelism in a domain quite different from music. In fact, such effects are so common that there is hardly a convincing example of what Pylyshyn (1980) calls a "cognitively impenetrable" domain, a domain of mental activity that cannot be influenced to some extent by the coherence of its output within the overall scheme of things.

To sum up, we have shown that a preference rule system has the correct formal properties to account for the characteristics of word meanings—in particular, to cope with the gradation of judgments and with the existence of exceptions to many apparently defining conditions. We can thus include in word meanings all those conditions that people seem to consider crucial, such as stripedness in tigers, two-leggedness in humans, and competition in games; they are simply marked as typicality conditions rather than as necessary conditions.

A word meaning, then, is a large heterogeneous collection of such conditions dealing with form, function, purpose, personality, or whatever else is salient. Taxonomic information, to be discussed in section 8.5, also plays a role. As the importance of information for individuation and categorization drops off (as weighting, observability, or frequency of occurrence decreases), it shades toward "encyclopedia" rather than "dictionary" information, with no sharp line drawn between the two types.

In permitting conditions that have exceptions, we are not sanctioning total lack of constraint in word meanings. Rather, the fact that the conditions are embedded in a preference rule system, operating according to Wertheimer's principles of reinforcement and conflict, means that there is overall control over the degree to which a particular item may be exceptional. This control is embodied in a measure of stability that encompasses all the conditions in a word meaning. Items that satisfy all or most conditions receive the most stable analyses and are judged more stereotypical instances of the concept in question. Items that fail more conditions receive less stable analyses; depending on what other analyses are possible, such items may be judged dubious instances or noninstances of the concept.[5]

On the other hand, we have found that the measure of stability has problematic computational characteristics. I believe that attempts in the literature to deal with this difficulty have not recognized the full generality of the problem, and so have been less than adequate. Section 8.7 will return to this issue, showing how basic the notion of preference rule system is to psychology.

8.4 Default Values and Prototype Images

An important contribution of computational theories of cognition is the notion of a *default value*. It is often the case that a particular [TOKEN] is missing certain information from which one wishes to draw an inference. For example, with visual inputs, one generally has no information about the back of an object; but one generally has a strong hypothesis or "best guess" about it, and one is most often not even aware that this hypothesis is an assumption. Similarly, with linguistic inputs, one is constantly disambiguating lexical items and syntactic structures. The degree to which this takes place unawares was not noticed until attempts at machine translation revealed rampant potential ambiguity in sentences, suppressed by semantic and pragmatic factors.

Approaches to this problem are found in Charniak's (1972) "demons," Schank and Abelson's (1975) "scripts," and Minsky's (1975) "frames" (and from a much broader perspective, Goffman's (1974) similar notion of frames). All of these are sets of conditions, often of great complexity, specifying what a typical member of some [THING

TYPE] or [EVENT TYPE] is like. These conditions are used as default values, to fill in or anticipate information not present in a visual or textual input—for example, that rooms usually have walls and ceilings, that one usually gives presents at a birthday party, and that at a restaurant one often decides what to eat after looking at a menu. One presumably uses this information not just to understand stories, but also to structure one's own action at birthday parties and in restaurants (this is the aspect that Goffman stresses).

In effect, these sets of conditions are preference rule systems for concepts more complex than we have considered so far. Their importance here lies not in their details but in what they show about preference rule systems. Up to this point we have considered conceptual structure primarily as a means for identifying and categorizing [TOKENS]: the rules specify ways of checking input against an internal standard. But one of the virtues of a preference rule system, as opposed to a system of necessary and sufficient conditions, is that one does not have to check *all* the conditions to arrive at a judgment. Rather, only enough need to be checked to establish a satisfactory degree of stability. Once one has arrived at a judgment, then, there are often preference rules that have not been (or cannot be) checked against the input at hand. The essence of frame/script theory is that one can turn around and employ these unused preference rules to supply default values for features of the concepts that have not been established during identification or categorization.

This way of looking at frame/script theory captures a generalization that appears to have been missed by most practitioners of the notion: the essential connection between the frame selection task (how one categorizes novel things and events) and the use of a frame for its default values. I am claiming here that these two tasks use the *very same* information. For instance, suppose that we were to watch a segment of a movie (or walk into someone's house) in which people were wearing funny hats, giving someone presents, etc. We would use the same information to decide that we were witnessing a birthday party in such a case (to select the "birthday party frame") as we would to anticipate what would happen at a birthday party to which we had been invited. We just use this information differently.

The use of preference rules to supply default values should not be too surprising. It is simply an extension of the principle of the syllogism to less fully determined cases. For example, a typical person has kidneys; you are a person; therefore, you probably have kidneys and I will act as though you do until I have evidence to the contrary. In the formal framework of chapter 6, such "invited inferences" are expressed as follows: We permit inference rule (6.11), repeated here as (8.12), to apply when Y is a typicality condition as well as a necessary condition.

$$(8.12) \quad \begin{bmatrix} X \\ \text{INSTANCE OF } (\begin{bmatrix} \text{TYPE} \\ Y \end{bmatrix}_j) \end{bmatrix}_i \leftrightarrow \begin{bmatrix} X \\ Y \end{bmatrix}_i$$

With the arrow going from left to right, this rule extracts a preference rule from a [TYPE] and embeds it in a [TOKEN] that is an instance of the [TYPE]. In addition, we need a rule that chooses satisfaction of the preference rule as a default value for the [TOKEN]. Let P(Y) be a preference rule, of which Y is the maximally stable or preferred condition; and let "$\overset{P}{\rightarrow}$" be the sign for invited inference, that is, an inference that can be canceled by contradictory evidence. Then the use of a preference rule as a default value is formalized as (8.13).

$$(8.13) \quad \begin{bmatrix} X \\ P(Y) \end{bmatrix} \overset{P}{\rightarrow} \begin{bmatrix} X \\ Y \end{bmatrix}$$

This use of preference rules explains the intuitive appeal of the notion that the meaning of a category word is an image of a stereotypical instance of the category. Certainly one does often experience a mental image of a typical tiger when thinking about tigers or about the word "tiger." However, as Fodor (1975) points out, there are terrible problems in stating how one relates the stereotype to anything else. In particular, it is impossible to use it to make categorization judgments. Moreover, Rosch et al. (1976) undermine the generality of a stereotype theory by pointing out that one does not form an image of a stereotype for every category. They pick out a class of "basic objects," the most inclusive categories whose instances, among other things, have similar shapes. (Chairs, for example, are basic objects; furniture is not.) They show experimentally that basic objects are the most inclusive [TYPES] for which a concrete image for the [TYPE] as a whole can be formed (i.e., for which the image-of-stereotype theory is plausible) and that, essentially, basic categories are the easiest to learn.

Now recall what was said about mental images in chapter 2: they are projected #entities# generated from conceptual structure, which resemble in many respects the #real objects# they are images of. In particular, they share most conceptual features that concern visual appearance, differing only in some feature like REAL/IMAGINED. Now suppose that one wants to imagine a [TYPE]. Since, as argued in chapter 5, a [TYPE] has no visual projection, the best one can do is imagine a [TOKEN, INSTANCE OF TYPE]. What information does one put into the #image# of the [INSTANCE]? Since the environment in this case provides no data at all, default values will be chosen for all typicality and centrality conditions, resulting in a maximally stereotypical conceptual structure for the #image#. Hence the experience of an #image of a stereotypical instance of a type# is just about what one would expect. Nonetheless, the #image# is not compared against #exemplars#: the [TYPE] projecting the #image# is. Hence Fodor's objection to the image theory is avoided without neglecting the intuition behind it.

Now suppose that a [TYPE] is such that a number of its preference rules concerning visual appearance are equally salient and mutually exclusive, because exemplars fall into groups of radically different shapes. "Furniture" expresses such a [TYPE]; the commonality of its members is found mainly in their function, not their shape. In such a case, it will be impossible to generate an #image# that incorporates default values for all preference rules, and hence there will be no possible #image of a stereotypical instance#. This is just the result obtained by Rosch et al.: the categories for which one can form images are those for which most instances have more or less similar shapes. The use of preference rules as default values thus accounts for the limitations of generality in the stereotype-image theory, again without denying the intuition behind its appeal.[6]

8.5 Preference Rules in Taxonomies

It is a commonplace of semantic and cognitive theory to use taxonomic information to reduce redundancy in conceptual structure. When a concept C contains a feature f, no concept that is an instance of or contained in C need be marked for f; all subordinates inherit f as a default value. (In fact, one can think of meaning postulate/ network theories as carrying this practice to an extreme, so that a concept need contain no features at all.) In the present theory, this possibility is stated in terms of inference rule (8.12).

Things become more interesting when exceptionality enters the picture. Raphael (1968) permits concepts subordinate to a concept C to be marked as exceptions to a feature f of C, and specifies that only the exceptional cases are marked. In present terms, since the feature f permits exceptions, it would be regarded as a typicality condition of C. Raphael's treatment corresponds to the intuition that once one learns the rule for the concept C, only the exceptions to f need be learned and stored among C's subordinates.

Extending this approach, we can account for the source of different sorts of exceptionality in a single word meaning. For example, one of the typicality conditions on [BIRD] is [CAN FLY]. [ROBIN], being subordinate to [BIRD], inherits this feature from it. Now suppose Roberts the robin has a broken wing and can't fly. Then his representation will be marked exceptional with respect to the feature in question; the exceptionality will be at the level of the individual. On the other hand, since it is typical of ostriches not to fly, [OSTRICH] must be marked an exception to the feature [CAN FLY] at the level of species; individual ostriches will be atypical birds, inheriting this exceptionality as a default value in their representations. But suppose Ollie the ostrich has somehow learned to fly. This does not cancel out the exceptionality of ostriches within his representation, making him a more typical bird. Rather, he must be marked an exception to the typicality condition [CANNOT FLY] that he would otherwise inherit from [OSTRICH]. Thus he is doubly exceptional. The diagram in (8.14) sums this up. (As in (8.13), P(x) means that x is a preferred or typical condition.)

(8.14)

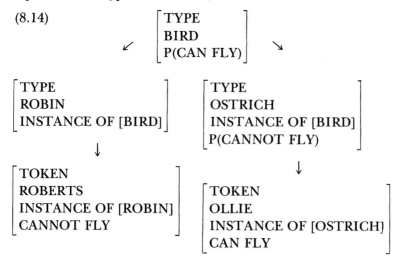

Consider also our old friend "bachelor," whose meaning presumably consists of the necessary conditions [MAN, ADULT, NEVER MARRIED]. This too inherits exceptions and dubious judgments from its superordinates. A one-legged bachelor is still a bachelor, but exceptional as a [MAN]. [ADULT] has a graded condition of age, by virtue of which we are dubious about whether to call a 12-year-old a bachelor, less dubious about a 16-year-old, and fully confident about a 21-year-old. [MARRIED] has nasty little problems about time, as well: at what precise moment during the marriage ceremony does one cease to be a bachelor? (This seemingly absurd question might even have practical repercussions, for instance for a probate court that had to dispose of the estate of someone who died during his wedding.) What these examples show is that the use of typicality conditions as default values in a taxonomic hierarchy is of utility in sorting the welter of imaginable atypical cases into some coherent order.

A different property of taxonomies emerges from an observation of Putnam (1975). He claims that his own personal conceptual structures for "elm" and "beech" must be the same—a stereotypical deciduous tree—since he cannot distinguish instances of the two. Yet their representations must differ, since the words are not synonyms.

But Putnam knows more than he claims to. What he overlooks is that if he were told that a particular tree was a beech, he would most likely judge that it is not an elm, and vice versa. This suggests a general preference rule over taxonomies, whereby members at a particular level of a taxonomy are typically disjoint. One feels uncomfortable, for example, with the notion that a color can be both red and purple, or that some object is both a cup and a bowl, or that a photon is both a wave and a particle. Such analyses are unstable because they violate this condition over taxonomies.

To begin to state the principle formally, we need to express taxonomic relations in conceptual structure. The functions INSTANCE OF and EXEMPLIFIED BY express subordination and superordination, respectively, but there is as yet no way to express the notion of two subordinates being "at the same level" in the taxonomy. The notation developed so far permits indiscriminate mixing of exemplars and subordinates at all levels, as in (8.15).

(8.15) $\begin{bmatrix} \text{TYPE} \\ \text{BIRD} \\ \text{EXEMPLIFIED BY [TYPE ROBIN]} \\ \text{EXEMPLIFIED BY [TYPE OSTRICH]} \\ \text{EXEMPLIFIED BY [TYPE DUCK]} \\ \text{EXEMPLIFIED BY [TYPE MALLARD]} \\ \text{EXEMPLIFIED BY [TYPE FLIGHTLESS BIRDS]} \\ \text{EXEMPLIFIED BY [TOKEN ROBERTS]} \end{bmatrix}$

While unstructured concepts like this must be permitted in conceptual structure, since they are the raw material out of which taxonomies can be built, there must be a way to express more highly organized concepts.

Toward this end, let us extend the operator EXEMPLIFIED BY to take more than one argument, as in (8.16). This notation will be taken to mean that $[Y_1]$, $[Y_2]$, ..., $[Y_n]$ are at the same level of subordination to the type X.

(8.16) $\begin{bmatrix} \text{TYPE} \\ \text{X} \\ \text{EXEMPLIFIED BY } ([Y_1], [Y_2], ..., [Y_n]) \end{bmatrix}$

In particular, [TYPES] and [TOKENS] cannot be simultaneously entered as arguments of a single EXEMPLIFIED BY operator. This distinguishes the last entry in (8.15) from the rest.

With this formalism, we can state a preference rule (8.17) that expresses Putnam's taxonomic knowledge about elms and beeches. (The function BE is as used in chapter 6.)

(8.17) $\begin{bmatrix} \text{TYPE} \\ \text{X} \\ \text{EXEMPLIFIED BY } (\begin{bmatrix} \text{TYPE} \\ Y_1 \end{bmatrix}, \begin{bmatrix} \text{TYPE} \\ Y_2 \end{bmatrix}) \end{bmatrix} \rightarrow$

$\begin{bmatrix} \begin{bmatrix} \text{STATE} \\ \text{BE } (Z, \begin{bmatrix} \text{TYPE} \\ Y_1 \end{bmatrix}) \end{bmatrix} \xrightarrow{\text{P}} \begin{bmatrix} \text{STATE} \\ \text{NOT BE } (Z, \begin{bmatrix} \text{TYPE} \\ Y_2 \end{bmatrix}) \end{bmatrix} \end{bmatrix}$

According to (8.17), the fact that two [TYPES] are arranged as sister subordinates leads to an invited inference that the [TYPES] are disjoint. In the case of Putnam's judgment, this rule supplies a default value in the absence of other evidence: if it's an elm, then by default it's not a beech.

On the other hand, the rule can be actively used to structure taxonomies: it creates pressure toward modifying sister [TYPES] so that they are indeed disjoint. For example, the primary color names in a language will tend to adopt nonoverlapping ranges of application, together exhausting the color solid (Miller and Johnson-Laird (1976, section 5.1)). Similarly, if [TYPE FRUIT] is expanded to include [TYPE TOMATO], then [TYPE VEGETABLE] will tend to contract to avoid overlap; this in turn may prompt some internal reorganization in other features of [TYPE VEGETABLE] so as to exclude [TYPE TOMATO] on principled (that is, stable) rather than arbitrary grounds.

Rule (8.17) is roughly equivalent to Sommers's (1965) *M Constraint*, utilized in Keil's (1979) study of conceptual development. In present terms, Keil finds that children's concepts, like adult concepts, tend to form a well-ordered taxonomy, even if the relations of concepts in the taxonomy differ from the adult's. The rule must be a preference rule rather than an absolute condition (despite Sommers's claims), because there are numerous counterexamples. For instance, "book" has features of both a physical object and a body of information; "university" has features of both a physical object and a social organization. That these are not lexical ambiguities but simultaneous possibilities is shown by sentences such as (8.18a,b), in which the words are used nonanomalously in both senses at once.

(8.18) a. The book, which weighs ten pounds, ended sadly.
       b. The university, which was built in 1896, has a left-wing orientation.

(These counterexamples, among others, are pointed out by Bierwisch (1981).)

While (8.17) states the consequence of two [TYPES] being sister subordinates to another [TYPE], it does not give reason for establishing the sister relationship. The preference rules (8.19a,b) address this issue.

(8.19) a. $\begin{bmatrix} \text{TYPE} \\ \text{X} \\ \text{EXEMPLIFIED BY} \left(\begin{bmatrix} \text{TYPE} \\ \text{Y}_1 \end{bmatrix} \right) \\ \text{EXEMPLIFIED BY} \left(\begin{bmatrix} \text{TYPE} \\ \text{Y}_2 \end{bmatrix} \right) \end{bmatrix} \xrightarrow{\text{P}}$

$$\begin{bmatrix} \text{TYPE} \\ \text{X} \\ \text{EXEMPLIFIED BY} \left(\begin{bmatrix} \text{TYPE} \\ \text{Y}_1 \end{bmatrix}, \begin{bmatrix} \text{TYPE} \\ \text{Y}_2 \end{bmatrix} \right) \end{bmatrix}$$

b. $\begin{bmatrix} \text{TYPE} \\ \text{X} \\ \text{EXEMPLIFIED BY} \left(\begin{bmatrix} \text{TYPE} \\ \text{Y}_1 \end{bmatrix} \right) \\ \text{EXEMPLIFIED BY} \left(\begin{bmatrix} \text{TYPE} \\ \text{Y}_2 \end{bmatrix} \right) \end{bmatrix} \xrightarrow{\text{P}}$

$$\begin{bmatrix} \text{TYPE} \\ \text{X} \\ \text{EXEMPLIFIED BY} \left(\begin{bmatrix} \text{TYPE} \\ \text{Y}_1 \\ \text{EXEMPLIFIED BY} \left(\begin{bmatrix} \text{TYPE} \\ \text{Y}_2 \end{bmatrix} \right) \end{bmatrix} \right) \end{bmatrix}$$

These rules say that a taxonomic arrangement of [TYPES] is more stable than a heterogeneous collection of subordinates: given two subordinates, it is preferable to organize them either as sisters (8.19a) or as hierarchically embedded (8.19b).

Notice that since (8.19a) and (8.19b) are *preference* rules rather than logical *inference* rules, they may have the same antecedent but logically incompatible consequents. Neither rule is necessary, but the application of either improves stability over the heterogeneous situation.

The preference rules in (8.19), like symmetry in musical grouping, are preferences over the abstract structure of concepts and may be overridden by empirical evidence (say, if the instances of [TYPE Y_1] and [TYPE Y_2] neither are disjoint nor satisfy an inclusion relation). Alternatively, such counterevidence may lead to internal restructuring of [TYPE Y_1] and [TYPE Y_2] so that they come to satisfy proper taxonomic relations. Which alternative is chosen depends on the resulting stability of the system as a whole.

From these preference rules over taxonomies emerges a programmatic view of a formal theory of conceptual development and change, reminiscent of remarks of Quine (1969). In response to environmental input, not only are new concepts formed, but in addition these new concepts create pressures on existing concepts in an effort to make their own niche in the taxonomy. An accumulation of instabilities here and there in a conceptual system may upon occasion be relieved by a more global restructuring—if the organism has sufficient computational capacity to measure relative stability of two or more competing global organizations. Alternatively, one may simply learn to live with local instabilities (or deny them, as in a neurosis). In short, a processing model of cognition must include an active component that continually seeks to adjust and reorganize conceptual structure in an effort to maximize overall stability. This component would play a crucial role both in the child's development and, at a more fully conscious level, in the conduct of science.

8.6 Preference Rules in a Verb Meaning

Most discussion of stereotypes, fuzziness, and family resemblances here and elsewhere in the literature has concerned the meanings of nouns and adjectives. Continuing the argument of chapter 4 for the structural parallelism of the major ontological categories, this section will show that verb meanings display similar characteristics. Thus they too are incapable of being described by exhaustive decomposition into necessary and sufficient conditions.

First consider graded conditions. There are many classes of verbs whose members differ primarily by information about manner— for example, the verbs of locomotion "walk," "run," "lope," "jog," "sprint," "scurry," etc. The differences among these verbs are not of particular grammatical import, but they do make semantic distinctions that are hard to tie down more than impressionistically. In this respect they resemble the color words, which also are grammatically homogeneous and can be really distinguished only by ostension. This suggests that these verbs share a set of necessary conditions having to do with traveling in physical space (and perhaps a typicality condition "traveling *on foot*," so that talk of cars sprinting is sensed as an extension of the use of the verb). However, each will have its own centrality condition of manner, containing a central visual and/or motor pattern that specifies a characteristic gait and speed. This use of centrality conditions seems the correct way to capture these very common shades of difference among verb meanings.

A rather clear example of the need for typicality conditions is provided by the verb "see."[7] Consider the sentences in (8.20), which make roughly identical observations.

(8.20) a. I must have looked at that a dozen times, but I never *saw* it.
        b. I must have seen that a dozen times, but I never *noticed* it.

If we assume that "see" has a unified meaning, (8.20) raises a serious problem, since the sense of "see" in (8.20a) is used to deny its sense in (8.20b). The standard response to such a problem is to say that there are two distinct but homophonous verbs "see_a" and "see_b" in (8.20a) and (8.20b), respectively. Taking this tack for the moment, let us find out what each of these might mean.

"See_b" has the sense proposed by Gruber (1967), attacked by Van-Develde (1977), and defended by Goldsmith (1979): "x $sees_b$ y" means something like "x's gaze goes to y." (The reader who feels queasy at this analysis of "see" should recall that we are not concerned with what seeing *really* is, but with what SEEING and #seeing# are, that is, with how one's mind encodes seeing into experience.) In this sense of "see," the direct object alternates with prepositional phrases, as in (8.21).

(8.21) a. Bill saw into the room.
        b. Bill saw under the table.

Note that the ambiguity of (8.21b) parallels that of "Bill ran under the table": it may mean that his gaze terminated at a point under the table or that his gaze passed under the table to a point beyond (see section 9.1). This sort of evidence, presented in more detail by Gruber, motivates the analysis of "see_b" as a verb of motion.[8] Moreover, as Goldsmith points out, "from" fixes the origin of the gaze in (8.22a), just as it fixes the origin of motion in (8.22b).

(8.22) a. Bill saw the flying saucer from his living room.
        b. Bill ran into the yard from his living room.

Notice that this sense says nothing about whether the subject of the sentence has derived any information from his gaze; it is rather like

"x's glance fell upon y," which indeed can be substituted for "x saw y" in (8.20b) but not in (8.20a).

Now consider "see$_a$." In (8.20a), the assertion is that I never became aware of the object. Roughly, then, we might suggest an analysis of "x sees$_a$ y" as "y comes to x's visual awareness." ("Notice" would omit the marker "visual," since it can be used for input through any sensory channel.) It is precisely this awareness that is not necessary for the assertion of "see$_b$." Thus, both sentences in (8.20) say that I made visual contact, but the contents of my visual field did not enter my awareness.

Now examine the premise that "see$_a$" and "see$_b$" are separate lexical items. If they are distinct, which one is intended in (8.23)? Or is (8.23) ambiguous?

(8.23) I saw Bill.

In typical ambiguous sentences such as "Flying planes can be dangerous" or "We went to the bank," the speaker has one reading or the other in mind. If he has both in mind, a pun is usually intended. But (8.23), like most ordinary descriptions of seeing, appears to intend both that my gaze went to Bill and that Bill entered my awareness. Thus, there is something wrong with claiming that "see$_a$" and "see$_b$" are distinct lexical items.

However, suppose we claim that the senses of "see$_a$" and "see$_b$" are typicality conditions in the reading of a single verb "see." Either alone suffices for calling an act "seeing." (8.20b) asserts "see$_b$" alone. When one speaks of seeing mental images or hallucinations, "see$_a$" alone is asserted; in (8.20a), "see$_a$" is denied. In normal, stereotypical, veridical seeing, though, both conditions are satisfied. With this analysis it is possible to say that (8.23) is unambiguous: it conveys information about an act of #seeing# that includes both "seeing$_a$" and "seeing$_b$" by default, unless there is further information to the contrary.

In short, we have recapitulated the discussion of "game" in section 7.4. We have found that "see" has a family resemblance character, and we have tried and rejected the ambiguity gambit. Again the solution lies in a preference rule system, showing that verb meanings as well as noun meanings must permit such analyses.

8.7 The Ubiquity of Preference Rule Systems

Let us review the symptoms of preference rule systems: (1) judgments of graded acceptability and of family resemblance; (2) two or more rules, neither of which is necessary, but each of which is under certain conditions sufficient for a judgment; (3) balancing effects among rules that apply in conflict; (4) a measure of stability based on rule applications; (5) rules that are not logically necessary used as default values in the face of inadequate information. These characteristics crop up time after time in the psychological literature, but it is my impression that their ubiquity has never been recognized. Here are a few examples, presented only very sketchily. The details should be obvious to anyone familiar with the phenomena in question.

Regan, Beverley, and Cynader (1979) investigate the visual cues for motion of an object toward and away from the observer. Two prominent candidates are change in size on the retina and oppositely-directed motion on the two retinas (if moving directly toward the observer, an object moves rightward in the left retina and leftward in the right retina). Manipulating these cues independently by means of computer-generated stereoscopic displays, they find that either alone is sufficient to produce a judgment of motion. Thus neither is *the* necessary cue. They then place the cues in conflict, offsetting increasing size with outwardly-directed motion. They find that the two can balance one another; with the right proportion of magnitudes for the cues, the observer perceives no motion, just as a preference rule theory would predict.

It is interesting that the subjects in these experiments differed drastically in the proportions of the two conflicting cues necessary to achieve experienced stasis. And this is in a low-level system where one might expect a relatively high degree of "hard-wiring." If such interpersonal differences are characteristic of preference rule systems in general, the prospects for a fully quantified theory of preference rules are discouraging.

At a higher level in the visual system, we used the Gestalt laws of "good form" to motivate preference rule systems in the first place. We need only add to the discussion in section 8.1 that these rules are clearly used as default values in the absence of specific information. For instance, in (3.1) we see the occluded portion of the #shaded thing# most naturally in the way indicated by the dotted lines (8.24a), following the laws of good form applied as default values. We would be surprised if removal of the occlusion revealed its shape and pattern to be (8.24b).

(8.24)

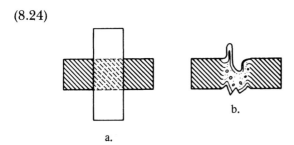

a.   b.

Similarly, in (3.2), the #dot passing behind the rectangle#, we use the laws of good form as default values to generate the hypothesis that there is a #dot# behind the #rectangle# and to generate expectations about when #it# will appear.

Turn next to language. Liberman and Studdert-Kennedy (1977) speak of a "trading relation" among the phonetic cues that distinguish the phrases "gray ship," "gray chip," and "great ship." Arguing against a simple feature detector model (in present terms, a necessary and sufficient condition), they show that the perceived features—continuant "sh" vs. affricated stop "ch" vs. stop plus continuant "t-sh"—depend in a complex way on the duration of the silence after the vowel of the first word (0–100 milliseconds) and the duration of the fricative "sh" noise (60–180 milliseconds). In particular, the duration of silence necessary to turn "gray ship" into "gray chip" is greater if the duration of the fricative is greater, a typical balancing effect. A similar and better-known case is the perception of the voiced-unvoiced distinction in stop consonants, which is affected by the interaction of aspiration, prevoicing, duration of silence, and length of the formant transitions in the following vowel.

Among the correspondence rules relating syntax and semantics, there is a subsystem dealing with the interpretation of quantifier scope. Ioup (1975) shows that this subsystem involves what in the present context appear to be preference rules. She takes seriously the observation, made occasionally in the literature, that multiple quantifiers in a single clause often create scope ambiguities, of which one reading is preferred. Her preference rules can be stated as follows:

(8.25) a. Given two quantifiers in the same surface clause, preferably assign larger scope to that quantifier which is higher on the following scale:

each > every > all > most > many > several > some > a few

b. Given two quantifiers in the same surface clause, preferably assign larger scope to the one in most salient surface position, defined by the scale:

topic > deep and surface subject > deep or surface subject but not both > indirect object > object of preposition > direct object

Ioup shows these preferences to hold over a wide range of languages (where the scale in rule (8.25a) is defined over the closest translation of the quantifiers) and thus feels confident in claiming that they are universal. Though Ioup does not work out the full interaction of the two rules, the overall pattern is that of a preference rule system: rule application of variable strength, which yields strongly preferred interpretations when rule applications reinforce, ambiguity when rule applications of commensurate strength conflict, and exceptions to a rule when its weak application is overridden by strong application of another rule.

An aspect of linguistic theory that has largely resisted successful formalization is the notion of *markedness conventions*: conditions that establish preferred forms for rules of grammar, but may be violated by particular grammars. Principles of markedness have been appealed to especially in phonology (e.g., Trubetzkoy (1939), Chomsky and Halle (1968)), but syntactic theory has also made frequent use of the "marked" vs. "unmarked" distinction, especially in recent work. Markedness conventions are seen not only as establishing a measure of relative stability over competing grammars, but also as supplying the language learner with default values for principles of grammar that are underdetermined by the primary linguistic evidence. Thus, some of the symptoms of preference rules appear in Chomsky's (1965) notion of *evaluation metric*, a fundamental component of contemporary linguistic theory. (I know of no evidence for reinforcement and conflict among markedness conventions; this may, however, be due to the fact that no one has thought to look for them.)

In the study of linguistic performance, the theory of syntactic parsing strategies (e.g., Kimball (1973), Wanner and Maratsos (1978), Janet D. Fodor (1978), Marcus (1980)) has frequently made use of heuristic principles that make a "best guess" about the structure of a sentence being processed. In present terms, these heuristics are preference rules that supply a default structure for incoming input. The interaction of syntactic and semantic cues to determine which of many potential structures is to be selected is typical of a preference rule system. For example, we find in the notorious "garden path" sentences such as (8.26) the characteristic conflict between local preferences and global requirements.

(8.26) The horse raced past the barn fell.

The difficulty of this sentence lies in the preference to read "raced" as the main verb, strongly reinforced by other local cues, but in conflict with the global need to integrate "fell" into the interpretation of the sentence. This global requirement can be sustained only by choosing the much less stable participial interpretation of "raced."

In pragmatics, the conversational maxims of Grice (1975) can be recast as preference rules. Although Grice states his principles as instructions to the speaker, Bach and Harnish (1979, chapter 8) point out that they apply equally to the process of interpretation by the hearer, where they appear as preferences in how to construe the speaker's intended meaning. In this form, five of Grice's maxims can be stated as (8.27a–e).

(8.27) a. Prefer to assume that the speaker is telling you all he knows. (Maxim of quantity)

  b. Prefer to assume that the speaker believes what he intends to convey. (Maxim of quality)

  c. Prefer to assume that the speaker has only one meaning in mind.

  d. Prefer to assume that the speaker is conveying something relevant. (Maxim of relevance)

  e. Prefer to assume that the speaker is speaking literally. (Presumption of literalness)

Grice works through a number of cases where the speaker violates maxims for special effects of various sorts (politeness, sarcasm, and puns, for example). The problem for the hearer is to decide what the speaker intends. In particular, if the speaker's literal meaning is irrelevant or supplies less information than the hearer believes he is entitled to, the hearer must construct a plausible intended message that is in some way related to what is uttered. This construction is what Grice calls a *conversational implicature*. For example, the question "May I ask you to pass the salt?" is usually taken as a request to pass the salt, because an answer to the literal interpretation of the sentence would infringe on the maxim of relevance.

In order to keep possible violations under control, Bach and Harnish propose the Principle of Charity: "Other things being equal, construe the speaker's remark so as to violate as few maxims as possible." As a refinement, they suggest that maxims may carry different weights in the Principle of Charity, so that the most stable analysis is determined by cumulative weight rather than merely by counting maxims. Thus the rules of conversational implicature not only display the reinforcement and conflict patterns of preference rules; they also require a characteristic weighted measure of stability.

Finally, consider three examples from real life: Shall I buy the one I like, or the one that's cheapest? Shall I answer the telephone, or finish what I'm doing? Should I make more profit, or better preserve natural resources? In each case, two incommensurate preferences are in conflict, and one must determine a course of action that balances them. Of course, if the two preferences reinforce each other—the one I like best happens to be cheapest, answering the telephone helps me finish what I'm doing, or the most profit can be made by maximally preserving natural resources, there is no difficulty in making a judgment. Thus these conscious preferences have the reinforcement-conflict patterns of preference rules. I need not comment on the insanity of attempting to devise an "objective" measure of stability for such cases (even if, as in the third case, social necessity forces us to try). Nonetheless, we can and do make such decisions all the time, intuitively.

We have seen, then, that the characteristics of preference rule systems are found everywhere in psychological processes, all the way from low-level perceptual mechanisms to problems so prominent in our conscious life as to be of social and political concern. Thus there is no obstacle in principle to adopting them as part of a theory of word meanings. Yet the notion of a preference rule system has not been recognized as a unified phenomenon, except perhaps by the

Gestalt psychologists. The reason for this, I think, is that the kind of computation a preference rule system performs is quite alien to prevalent ideas of what a formal theory should be like. Formal logic, generative grammar, and computer science all have their roots in the theory of mathematical proof, in which there is no room for graded judgments, and in which conflict between inferences can be resolved only by throwing the derivation out. Although graded judgments and amicable resolution of conflicting inferences are endemic in psychological computation, statistical adaptations of traditional computational techniques to simulate these characteristics always have an air of artificiality about them. Thus, when preference rule phenomena emerge within a theory, there is a strong tendency to downplay them, to minimize their significance. I hope the present chapter can begin to alter the perspective of the field.

I see a preference rule system as a way to accomplish what psychological systems do well but computers do very badly: deriving a quasi-determinate result from unreliable data. In a preference rule system there are multiple converging sources of evidence for a judgment. In the ideal (stereotypical) case these sources are redundant; but no single one of the sources is essential, and in the worst case the system can make do with any one alone. Used as default values, the rules are invaluable in setting a course of action in the face of insufficient evidence. At higher levels of organization, they are a source of great flexibility and adaptivity in the overall conceptual system.

It is also not hard to imagine neurons as performing preference-rule-like computations. The McCulloch-Pitts (1943) idealization of a binary neuron leads to neural nets with the computational power of a Turing machine. Suppose that instead of neural inputs and outputs having only the values 0 and 1, we were to allow them continuously graded values based on rate or pattern of firing. Then a neuron's rate of firing (that is, strength of judgment) would be based on some weighted function of the excitatory and inhibitory inputs (relative strength of application of preference rules). Thus, on both formal and physiological grounds, preference rule systems would appear to be a pervasive hallmark of natural intelligence, something whose computational properties deserve exploration.

8.8 Goals Revisited

We have found in preference rule systems a solution for two of the serious problems facing necessary and sufficient conditions as a theory of word meaning: fuzziness and family resemblances. It remains to be seen whether with preference rule systems it is possible to exhaustively decompose word meanings into primitives.

However, we have made some progress. The enlargement of the ontology argued for in chapter 3 provides a much richer range of dimensions in which concepts can be situated. In the next three chapters, moreover, we will break out of [PHYSICAL SPACE] into an even richer ontology of what still can be regarded as primitive conceptual features.

A different sort of expansion of possibilities comes from centrality conditions. Within a semantic field that includes continuous variation in one or more dimensions—for instance, color, shape, or gait—any value can be chosen as focal value for a new concept, subject only to one's ability to discriminate one focal value from the next. Moreover, one can add typicality conditions of various weights, the choice of weighting affecting shades of meaning as well. Thus a preference rule system provides a whole panoply of combinatorial possibilities that give any fixed set of primitives a far greater expressive power than they would have in a simple feature system.

Finally, it should be pointed out that a theory of primitives does not require that each primitive be individually capable of lexical realization. It might be that some primitives fall into feature systems like that in phonology. Then, just as [+voiced], for example, cannot be realized except as part of a fully specified phonological matrix, a semantic primitive within such a feature system could not appear alone as the meaning of a word. This again opens up the range of possibilities.

But to determine whether these enrichments are enough to achieve exhaustive decomposition into primitives, or whether still more formal power is needed—or whether there is some entirely different way to think about the problem of word meanings—requires a concerted attack on the lexicon. We now turn to some representative problems of lexical analysis, showing how they reflect on the theory of cognition.

Part IV

APPLICATIONS

Chapter 9
Semantics of
Spatial Expressions

These last three chapters move away from fundamental theoretical issues toward more detailed linguistic description. They are intended as illustration of the benefits to be gained from adopting the theoretical stance developed in the preceding chapters.[1]

9.1 The Semantics of Spatial Prepositional Phrases

Chapter 3 argued that prepositional phrases such as "here," "thataway," "on the table," and "in the park" can function referentially, being used to pick out #places# and #paths# in the projected world. This section will develop these notions at somewhat greater length, in order to arrive at a rough taxonomy of #places# and #paths# and their relationship to the prepositional phrases (PPs) of English. (For the rest of this and the next chapter, I will drop ## when speaking of reference, for the sake of typographical sightliness.)

First consider the internal structure of simple PLACE concepts. As observed in chapter 4, a PP in English may consist of an intransitive preposition alone, such as "here," "thataway," "forward," or "downstairs." Alternatively, it may explicitly mention a *reference object* as the object of the preposition, as in "on the table," "under the counter," or "in the can." It may even mention two reference objects, as in "between the square and the circle" and "across the road from the firehouse." (Both of these examples function as unitary PPs—see Jackendoff (1977a).) The place referred to is distinct from the reference object, since one can refer to a variety of places, such as "under the table," "near the table," "on the table," and "inside the table," holding the reference object constant.

We can express this conceptual possibility formally in terms of a phrase-structure-like rule for the functional composition of a conceptual structure. (We ignore multiple reference objects for the moment.)

(9.1)
$$[\text{PLACE}] \rightarrow \begin{bmatrix} \text{PLACE} \\ \text{PLACE-FUNCTION ([THING])} \end{bmatrix}$$

For convenience, we will introduce an alternative notation, which treats the ontological category feature as a subscript on the bracketing, or omits it when clear from context. Thus we use (9.2) interchangeably with (9.1).

(9.2) $[_{\text{Place}} \, x] \rightarrow [_{\text{Place}} \, \text{PLACE-FUNCTION} \, ([_{\text{Thing}} \, y])]$

Different PPs correspond to place-concepts in different ways. The intransitive preposition "here" expresses a [PLACE] all by itself, so the expansion (9.2) does not apply. The transitive preposition "on," by contrast, expresses a place-function, and its strictly subcategorized object NP has the role of expressing the reference object, the argument y of the place-function.

Each place-function imposes conceptual constraints on the nature of the reference object. These appear in the language as selectional restrictions on the corresponding preposition. For instance, the place-function IN requires its reference object to be regarded as a bounded area or volume; this is why "The dog is in the dot" is odd. The most salient place-function expressed by "on" requires its reference object to have an upper surface. Another sense of "on" occurs in "the fly on the ceiling," in which the place-function involves the *outer* (i.e., visible) surface of the reference object. These two senses seem to be typicality conditions in a preference rule system in the lexical entry for "on." (See Miller and Johnson-Laird (1976, section 6.1) for interesting discussion of various spatial prepositions.)

The most important distinction within the class of senses of spatial PPs is the distinction between [PLACES] and [PATHS]. [PLACES] are the simpler of the two: a [PLACE] projects into a point or region, as illustrated in the examples above. Within the structure of an event or state, a [PLACE] is normally occupied by a [THING], as seen in sentences like those in (9.3).

(9.3)   ([THING] occupies [PLACE])
  a. John is in the room.
  b. The lamp is standing on the floor.
  c. The mouse stayed under the table.

Alternatively, a PP of location can express the location of the event or state described by the sentence. This PP may come at either the beginning or the end of the sentence, and is attached higher on the tree than strictly subcategorized arguments (see the trees in section 4.2).

(9.4) a. In Cincinnati, Max met a cockroach.
      b. Jean ate breakfast in her bedroom.

[PATHS] have more varied structure than [PLACES] and play a wider variety of roles in [EVENTS] and [STATES]. The internal structure of a [PATH] often consists of a path-function and a reference object, as expressed by phrases like "toward the mountain," "around the tree," and "to the floor." Alternatively, the argument of a path-function may be a reference *place*. This possibility is most transparent in a phrase like "from under the table," where "from" expresses the path-function and "under the table" expresses the reference place. Prepositions such as "into" and "onto" express both a path-function and the place-function of the reference place, meaning roughly "to in" and "to on," respectively. Thus we have such conceptual structures as these:

(9.5) a. The mouse ran from under the table.
         $[_{Path} \text{FROM} ([_{Place} \text{UNDER} ([_{Thing} \text{TABLE}])])]$
      b. The mouse ran into the room.
         $[_{Path} \text{TO} ([_{Place} \text{IN} ([_{Thing} \text{ROOM}])])]$

Many prepositions in English—for example, "over," "under," "on," "in," "above," and "between"—are ambiguous between a pure place-function and TO + place-function, as illustrated in (9.6).

(9.6) a. The mouse is under the table.
         $[_{Place} \text{UNDER} ([_{Thing} \text{TABLE}])]$
      b. The mouse ran under the table.
         $[_{Path} \text{TO} ([_{Place} \text{UNDER} ([_{Thing} \text{TABLE}])])]$

To avoid ambiguity in the notation for conceptual structure, we will henceforth use such prepositions in capitals exclusively to denote the place-function reading; the path-function reading will be notated as in (9.6b).

One might consider claiming that there is no ambiguity in these prepositions and that it is a mistake to distinguish [PATHS] from [PLACES]. As this section continues, we will provide further evidence for the distinction. As a preliminary bit of evidence, though, we observe that there are other languages in which the distinction between the path and place readings receives systematic grammatical treatment. For example, certain German prepositions take dative case when used as place-functions and accusative when used as path-functions. In Hungarian, postpositions (prepositions that occur after their object) take an extra suffix -n when used as place-functions that is not present when they express path-functions. For these grammatical distinctions to be properly based in semantic distinctions, both conceptual structures in (9.6) are essential, and we must treat prepositions like "under" as ambiguous. Thus we find three-way patterns in English like (9.7).

(9.7) a. [$_{Place}$ PLACE-FUNCTION ([THING])]

   in the room, on the table, between the trees, under the house

   b. [$_{Path}$ PATH-FUNCTION ([$_{Place}$ PLACE-FUNCTION
                                                          ([THING])])]

   (*functions lexicalized separately*)

   from in the room, from on the table, from between the trees, from under the house

   c. [$_{Path}$ PATH-FUNCTION ([$_{Place}$ PLACE-FUNCTION
                                                          ([THING])])]

   (*functions lexicalized together*)

   in(to) the room, on(to) the table, between the trees, under the house

In addition, a number of intransitive place-prepositions fall into a similar (though slightly less regular) pattern, except that the reference object is not expressed separately as an NP. (9.8a,b,c) correspond to (9.7a,b,c), respectively.

(9.8) a. here, there, (at) home
       b. from here, from there, from home
       c. here, (to) there, home

Paths can be divided into three broad types, according to the path's relationship to the reference object or place. The first class, *bounded paths,* includes source-paths, for which the usual preposition is "from," and goal-paths, for which the preposition is "to." In bounded paths, the reference object or place is an endpoint of the path—the beginning in a source-path and the end in a goal-path. As already observed, "from" can be followed by many place-prepositions to express conceptually complex sources, whereas the path-function TO tends to combine with place-functions into a single lexical item.

In the second class of paths, *directions,* the reference object or place does not fall on the path, but would if the path were extended some unspecified distance. "Away from" and "toward" are the most common transitive prepositions expressing directions. To see the distinction between bounded paths and directions, notice that in (9.9a) John is claimed to have reached the house, while in (9.9b) he quite possibly has not. Similarly, in (9.9c) he began running at a point adjacent to or inside the house, while in (9.9d) his initial distance from the house is inexplicit.

(9.9) a. John ran to the house. (bounded path)
　　　 b. John ran toward the house. (direction)
　　　 c. John ran from the house. (bounded path)
　　　 d. John ran away from the house. (direction)

In addition to the transitive prepositions "toward" and "away from," there are several intransitive prepositions of direction, such as "up(ward)," "down(ward)," "forward," "backward," "homeward," and "north(ward)." We will use the expressions TOWARD and AWAY-FROM for the basic path-functions of direction. Like TO and FROM, these differ in polarity.

In the third class of paths, *routes,* the reference object or place is related to some point in the interior of the path. (9.10) gives some examples; the verb used there, "pass," occurs only with a PP that expresses a route.

(9.10)　　　　　　　　　　　　 by the house.
　　　　　　　　　　　　　　　 along the river.
　　　　The car passed 　　　 through the tunnel.
　　　　　　　　　　　　　　　 *to the garage. (PP is goal)
　　　　　　　　　　　　　　　 *toward the truck. (PP is direction)

In the traversal of a route, nothing is specified about the endpoints of the motion. All that we know is that at some point in time along the trip, the car in (9.10) was located by the house, along the river, or inside the tunnel.

We will use VIA as the basic path-function for routes, to be further differentiated by features that we will not explore here. Many route expressions of English use place-prepositions such as "by," "along," and "over" to express VIA + place-function. "Through" expresses roughly VIA INSIDE. "Under" has, in addition to the place and goal readings illustrated in (9.6), a route reading that appears in "The mouse passed under the table." Thus "The mouse went under the table" is actually ambiguous between the goal and route readings.

(9.11) a. The mouse went under the table.
$$[_{\text{Path}} \text{ TO } ([_{\text{Place}} \text{ UNDER } ([_{\text{Thing}} \text{ TABLE}])])]$$

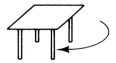

   b. The mouse went under the table.
$$[_{\text{Path}} \text{ VIA } ([_{\text{Place}} \text{ UNDER } ([_{\text{Thing}} \text{ TABLE}])])]$$

The need for this distinction provides further evidence for the ambiguity in (9.6), between "under" of place and of path.

A wide range of paths, then, can be expressed by the well-formedness rule (9.12), which is analogous to rule (9.2) for places.

(9.12)

$$[\text{PATH}] \rightarrow \left[\left[\begin{matrix} \text{TO} \\ \text{FROM} \\ \text{TOWARD} \\ \text{AWAY-FROM} \\ \text{VIA} \end{matrix} \right]_{\text{Path}} \left(\left\{ \begin{matrix} [_{\text{Thing}} \, y] \\ [_{\text{Place}} \, y] \end{matrix} \right\} \right) \right]$$

To complete this rough taxonomy of place- and path-concepts, we must introduce a class of place-concepts that appear to be based on reference *paths*. For example, "The house is up the hill" seems to imply "on a (distal) point of a path up the hill." "Ahead" and "through" used as place-expressions have a similar effect, as in

"There's a train ahead" and "The train is through the tunnel." This suggests an additional well-formedness rule (9.13a) for [PLACE], giving the place-expression "up the hill" the conceptual structure (9.13b), in which UP is a variety of direction-function ("toward the top of" or the like).[2]

(9.13) a. [PLACE] → [Place ON ([Path x])]

  b. [Place ON ([Path UP ([Thing HILL])])]

The construction of a place-concept from a reference path permits two more options, which can be added to (9.13a). Consider the examples in (9.14).

(9.14)

The firehouse is
{
  a. across the street from the library.
  b. two miles down the road (from here).
  c. far/way north of/from here.
  d. two miles from my house.
}

In (9.14a) the location of the firehouse is given in terms of a reference path, "across the street," whose origin is specified in the "from"-phrase. If the reference path is unbounded (for instance, "down the road" or "north"), then a distance along the reference path can be added, as in (9.14b,c). Finally, one can specify just the origin and the distance, leaving direction inexplicit, as in (9.14d). (9.15) makes this construction more graphic.

(9.15)

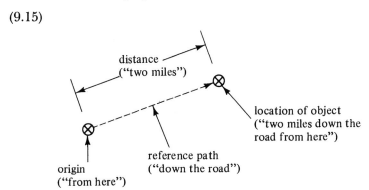

distance ("two miles")

location of object ("two miles down the road from here")

reference path ("down the road")

origin ("from here")

An amplification of (9.13a) that permits these possibilities is (9.16a). (9.16b) and (9.16c) are then approximate representations of the [PLACES] in (9.14a) and (9.14b), respectively. (The connection of the components in (9.16a) is looser than it should be, but it will suffice for present purposes.)

(9.16)

a. [PLACE] →
$$\left[\begin{array}{l} \text{ON}\left(\left[\begin{array}{l} \text{FROM } ([\left\{\begin{array}{l}\text{THING}\\\text{PLACE}\end{array}\right\}]) \\ \left\{\begin{array}{l}\text{TO } ([\begin{array}{l}\text{THING}\\\text{PLACE}\end{array}]) \\ \text{DIRECTION}\end{array}\right\} \\ \text{[DISTANCE]} \end{array}\right]_{\text{Path}}\right) \end{array}\right]_{\text{Place}}$$

b.
$$\left[\begin{array}{l}\text{ON}\left(\left[\begin{array}{l}\text{FROM } ([_{\text{Thing}} \text{ LIBRARY}]) \\ \text{TO } ([_{\text{Place}} \text{ OTHER SIDE OF } ([_{\text{Thing}} \text{ ROAD}])])\end{array}\right]_{\text{Path}}\right)\end{array}\right]_{\text{Place}}$$

c.
$$\left[\begin{array}{l}\text{ON}\left(\left[\begin{array}{l}\text{FROM } ([_{\text{Place}} \text{ HERE}]) \\ \text{DOWN } ([_{\text{Thing}} \text{ ROAD}]) \\ [_{\text{Distance}} \text{ TWO MILES}]\end{array}\right]_{\text{Path}}\right)\end{array}\right]_{\text{Place}}$$

Now let us turn to the roles that paths may play in an event or state. First, a [PATH] may be *traversed* by a [THING], as in (9.17a). Second, a [THING] may *extend* over a [PATH], as in (9.17b); here the subject of the sentence is not understood as being in motion. Third, a [THING] may be *oriented* along a [PATH], as in (9.17c); here the subject, if in motion, is understood to be adopting an orientation, not traversing the path.

(9.17) a. ([THING] traverses [PATH])
      John ran into the house.
      The mouse skittered toward the clock.
      The train rambled along the river.

    b. ([THING] extends over [PATH])
      The highway extends from Denver to Indianapolis.
      The flagpole reaches (up) toward the sky.
      The sidewalk goes around the tree.

    c. ([THING] is oriented along [PATH])
      The sign points to Philadelphia.
      The house faces away from the mountains.
      The cannons aim through the tunnel.

The next section will discuss how [PATHS] come to play these roles as a consequence of the choice of other elements in the sentence.

To sum up the taxonomy of [PATHS], there are nine possible combinations of path type with path role. (9.17) illustrates each path role with one example of each path type (bounded paths, directions, routes), thus exhibiting the full range of paths.

Many accounts of the structure of spatial concepts have not recognized the generality of path-concepts. Schank (1973), for example, encodes the source and the goal of a physical motion as two arguments of the "primitive act" PTRANS, which means roughly "object is in one place (source) at the beginning of the event and in another (goal) at the end." Such an account allows for only one of the nine possible combinations of path type with path role, the one in the first sentence of (9.17a).[3] Similarly, Jackendoff (1976) treats source and goal as the second and third arguments of the function $GO(x,y,z)$; there is no way to represent directions, routes, or even complex goals like those in (9.6b). The formulation is a slight improvement on Schank's, in that the function GO can express extension as well as transition, but the orientation role of paths still cannot be represented. Miller and Johnson-Laird (1976) have a notion of path as a distinct conceptual category and are thus able to treat the three path types uniformly. However, they describe paths in terms of a temporal succession of points, for example (p. 406):

$TO(x,y)$: A referent x is "to" a relatum y if, for an interval ending at time $t - 1$, $notAT(x,y)$ and: (i) $AT(x,y)$ at time t.

Though such a definition suffices for the traversal role of paths, it cannot be adapted to the extensional role (9.17b) or the orientation role (9.17c).

By contrast, the present account provides a uniform set of conceptual structures for PPs that express paths. These conceptual structures are organized spatially and nontemporally. They are therefore equally available for any of the three roles that paths may play in larger conceptual structures.

An interesting bit of nonverbal evidence for the psychological reality of paths comes from the observations of Köhler (1927, chapter 1). He points out that a sufficiently intelligent animal (e.g., a dog but not a chicken), confronted with food behind a transparent barrier, will "run in a smooth curve, without any interruption, out of the blind alley, round the fence to the new food," as in (9.18).

(9.18)

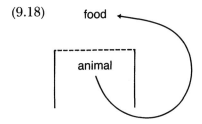

The execution of such a smooth curve requires its being planned in advance—not as a finite sequence of points joined by straight lines, but as an entire path. For this plan to be present all at once, it must be stored nontemporally; the animal then plays out the plan over time. Thus, if an animal can perform such an action as Köhler describes, it must be able to formulate concepts of spatial organization that fall under what we have called here the major ontological category of paths. In other words, not only language but the theory of action as well requires a notion of path, and it is pointless to try to eliminate it from language on grounds of parsimony.

9.2 Verbs of Spatial Location and Motion

We next turn to sentences that describe spatial location and motion. For the moment let us restrict ourselves to sentences of the form NP V PP; we will extend the analysis to the more general case shortly. Within this restricted class, the correspondence of syntax and semantics is transparent: the PP refers to a place or path, the subject NP refers to a thing, and the sentence as a whole refers to a situation or event in which the thing is located or moving in some way with respect to the place or path. The verb specifies exactly what the thing is doing with respect to the place or path. For example, in "Bill flew around the pole," the sentence refers to an event in which Bill traverses a path specified as being around the pole. The verb "fly" specifies both that Bill traverses the path (rather than occupying it, for instance) and that Bill traverses it in a particular manner.

In general, the thing whose motion or location is asserted is not always in subject position; hence we need a technical term for the NP that fulfills this semantic function. Following Gruber's (1965) analysis, we will call the NP whose motion or location is asserted the *theme*. Thus "Bill" is the theme of the example above.[4]

A major division in the class of spatial sentences, already alluded to in chapter 4, is between those that express [EVENTS] and those that express [STATES]. A clear linguistic test for the distinction is the possibility of occurring after "What happened/occurred/took place was (that) . . ."; events happen, while states do not. Thus we find contrasts like these:

(9.19) a. (Events)

What happened was that $\left\{\begin{array}{l}\text{Bill flew around the pole.}\\\text{the rock fell off the table.}\\\text{the mouse ran up the clock.}\\\text{a bee buzzed in the window.}\end{array}\right\}$

   b. (States)

?What happened was that $\left\{\begin{array}{l}\text{Max was in Africa.}\\\text{the rug lay on the floor.}\\\text{the statue stood in the park.}\\\text{a vine clung to the wall.}\end{array}\right\}$

Another relevant grammatical distinction, idiosyncratic to English, concerns the use of the simple present tense. With states, simple present can be used to express present time (9.20a). With events, however, present time must be expressed by present progressive aspect (9.20b); simple present may only be used to express generic events, future time, and various less common sorts of speech acts such as stage directions and newspaper headlines.

(9.20) a. (States)
   Max is in Africa.
   The rug lies/is lying on the floor.
   The statue stands/is standing in the park.
   The picture hangs/is hanging on the wall.

   b. (Events)
   Bill is flying/*flies around the pole.
   The rock is falling/*falls off the table.
   The mouse is running/*runs up the clock.
   A bee is buzzing/*buzzes in the window.

   c. Bill flies around the pole tomorrow. (future)
   Bill flies around the pole every day. (generic)
   Bill flies around the pole, and then says, ". . ." (stage direction)
   BILL FLIES AROUND THE POLE! (headline)

All the sentences in (9.19a) describe motion of the theme along a path. We will express this commonality with conceptual structure (9.21a), a necessary condition for the verbs of motion in (9.19a) as well as for several hundred others of the same character (see Miller and Johnson-Laird (1976) for a larger sample). The sentences in

(9.19b), by contrast, express the location of the theme in a place; we will express this with conceptual structure (9.21b). (The relation of this BE to the BE of chapters 5 and 6 will be discussed in section 10.2.)

(9.21) a. [$_{Event}$ GO ([$_{Thing}$ x], [$_{Path}$ y])]

      b. [$_{State}$ BE ([$_{Thing}$ x], [$_{Place}$ y])]

The variables x and y in (9.21) represent the information to be filled in from the subject and PP of the sentence, respectively.

GO is not the only event-function. A much smaller class of verbs such as "stay" and "remain" express the maintenance of position over time. The tests of (9.19) and (9.20) reveal these as expressions of events.

(9.22) a. What happened was that $\begin{cases} \text{the bird stayed in its nest.} \\ \text{Bill remained on the floor.} \end{cases}$

      b. The bird is staying/*stays in its nest.

      c. Bill is remaining/*remains on the floor.

We will assign these verbs the partial conceptual structure (9.23).[5]

(9.23) [$_{Event}$ STAY ([$_{Thing}$ x], [$_{Place}$ y])]

Nor is BE the only state-function. In the previous section we discussed the use of paths as arguments of functions of extent (9.17b) and orientation (9.17c), repeated here.

(9.17) b. The highway extends from Denver to Indianapolis.
         The flagpole reaches (up) toward the sky.
         The sidewalk goes around the tree.

      c. The sign points to Philadelphia.
         The house faces away from the mountains.
         The cannons aim through the tunnel.

These sentences pass the tests for state rather than event expressions: they are in the simple present tense, and in past tense they cannot be preceded by "What happened was" (as in *"What happened was that the highway extended from Denver to Indianapolis").

Let us examine the orientation sentences first. These describe not the location of the subject but the direction it is pointing (as a result, the subject is restricted to orientable things—featureless spheres cannot point). The prepositional phrase is a path-function, usually a direction or route, that specifies the orientation of the subject. Thus we need a new function *ORIENT,* with the functional structure (9.24).

(9.24) [State ORIENT ([Thing x], [Path y])]

There are also orientation *events,* such as that described in "John spun around," but we will not go into further details here.

Now turn to the extent sentences (9.17b). Notice how they differ from motion sentences such as "Amy went from Denver to Indianapolis." In a motion sentence, the subject is asserted to have traversed the path, covering each point of the path in order over time. By contrast, in "Highway 36 goes from Denver to Indianapolis," the subject is asserted to occupy the entire path at a single point in time. I will call the function expressed by extent sentences GO_{Ext}, as in (9.25).

(9.25) [State GO_{Ext} ([Thing x], [Path y])]

It is significant that most verbs of extent, like those in (9.17b), can also be used as verbs of motion. With such verbs, the possibility of a motion or extent interpretation is determined by the motility of the subject (people travel, roads don't) and sometimes by the tense (simple present for extent, a state, and progressive for traversal, an event). With the proper choice of subject and tense, one can produce an ambiguous sentence such as "The giant reached to the ceiling," which may describe either a movement by the giant or the giant's extreme height.

This lexical generalization between verbs of motion and verbs of extent is of the sort that the Grammatical Constraint encourages us to incorporate into semantic theory. One plausible way is to claim that GO and GO_{Ext} are not distinct functions, but that the difference between a traversal and an extent interpretation depends only on whether the GO function is a feature of an [EVENT] or a [STATE]. Alternatively, one could claim that the functions are distinct but share a great deal of internal structure. At the moment I do not know how to distinguish these two positions; for clarity I will retain the term GO_{Ext}, using GO for traversal only.

Stepping back from the formal issues, we see from this lexical generalization that there is a close relation between the means for mentally representing temporal sequence (motion along a path) and spatial sequence (objects extending along a path). Thus semantic theory provides a surprisingly direct corroboration of Lashley's (1951) argument that temporal ordering must be mentally represented in spatial terms.

As mentioned in the previous section, the function GO has often been treated as expressing a change of state from one position to another, in effect reducing the event GO to a succession of two states and apparently eliminating one primitive spatial function. Here are three arguments against such a treatment. First, GO can occur not only with bounded paths (sources and goals) but also with directions and routes, where the endpoints are left inexplicit. This shows that the stipulation of beginning- and end-states is not essential to the use of a GO function. Rather, whatever the particulars of the path, GO expresses the traversal of every point of it. Second, the reduction of GO to a change of state is incompatible with the generalization of GO to expressions of extent. "The road goes from A to B" does not merely inform us about the endpoints; it tells us about the continuity of the road between A and B. For GO_{Ext} to be related in any sensible way to motional GO, the latter must encode continuous transition. Third, it is clear that perception must include representations of motion: we are aware not just of things being in one place and then being somewhere else—they might as well be jumping discontinuously—but also of their moving. Why should natural language semantics not permit us to encode this? Thus the Expressiveness Constraint, the Grammatical Constraint, and the Cognitive Constraint all converge on the position that there must be an event-function GO that is not reducible to a succession of BEs.

To sum up, the well-formedness rules (9.26a,b) express the functional decomposition of [EVENTS] and [STATES].

(9.26) a. [EVENT] $\rightarrow$ $\begin{Bmatrix} [_{Event} \text{ GO } ([_{Thing} x], [_{Path} y])] \\ [_{Event} \text{ STAY } ([_{Thing} x], [_{Place} y])] \end{Bmatrix}$

b. [STATE] $\rightarrow$ $\begin{Bmatrix} [_{State} \text{ BE } ([_{Thing} x], [_{Place} y])] \\ [_{State} \text{ ORIENT } ([_{Thing} x], [_{Path} y])] \\ [_{State} \text{ GO}_{Ext} ([_{Thing} x], [_{Path} y])] \end{Bmatrix}$

9.3 Causative Functions

A further element in our survey of spatial functions is the notion of causation, involved in the relation between the sentences in (9.27a) and those in (9.27b).

(9.27) a. Sim came into the room.
The ball flew out the window.
The books stayed on the shelf.

b. The wind pushed Sim into the room.
Beth threw the ball out the window.
Suzanne kept the books on the shelf.

Roughly, the (b) sentences describe an agent bringing about the events described in the (a) sentences. We will represent the role of the agent by means of a binary function CAUSE, with structure (9.28a). Thus the sentences in (9.27b) have the representations shown in (9.28b); the embedded [EVENT] in each of these is the representation of the corresponding noncausative in (9.27a).

(9.28) a. [Event CAUSE ([Thing x], [Event y])]

b. [Event CAUSE ([Thing WIND], [Event GO ([Thing SIM],
[Path INTO ROOM])])]

[Event CAUSE ([Thing BETH], [Event GO ([Thing BALL],
[Path OUT WINDOW])])]

[Event CAUSE ([Thing SUZANNE],
[Event STAY ([Thing BOOKS], [Place ON SHELF])])]

A number of points about this representation merit discussion. First, consider the syntactic relation between the (9.27a) sentences and the (9.27b) sentences. The noncausative sentences, like all the sentences of the previous subsection, have the form NP_1 V PP, with the theme in the subject. The causative sentences have the form NP_2 V NP_1 PP, with the agent in the subject and the theme in the direct object. In an earlier period of generative grammar, various attempts were made to treat this relationship by means of syntactic transformations. This was the hallmark of case grammar (Fillmore (1968)) and generative semantics (McCawley (1968), Lakòff (1970, 1971)), for example. Such an account was especially appealing in light of verbs that have both causative and noncausative forms, such as "fly" and "grow."

(9.29) a. Amelia flew the plane.
The plane flew.

b. Luther grew the peas.
The peas grew.

But since the introduction of lexical rules as a means of expressing morphological and semantic relations among similar lexical items (Chomsky 1970)), it has come to be widely accepted that the causative-noncausative relation in English is not a syntactic relationship but a lexical one. That is how it will be treated here; I will assume that there is no "deeper" word order underlying either set of sentences in (9.27). (See Jackendoff (1975a) and Bresnan (1978) for details.)

Let us consider now some aspects of semantic structure (9.28a) itself. Notice that the agent is not necessarily acting willfully; for example, "the wind" is agent in the first sentence of (9.27b). The possibility of willfulness arises from the fact that an event of causation can be reanalyzed as an actor performing an action, as will be discussed in the next section. We will see there that willfulness or intentionality is an optional property of an *actor*, and need not be represented in addition as part of the function CAUSE.

Some analysts (for example, Schank (1973), Davidson (1967b), and Miller and Johnson-Laird (1976)) have treated CAUSE as a function over two events. Instead of (9.28a), they propose something like (9.30). (I have translated their notations into my formalism.)

(9.30) [$_{Event}$ CAUSE ([$_{Event}$ DO([$_{Thing}$ x], [$_{Action}$ z])], [$_{Event}$ y])]

(9.30) can be expressed in English roughly as "x did something z that caused y." This analysis has been justified on the basis of sentences like "John's blowing bubbles made us laugh," in which an event, expressed by an NP, appears in subject position and therefore appears to be fulfilling the role of agent. The claim is that greater generality is achieved by requiring the first argument of CAUSE always to be an event; the representation in (9.30) then automatically expresses the fact that x is performing some action in bringing y about. Furthermore, this analysis easily accommodates an expression such as the "by"-phrase in "John made us laugh by blowing bubbles": such an expression of means simply fills in the action z in (9.30).

However, according to the Grammatical Constraint, we should be wary of positing a semantic structure such as the DO...[$_{Action}$ z] in (9.30) and of assigning the same semantic structure to such radically different syntactic structures as subjects and means expressions. Indeed, this wariness is justified by the existence of means expressions in sentences whose subject is an [EVENT], such as "John's blowing bubbles made us laugh by making us realize how drunk we all were." This example shows that the means expression cannot be taken to fill the variable z in (9.30): in this example z has already putatively been filled by "blowing bubbles." Thus the alleged syntactic generality of (9.30) is illusory. (A related argument appears in Fodor, Garrett, Walker, and Parkes (1980).)

In the present theory, we will claim instead that the function CAUSE permits either a [THING] or an [EVENT] as its first argument and that this argument appears invariably in subject position. Then "John made us laugh" is represented roughly as (9.31a); "John's blowing bubbles made us laugh" as in (9.31b).

(9.31) a. [Event CAUSE ([Thing JOHN], [Event WE LAUGH])]

b. [Event CAUSE ([Event JOHN BLOW BUBBLES],
                                            [Event WE LAUGH])]

The fact that John did something will be expressed by the reanalysis of (9.31a) and the first argument of (9.31b) as actor-action pairs (see next section). The fact that John may have been willful but John's blowing bubbles (taken as a whole) could not be follows from the fact that only animate actors can be willful. Finally, a means expression, like all such syntactic modifiers, corresponds to a restrictive modifier of the conceptual constituent that dominates it—in this case the CAUSE function. In other words, the means expression expresses *how* John, or John's blowing bubbles, caused the event in the second argument. Thus the present analysis, by simply extending the first argument of CAUSE to include [EVENTS], incorporates all the evidence for (9.30) at no cost to the generality of the syntax-semantics correspondence.

Finally, consider the second argument of CAUSE. This is explicitly an [EVENT], not a [STATE], for agents make things *happen*. For example, (9.32) presents two alternative analyses of "Amy put the flowers in the vase."

(9.32) a. [Event CAUSE ([Thing AMY], [Event GO ([Thing FLOWERS],
                                                          [Path INTO VASE])])]

b. [Event CAUSE ([Thing AMY], [State BE ([Thing FLOWERS],
                                                          [Place IN VASE])])]

(9.32a) may be read "Amy made it happen that the flowers went into the vase"; (9.32b), "Amy made it be the case that the flowers were in the vase." Either is superficially plausible. However, notice that the latter is somewhat odd-sounding: what Amy really did was bring about an event whose end-state is the situation in question. This is invariably the case in causative sentences that appear to have a [STATE] as a second argument. Thus I will maintain that the second argument of CAUSE is an [EVENT]. (For further discussion, see Jackendoff (1976).)

Gruber (1965) motivates a second kind of agency, called *permissive* agency, using contrasts like those in (9.33).

(9.33) a. The rock went down the cliff.
    The bird flew out of the cage.
    Sam ran around the tree.

   b. Bill pushed the rock down the cliff.
    Bill removed the bird from the cage.
    Bill made Sam run around the tree.

   c. Bill dropped the rock down the cliff.
    Bill released the bird from the cage.
    Bill let Sam run around the tree.

The sentences in (9.33b) express the familiar causative versions of those in (9.33a). The sentences in (9.33c), however, involve a different relation between the agent and the event, which we will call the function *LET*. The fundamental structure is (9.34).

(9.34) [$_{Event}$ LET ([$_{Thing}$ x], [$_{Event}$ y])]

It has been suggested from time to time that LET means something like "cease to prevent" and therefore may be reducible to NOT CAUSE...NOT. For instance, the first example in (9.33c) might be taken to mean "Bill ceased preventing the rock from going down the cliff." However, the differences between CAUSE and LET, when examined in detail, do not support such a reduction, at least with particular ease. (See Gruber (1965), Jackendoff (1976), Miller and Johnson-Laird (1976, section 6.3).) I will therefore assume that LET represents a distinct type of causative function.

We therefore add the following two event types to the taxonomy of (9.26), establishing the basic syntax of causal concepts.

(9.35)

$$[\text{EVENT}] \rightarrow \left\{ \begin{array}{l} [_{Event}\ \text{CAUSE}\ ([\substack{Thing \\ Event}\ x],\ [_{Event}\ y])] \\ [_{Event}\ \text{LET}\ ([\substack{Thing \\ Event}\ x],\ [_{Event}\ y])] \end{array} \right\}$$

Further refinement of the semantics of causation is possible. I will mention only one example from Talmy's (1976) interesting study.

Talmy observes that some verbs, such as "throw" and "send," express events in which the agent acts only as initiator; after the inception of the event, the theme takes its course without the agent's further intervention. By contrast, the agents of verbs such as "drag" and "bring" participate throughout the theme's motion. Among verbs of permissive agency, "drop" and "lower" contrast along the same dimension. I leave the formalization of this distinction and of others like it for future research.

9.4 VPs and ACTIONS

The formal treatment developed in chapter 4 and elaborated here has so far ignored one of the major ontological categories discussed in chapter 3: [ACTIONS]. As pointed out in section 4.4, [ACTIONS] correspond to the double-primed syntactic category VP and are thus an exception to the generalization that major ontological categories are expressed by major (triple-primed) syntactic categories. This leads to a descriptive inadequacy in a representation like (9.36) for "The man put the book on the table," for this representation contains no constituent identified as an [ACTION].

(9.36) [$_{Event}$ CAUSE ([$_{Thing}$ MAN], [$_{Event}$ GO ([$_{Thing}$ BOOK],

[$_{Path}$ TO ON TABLE])])]

As a first step in solving this problem, notice that sentences that express [ACTIONS] are a subset of those that express [EVENTS]. (9.37) illustrates this; "what happened was" is a diagnostic for [EVENTS] and "what x did" is a diagnostic for [ACTIONS].

(9.37) a. What happened was that

the pig ran away.
she put the book on the table.   ⎫
Fred heard about the accident.   ⎬ EVENTS
Louise received a letter.   ⎭
*the fire truck was red.   ⎫ STATES
*Fred loved Louise.   ⎭

b. What Fred did was

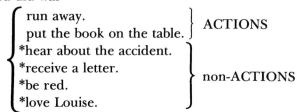

$$\left\{ \begin{array}{l} \text{run away.} \\ \text{put the book on the table.} \end{array} \right\} \text{ACTIONS}$$

$$\left\{ \begin{array}{l} \text{*hear about the accident.} \\ \text{*receive a letter.} \\ \text{*be red.} \\ \text{*love Louise.} \end{array} \right\} \text{non-ACTIONS}$$

An [EVENT] that is also an [ACTION] involves a character with a special role—the one who is performing the [ACTION]. We will call this character the [ACTOR]. The linguistic evidence of chapter 3 shows that an [ACTION] can be identified independently of who is carrying it out (for instance, "Joe did the same thing Harry did"). Thus an [ACTION] is an [EVENT] from which one argument is missing, the one corresponding to the [ACTOR].

These considerations suggest a representation for "The man put the book on the table" something like (9.38).

(9.38) $\left[_{\text{Event}} \begin{array}{c} \text{ACTOR} \\ _{\text{Thing}}\ \text{MAN} \end{array} \right]_i$, $[_{\text{Action}}$ CAUSE $(i,$

$[_{\text{Event}}$ GO $([_{\text{Thing}}$ BOOK], $[_{\text{Path}}$ TO ON TABLE])])]]

In this expression, the first argument of CAUSE is occupied by i, the index of the [ACTOR] constituent. Formally, one can think of this argument place as bound by the [ACTOR]; conceptually, this role is what the [ACTOR] does in performing this [ACTION].

(9.38) deviates from the usual function-argument structure we have employed so far. It is therefore necessary to sanction the possibility of this expression by means of a special well-formedness rule (or rule of conceptual reanalysis):

(9.39) $[_{\text{Event}}$ F$(X_i, Y_j, Z_k,...)] \leftrightarrow$

$[_{\text{Event}} \left[\begin{array}{c} \text{ACTOR} \\ \text{X} \end{array} \right]_i$, $[_{\text{Action}}$ F$(i, Y_j, Z_k,...)]]$

The double arrow in (9.39) means that the forms are interconvertible, so that (9.38) can be derived from (9.36) and vice versa.

Rule (9.39) must be amplified with conceptual conditions on what can count as an [ACTOR] and what as an [ACTION]. The conditions on [ACTOR] can be illustrated by a contrast like the one shown in (9.40).

(9.40) What $\left\{ \begin{array}{l} \text{Fred} \\ \text{?the mail} \end{array} \right\}$ did was go to Philadelphia.

Apparently an [ACTOR] must display a certain capacity for autonomy. Animacy is too strong a requirement, since (9.41a) and even (9.41b) are acceptable.

(9.41) a. What the rock did was roll down the hill.
b. What the clouds did was go over Philadelphia.

The mail seems even flabbier than the clouds, incapable of action; but I won't try to push the distinction further here.

The conditions on [ACTION] can be specified fairly precisely. First, when the variable of an [ACTION] is bound, the result must be an [EVENT]; this condition is incorporated into rule (9.39). This condition excludes "being tall" or "loving Louise" from expressing [ACTIONS], since binding the variable results in a [STATE] rather than an [EVENT]. Second, the semantic role of the variable position in an [ACTION] is limited to agents, as in (9.36), and themes, as in (9.41a). "Receive a letter" and "hear about Bill" do not express [ACTIONS] because the subject is a goal rather than an agent or theme.

Among the correspondence rules, there must be a rule relating the constituent VP to the [ACTION] constituent in conceptual structure:

(9.42) A VP may be construed as an [ACTION]; the argument position of the verb corresponding to the subject is occupied by the bound variable of the [ACTION].

This rule is necessary particularly for the interpretation of sentences like (9.37b), in which a bare VP expressing an [ACTION] appears to the right of "be." It may also prove useful elsewhere.[6]

This account requires no special lexical markings of verbs as action verbs (as does, for example, Ross's (1972) theory). Rather, this information is encoded in the general conditions on the nature of [ACTIONS], in the relation of [ACTIONS] to [EVENTS], and in the correspondence rule (9.42) that relates VPs to [ACTIONS]. A particular VP will be construed as an [ACTION] only if all these conditions are met.

An important subclass of actions is the class of *willful* or *intentional* actions. Consider the following pairs of sentences:

(9.43) a. The rock rolled down the hill.
b. John rolled down the hill.

(9.44) a. The rock broke the window.
        b. John broke the window.

The VPs of all these sentences express [ACTIONS] ("What John/the rock did was roll down the hill/break the window"). The subjects in (9.43a,b) are both themes, and those in (9.44a,b) are both agents. However, the (b) sentences are ambiguous: one can ask whether John acted on purpose or not. In the intentional sense, John performs the action as a result of his own will. In the unintentional sense, he is acting more or less as an inanimate object: he stumbles and falls down the hill or is pushed into the window. This ambiguity can be expressed by the presence or absence of a marker WILLFUL in the semantic structure of the sentence. This marker will be applicable to an animate actor such as "John," but anomalous if applied to an inanimate actor such as "the rock."

How should this marker be attached to the semantic structure? One possibility would be to make it a modifier of CAUSE. But this would not explain the possibility of willfulness when the subject is theme, as in (9.43b).[7] The alternative is to associate the marker WILLFUL with [ACTOR]-[ACTION] pairs, regardless of the thematic relation of the [ACTOR]. This analysis applies uniformly to (9.43) and (9.44) without further ado.

There is then the question of whether WILLFUL should be associated with the [ACTOR] or with the [ACTION]. One's first impulse is to attach it as a modifier of the [ACTOR], since this is the character exerting will. In fact, however, syntactic expressions of willfulness such as "deliberately" and "on purpose," as well as the denial of willfulness in "accidentally," are normally attached to the VP, not to the subject:

(9.45)
        a. What John did was roll down the hill $\begin{Bmatrix} \text{deliberately.} \\ \text{on purpose.} \\ \text{accidentally.} \end{Bmatrix}$

        b. Breaking windows $\begin{Bmatrix} \text{deliberately} \\ \text{accidentally} \\ \text{on purpose} \end{Bmatrix}$ is punishable by death.

Thus the Grammatical Constraint suggests that WILLFUL is a feature of an [ACTION], not of an [ACTOR].

This analysis leads to a simple treatment of imperative sentences like "Wash the dishes!" as bare VPs that express [WILLFUL AC-

TIONS]. Thus, for example, "Receive a letter!" and "Know the answer!" are not possible commands because they do not express [ACTIONS], and "Keep sleeping!" is odd because it expresses an [ACTION] over which it is hard to imagine exerting will.[8]

With this analysis, then, we can treat [ACTIONS] as independent conceptual constituents, in accordance with the linguistic evidence presented in chapter 3. A VP expressing an [ACTION] is a conceptual constituent that may be used referentially, filled in with information derived from pragmatic anaphora, questioned, or quantified over. Moreover, action sentences have a conceptual analysis containing both an [EVENT] and an [ACTION] constituent, as required for explicitness in conceptual representation. This dual analysis, created by rule (9.39), leads to formal and substantive advantages in the description of a number of linguistic constructions.

9.5 A Principle of Lexicalization

The verbs in the examples so far express only one event- or state-function, with the exception of causative verbs, which express two. All of the sentences have also expressed place- or path-functions explicitly as a preposition. However, this is only because I have selected examples in which the correspondence of semantics and syntax is maximally transparent.

In order to deal with the more general case, we must ask how a conceptual structure can be carved up into lexical items. The verb "enter" serves as a good preliminary example. "The dog entered the room" can be paraphrased by "The dog went into the room." Both sentences have the semantic structure (9.46a), in which "the dog" is theme and "the room" is the reference object of the path.[9] However, this structure is lexicalized differently in the two cases. (9.46b) shows how it is composed in "The dog went into the room"; (9.46c) shows how it is composed in "The dog entered the room."

(9.46) a. $[_{\text{Event}} \text{GO} ([_{\text{Thing}} \text{DOG}], [_{\text{Path}} \text{TO} ([_{\text{Place}} \text{IN} ([_{\text{Thing}} \text{ROOM}])])])]$

  b. "go": $[_{\text{Event}} \text{GO} ([_{\text{Thing}} x], [_{\text{Path}} y])]$
     "into": $[_{\text{Path}} \text{TO} ([_{\text{Place}} \text{IN} ([_{\text{Thing}} z])])]$

  c. "enter": $[_{\text{Event}} \text{GO} ([_{\text{Thing}} x], [_{\text{Path}} \text{TO} ([_{\text{Place}} \text{IN} ([_{\text{Thing}} z])])])]$

In other words, the verb "enter" itself lexicalizes the path- and place-functions instead of leaving them to be overtly expressed by a preposition. Since the open argument z is a thing rather than a place or a path, "enter" acts syntactically as a simple transitive verb.

A similar case is "approach," which also lexicalizes a path-function. This time the appropriate function is TOWARD:

(9.47) "approach": [$_{Event}$ GO ([$_{Thing}$ x], [$_{Path}$ TOWARD ([$_{Thing}$ y])])]

Slightly more complex is the verb "rise," which can occur either intransitively ("The balloon rose") or with a PP ("The balloon rose along the cliff"). The intransitive use lexicalizes the path UPWARD; the PP adds an additional component to the path, as in (9.48).

(9.48) [$_{Event}$ GO ([$_{Thing}$ BALLOON], $\begin{bmatrix} \text{UPWARD} \\ _{Path} \text{ ALONG ([}_{Thing}\text{ CLIFF])} \end{bmatrix}$)]

The structure of "rise" is therefore (9.49).

(9.49) "rise": [$_{Event}$ GO ([$_{Thing}$ x], $\begin{bmatrix} \text{UPWARD} \\ _{Path} \quad \langle y \rangle \end{bmatrix}$)]

The angle brackets around the variable y indicate that this argument is optional. When it is not present, we get the intransitive "rise," which takes only a single argument, the theme: the path is totally lexicalized by the verb. When y is present, we get the use of "rise" with a PP: the path given by the verb and that given by the PP combine as features of a more complex path.

The verb "raise" is the causative of "rise." Its structure, which is representative of causatives, is (9.50).

(9.50) "raise": [$_{Event}$ CAUSE ([$_{Thing}$ x], [$_{Event}$ GO ([$_{Thing}$ y],

$\begin{bmatrix} \text{UPWARD} \\ _{Path} \quad \langle z \rangle \end{bmatrix}$)])]

The bracketed variable z abbreviates two uses of "raise," with and without a PP after the direct object, as in "Max raised his hand to the ceiling" and "Max raised his hand," respectively.

Verbs may lexicalize more than just a path- or place-function. For example, "Nicky buttered the toast" has a component that may be paraphrased as "Nicky put butter on the toast"; "Sam dusted the furniture" means "Sam took (the) dust off the furniture." Thus the verbs "butter" and "dust" lexicalize not only the path-function but the theme as well, leaving the agent and the reference object as the two syntactically expressed arguments.

(9.51) a. "butter": [Event CAUSE ([Thing x], [Event GO ([Thing BUTTER],

[Path TO ([Place ON ([Thing y])])])])]

b. "dust": [Event CAUSE ([Thing x], [Event GO ([Thing DUST],

[Path FROM ([Place ON ([Thing y])])])])]

Notice that the two verbs have opposite path-functions. Each is representative of a class of English denominal verbs. Like "butter" are many verbs such as "paper (the walls)," "paint," and "water." Like "dust" are less numerous verbs such as "scale (a fish)," "milk" (with path FROM IN), and "skin."

The most extreme case arises when a verb lexicalizes both the theme and the path, leaving no arguments to be expressed syntactically. The verb "rain" is such a case: it strictly subcategorizes only a semantically empty "it" in the subject. In languages such as Spanish that do not require a syntactic subject, the parallel verb can form a sentence all by itself.

(9.52) "rain": [Event GO ([Thing RAIN], [Path DOWNWARD])]

From these examples emerges an important general principle of lexicalization, for which I have found no exceptions.

Lexical Variable Principle
A variable in the structure of a lexical item must be capable of being filled by a conceptual constituent.

This principle is true of every example given here (including the variable y in "rise" (9.49), which is a [PATH]). To understand its significance, let us see what it predicts must *not* happen.

(An initial caveat: I am generally put off by arguments purporting to demonstrate the nonexistence of a conceivable class of lexical items, since they rely essentially on the author's lack of imagination. Thus I present such an argument with a certain amount of diffidence. To keep myself honest, I will try to formulate as plausible an example as possible.)

Suppose that we take a conceptual structure like (9.53), which is lexicalized most transparently as "Joe put butter on the bread."

(9.53) [Event CAUSE ([Thing JOE], [Event GO ([Thing BUTTER],

[Path TO ([Place ON ([Thing BREAD])])])])]

(9.53) can also be lexicalized as "Joe buttered the bread," in which the verb includes the theme as well as the path- and place-functions, as shown in (9.51). However, one might imagine another lexicalization in which the verb includes the reference object instead. Suppose that, following approximately the pattern of the denominal verbs in (9.51), this verb were pronounced "bread." It would have the structure (9.54).

(9.54) "bread": [Event CAUSE ([Thing x], [Event GO ([Thing y],

[Path z ([Thing BREAD])])])]

We would expect this verb to occur in patterns like (9.55).

(9.55) a. Joe breaded the butter on. (= "Joe put butter on the bread.")

b. Joe breaded the jelly under. (= "Joe put jelly under the bread.")

c. Joe breaded some salami on top of. (= "Joe put some salami on top of the bread.")

Such a verb is plausible on pragmatic grounds: it means something that one can imagine actually wanting to say. Nevertheless, it is intuitively bizarre. This is clearer if we compare it to a hypothetical verb "mayonnaise" ("put mayonnaise on") that follows the formal pattern of "butter" in (9.51a). A sentence like "Joe mayonnaised the bread," though it uses a nonexistent verb, is altogether understandable, while "Joe breaded the butter on," in the sense intended in (9.55a), is nonsense.

There are two ways in which the hypothetical verb "bread" differs from the other verbs we have discussed. First, it violates the Lexical Variable Principle: the variable z is not a conceptual constituent, but a path-function whose argument position has been lexicalized. The second difference is a direct syntactic reflection of the first: in order to express the argument z, such a verb would have to subcategorize a transitive preposition occurring without its object. The reason one can feel fairly confident of the nonexistence of a verb like "bread" is that there are no verbs with such a subcategorization. One can produce the superficial syntactic pattern of (9.55) in two ways, illustrated in (9.56).

(9.56) a. John put the books down.
   Sally sent some sandwiches over.

b. Bill turned the light off.
   Alice looked the answer up.

In (9.56a), the verb subcategorizes a full PP, which happens in these instances to be filled by an (optionally) intransitive preposition. In these examples, the preposition specifies the path all by itself. In (9.56b), the verb occurs idiomatically with an intransitive preposition (or "particle"), and the meaning of the verb-particle combination is specified in the lexicon. In neither case does the preposition have the syntactic or semantic role called for by a verb like "bread," a bare preposition expressing a bare path-function. Thus the Lexical Variable Principle appears to be valid, at least for this case, which—given the wide range of combinations of functions and arguments seen in (9.46)–(9.52) that *can* lexicalize—is not a trivial one.

This argument has involved lexicalization of an event-function and parts of a path. Ross (1972) gives a similar argument with respect to embedded event-functions (interestingly, in a quite different theoretical framework). He observes that the semantic structure of "try to find" in (9.57a) can also be lexicalized as "look for," as in (9.57b); but there could not be a verb "trentertain" that lexicalizes the semantic structure of "try" and "entertainment" alone, as in (9.57c).

(9.57) (Ross's (88))
     a.   Fritz tried to find entertainment.
     b.   Fritz looked for entertainment.
     c.   *Fritz trentertained to find.

Though the pragmatics of Ross's hypothetical example may leave something to be desired, the verb "trentertain" is particularly implausible because the corresponding syntactic pattern—a verb that must be followed by an objectless transitive verb—is unknown. Ross argues from this example that if a verb lexicalizes multiple predicates (event- or state-functions), they must be adjacently embedded in semantic structure. Formally, his claim amounts to a special case of the Lexical Variable Principle, since lexicalization of nonadjacent functions would lead to a variable that is a bare event- or state-function rather than a full conceptual constituent. Again, this is a case of nontrivial interest.[10]

This is by no means all there is to say about lexicalization patterns. I have not mentioned, for instance, any of the fascinating material in Talmy's (1980) broad crosslinguistic survey. However, this much will serve for present purposes; it begins to provide some idea of how lexical and syntactic variety can be achieved within the expressive constraints imposed by a fairly rigid functional form in semantic structure.

Chapter 10
Nonspatial Semantic Fields and the Thematic Relations Hypothesis

The great insight of Gruber (1965), anticipated by others but never demonstrated in such detail (see references in Anderson (1971, 6), is that the semantics of motion and location provide the key to a wide range of further semantic fields.

In present terms, Gruber's hypothesis may be stated like this:

Thematic Relations Hypothesis (TRH)
In any semantic field of [EVENTS] and [STATES], the principal event-, state-, path-, and place-functions are a subset of those used for the analysis of spatial location and motion. Fields differ in only three possible ways:
a. what sorts of entities may appear as theme;
b. what sorts of entities may appear as reference objects;
c. what kind of relation assumes the role played by location in the field of spatial expressions.

Gruber develops this hypothesis by showing that similar grammatical and lexical patterns appear across apparently unrelated semantic fields; Jackendoff (1972, 1976) extends and formalizes Gruber's work. Here we will give only the flavor of this work and discuss its consequences, emphasizing improvements on the 1976 formulation.

The significance of this insight to the present undertaking cannot be overemphasized. It means that in exploring the organization of concepts that, unlike those of #physical space#, lack perceptual counterparts, we do not have to start *de novo*. Rather, we can constrain the possible hypotheses about such concepts by adapting, insofar as possible, the independently motivated algebra of spatial concepts to our new purposes. The psychological claim behind this methodology is that the mind does not manufacture abstract concepts out of thin air, either. It adapts machinery that is already available, both in the development of the individual organism and in the evolutionary development of the species.

10.1 Temporal and Possessive Fields

Let us begin with a particularly transparent illustration of the Thematic Relations Hypothesis. It has often been noticed (as in Anderson (1971), Clark (1973)) that prepositions of time are on the whole identical to spatial expressions (10.1) and that temporal PPs are attached to sentences in the same way as PPs of location (10.2).

(10.1) a. at 6:00
          from Tuesday to Thursday
          in 1976
          on my birthday

       b. at the corner
          from Denver to Indianapolis
          in Cincinnati
          on the table

(10.2) a. In 1976, Max met a cockroach.
          Jean ate breakfast at 8:00.

       b. In Cincinnati, Max met a cockroach. (= (9.4))
          Jean ate breakfast in her bedroom.

This suggests that temporal expressions define a one-dimensional "pseudospace," the well-known time-line. It is not [THINGS] that are located in time, but [EVENTS] and [STATES]. Thus we may define the temporal field as follows, according to criteria (a–c) of the Thematic Relations Hypothesis:

(10.3) Temporal field:
       a. [EVENTS] and [STATES] appear as theme.
       b. [TIMES] appear as reference object.
       c. Time of occurrence plays the role of location.

The TRH predicts a phenomenon not pointed out by Anderson or Clark: that verbs asserting temporal location will appear in patterns parallel to those of spatial verbs. Let us compare the temporal expressions in (10.4) to the spatial ones in (10.5).

(10.4) a. The meeting is at 6:00. (BE)
     b. We moved the meeting from Tuesday to Thursday. (GO)
     c. Despite the weather, we kept the meeting at 6:00. (STAY)

(10.5) a. The statue is in the park. (BE)
     b. We moved the statue from the park to the zoo. (GO)
     c. Despite the weather, we kept the statue on its pedestal. (STAY)

(10.4) shows that when the temporal location of an event is capable of being changed, the verbs used to express change or lack thereof are identical to verbs of spatial motion or lack thereof. Similarly, compare the temporal expressions in (10.6a) with the spatial expressions of extent in (10.6b).

(10.6) a. Ron's speech went/extended/lasted from 2:00 to 4:00.
     b. The road went/extended from Denver to Indianapolis.

Again, many of the same verbs occur.

To appreciate the force of the parallelism, consider the inference patterns of corresponding spatial and temporal expressions. The function GO_{Ext}, expressed in (10.6b), maps a [THING] and a [PATH] into a [STATE] and asserts that the [THING] occupies every point of the [PATH]. When shifted into the temporal domain, as in (10.6a), GO_{Ext} maps an [EVENT] and a temporal [PATH] into a [STATE] and asserts that the [EVENT] occupies all points in time within the temporal [PATH]. The verb "move" in (10.4b), while it loses the sense of continuous traversal, asserts that at the beginning of the event described, the meeting was on Tuesday, and at the end, on Thursday—a subset of the inference pattern expected of spatial GO. In other words, temporal expressions preserve much of the force of lexically parallel spatial expressions, relative to the definitions of theme and location in (10.3).

We will express this semantic parallelism formally by using subscripted spatial functions as conceptual structures for temporal functions. Thus, for example, (10.7a–d) will be the representations for (10.4a–c) and (10.6a).

(10.7) a. [State BE_{Temp} ([Event MEETING], [Place AT_{Temp} ([Time 6:00])])]

     b. [Event CAUSE ([Thing WE], [Event GO_{Temp} ([Event MEETING],

$$\begin{bmatrix} \text{FROM}_{\text{Temp}} \text{ ([Time TUESDAY])} \\ {}_{\text{Path}} \text{ TO}_{\text{Temp}} \text{ ([Time THURSDAY])} \end{bmatrix})])]$$

c. [$_{Event}$ CAUSE ([$_{Thing}$ WE], [$_{Event}$ STAY$_{Temp}$
([$_{Event}$ MEETING], [$_{Place}$ AT$_{Temp}$ ([$_{Time}$ 6:00])])])]

d. [$_{State}$ GO$_{Ext,Temp}$ ([$_{Event}$ SPEECH],
$$\begin{bmatrix} & \text{FROM}_{Temp} \ ([_{Time} \ 2{:}00]) \\ _{Path} & \text{TO}_{Temp} \ ([_{Time} \ 4{:}00]) \end{bmatrix})]$$

This is not the only way time can be conceptualized. As Clark (1973) observes, there is an alternative conceptualization in which times serve as theme instead of reference object. Compare (10.8a) and (10.8b).

(10.8) a. Tuesday crept by.
Christmas is fast approaching.
Our future lies ahead of us.

b. The freight train crept by.
The tiger is fast approaching.
The frontier lies ahead of us.

Here temporal periods, or events considered as temporal periods, are conceived of as moving relative to an observer or experiencer who is conceived of as reference object. Interestingly, expressions in this field often seem to be more emotionally loaded than those defined by (10.3). This is perhaps because these expressions are more closely related to the experience of time than (10.3), which abstracts time away from experience so that one can view time periods synoptically and move events around within them.[1]

Verbs of possession define an entirely different semantic field — actually a family of semantic fields, since there are several distinct notions of possession. A well-known difference is that between inalienable possession—the way one possesses one's nose, for instance—and alienable possession—the way one possesses a book. Alienable possession in turn divides into (at least) ownership and temporary control, so that one can, for example, distinguish a lender's from a borrower's rights over an object. (See Miller and Johnson-Laird (1976, section 7.2.2) for discussion.) Moreover, the kinds of things one can do with a disease such as a cold—have one, get one, give yours to someone else—pattern much like expressions of possession, suggesting yet another member of this family of fields.

Whichever notion of possession we consider, we find that it plays the role that location does in the spatial field, as the central element of a group of [STATE] and [EVENT] concepts. As illustration, we will treat alienable possession, ignoring its further subdivision. It satisfies the Thematic Relations Hypothesis in the terms stipulated in (10.9). Each of the other members of the family substitutes the appropriate notion of possession for "alienably possessed" in (10.9c).

(10.9) Alienable possession:
    a. [THINGS] appear as theme.
    b. [THINGS] appear as reference object.
    c. Being alienably possessed plays the role of location; that is, "y has/possesses x" is the conceptual parallel to spatial "x is at y."

The pseudospaces of all the possessive fields are discontinuous; there is no way to make sense of a continuous transition in possession from one individual to another. Thus [PATHS] degenerate essentially into their endpoints, and the function GO can be treated, in this special case, as a change-of-state function, if one desires.

The examples in (10.10) illustrate verbs in this field, displaying the full range of functional possibilities. (Subscripts that are obvious have been omitted; we use the subscript "Poss" to designate functions relativized to alienable possession.)

(10.10) a. Beth has/possesses/owns the doll.
        The doll belongs to Beth.
        [$_{State}$ BE$_{Poss}$ ([DOLL], [$_{Place}$ AT$_{Poss}$ ([BETH])])]

     b. Beth received the doll.
        [$_{Event}$ GO$_{Poss}$ ([DOLL], [$_{Path}$ TO$_{Poss}$ ([BETH])])]

     c. Beth lost the doll.
        [$_{Event}$ GO$_{Poss}$ ([DOLL], [$_{Path}$ FROM$_{Poss}$ ([BETH])])]

     d. Amy gave the doll to Beth.
        [CAUSE ([AMY], [GO$_{Poss}$ ([DOLL],
$$\left[\begin{array}{l} \text{FROM}_{Poss}\ ([AMY]) \\ _{Path}\ \text{TO}_{Poss}\ ([BETH]) \end{array}\right])])]$$

     e. Amy kept the doll.
        [CAUSE ([AMY], [STAY$_{Poss}$ ([DOLL],
                       [$_{Place}$ AT$_{Poss}$ ([AMY])])])]

     f. Amy gave up/relinquished the doll.
        [LET ([AMY], [GO$_{Poss}$ ([DOLL], [FROM$_{Poss}$ ([AMY])])])]

     g. Beth obtained the doll.
        [CAUSE ([BETH], [GO$_{Poss}$ ([DOLL], [TO$_{Poss}$ ([BETH])])])]

   h. Beth accepted the doll.
      [LET ([BETH], [GO$_{Poss}$ ([DOLL], [TO$_{Poss}$ ([BETH])])])]

   i. Amy sold the doll to Beth for \$5.
      [CAUSE ([AMY],

$$\left[\begin{array}{l} GO_{Poss} \text{ ([DOLL], } \left[\begin{array}{l} FROM_{Poss} \text{ ([AMY])} \\ TO_{Poss} \text{ ([BETH])} \end{array}\right]) \\ GO_{Poss} \text{ ([\$5], } \left[\begin{array}{l} FROM_{Poss} \text{ ([BETH])} \\ TO_{Poss} \text{ ([AMY])} \end{array}\right]) \end{array}\right])]$$

   j. Beth bought the doll from Amy for \$5.
      [CAUSE ([BETH],

$$\left[\begin{array}{l} GO_{Poss} \text{ ([DOLL], } \left[\begin{array}{l} FROM_{Poss} \text{ ([AMY])} \\ TO_{Poss} \text{ ([BETH])} \end{array}\right]) \\ GO_{Poss} \text{ ([\$5], } \left[\begin{array}{l} FROM_{Poss} \text{ ([BETH])} \\ TO_{Poss} \text{ ([AMY])} \end{array}\right]) \end{array}\right])]$$

Only a few verbs are shared between the spatial and possessive fields; the most prominent are "keep," a STAY verb in both fields, and "belong," which expresses BE of possession and something like SHOULD BE of location (as in "The cookies belong in the jar"). On the other hand, the use of "from" and "to" to express possessive source- and goal-function is quite general; and other languages such as French and Hebrew use the verb "be" for possession ("Le livre est à Jean," "Hasefer haya ləmoshe"). In addition, English has the possessive "The book is mine" and the spatial "The table has a book on it." Thus there is a certain amount of lexical justification for this analysis, though less for English than in the temporal field.

Causation plays a rich role in this field. "Receive" and "lose" express noncausative events, since the subject exercises no control. The contrasts between "give" and "relinquish" and between "obtain" and "accept" are prime examples of the distinction between CAUSE and LET. With transactional verbs such as "buy" and "sell," the subject is conceptualized as the initiator of the transfer of both the doll (primary theme) and the money (secondary theme). The activity of the other partner in the transaction is not described, though it may be inferred pragmatically (or perhaps there is further internal structure not represented here—see Miller and Johnson-Laird (1976, section 7.2.6)). Thus "buy" and "sell" describe similar transactions, and differ only with respect to which character is the initiator.

10.2 Identificational, Circumstantial, and Existential Fields

Another semantic field, called *identificational* by Gruber, concerns categorization and ascription of properties.

(10.11) Identificational field:
    a. [THINGS] appear as theme.
    b. [THING TYPES] and [PROPERTIES] appear as reference objects.
    c. Being an instance of a category or having a property plays the role of location.

This is the field in which we find the "be" of categorization that played such a prominent role in chapters 5 and 6. As observed there, NPs used as reference objects in this field appear grammatically as predicate nominals, and when indefinite are interpreted as [TYPES] rather than [TOKENS].

(10.12) gives examples of verbs in this field. (Again, subscripts are omitted where obvious.)

(10.12) a. Elise is a pianist.
$$[_{\text{State}} \text{BE}_{\text{Ident}} ([_{\text{Thing Token}} \text{ELISE}],$$
$$[_{\text{Place}} \text{AT}_{\text{Ident}} ([_{\text{Thing Type}} \text{PIANIST}])])]$$

    b. Elise became/turned into a mother.
$$[_{\text{Event}} \text{GO}_{\text{Ident}} ([_{\text{Token}} \text{ELISE}],$$
$$[_{\text{Path}} \text{TO}_{\text{Ident}} ([_{\text{Type}} \text{MOTHER}])])]$$

    c. The coach changed from a handsome young man into a pumpkin.
$$[_{\text{Event}} \text{GO}_{\text{Ident}} ([_{\text{Token}} \text{COACH}],$$
$$\begin{bmatrix} \text{FROM}_{\text{Ident}} ([\text{MAN}]) \\ _{\text{Path}} \text{TO}_{\text{Ident}} ([\text{PUMPKIN}]) \end{bmatrix})]$$

    d. The coach stayed/remained a pumpkin.
$$[_{\text{Event}} \text{STAY}_{\text{Ident}} ([_{\text{Token}} \text{COACH}],$$
$$[_{\text{Place}} \text{AT}_{\text{Ident}} ([_{\text{Type}} \text{PUMPKIN}])])]$$

    e. Sol made Gary a celebrity.
$$[\text{CAUSE} ([\text{SOL}], [\text{GO}_{\text{Ident}} ([\text{GARY}],$$
$$[\text{TO}_{\text{Ident}} ([\text{CELEBRITY}])])])]$$

    f. Sol kept Gary a celebrity.
$$[\text{CAUSE} ([\text{SOL}], [\text{STAY}_{\text{Ident}} ([\text{GARY}],$$
$$[\text{AT}_{\text{Ident}} ([\text{CELEBRITY}])])])]$$

  g. Sol left Gary a celebrity.
     [LET ([SOL], [STAY$_{Ident}$ ([GARY],
                                    [AT$_{Ident}$ ([CELEBRITY])])])]

The preposition "as" frequently appears as a marker of identificational location (i.e., categorization). (10.13) gives some representative constructions, most of which are too complex to be analyzed with the formalisms developed so far.

(10.13) a. I used to work as a musician.
        b. He imagined me as a celebrity.
        c. He treated me as a celebrity.
        d. He hired me as a janitor.
        e. As a citizen of Lower Bassadonia, I protest vehemently.

All the verbs in (10.12) can appear with an adjective phrase in place of the predicate nominal. (10.14) gives a few cases.

(10.14) a. The light is red.
           [BE$_{Ident}$ ([LIGHT], [AT$_{Ident}$ ([$_{Property}$ RED])])]
        b. The light changed from red to green.
           [GO$_{Ident}$ ([LIGHT], $\begin{bmatrix} \text{FROM}_{Ident} ([_{Property} \text{ RED}]) \\ \text{TO}_{Ident} ([_{Property} \text{ GREEN}]) \end{bmatrix}$)]
        c. Sol kept Gary famous.
           [CAUSE ([SOL], [STAY$_{Ident}$ ([GARY],
                                          [AT$_{Ident}$ ([$_{Property}$ FAMOUS])])])]

There are also adjectival analogues to some of the "as NP" constructions in (10.13), for instance, "He considered me famous," "He imagined me famous." And many [PROPERTIES] lexicalize with a GO$_{Ident}$ function to form so-called inchoative verbs, a few of which appear in (10.15).[2]

(10.15) a. The pages yellowed.
           [GO$_{Ident}$ ([PAGES], [TO$_{Ident}$ ([$_{Property}$ YELLOW])])]
        b. The metal melted.
           [GO$_{Ident}$ ([METAL], $\begin{bmatrix} \text{FROM}_{Ident} ([\text{SOLID}]) \\ \text{TO}_{Ident} ([\text{LIQUID}]) \end{bmatrix}$)]
        c. The flames blackened the building.
           [CAUSE ([FLAMES], [GO$_{Ident}$ ([BUILDING],
                                           [TO$_{Ident}$ ([BLACK])])])]

The identificational field, unlike the possessive field, shows signs of continuous [PATHS] as well as end-states. For instance, the verb "range" behaves like a GO_{Ext} function, specifying occupation of endpoints and all (or many) points in between. Note that it appears in simple present and with source- and goal-functions, the sign of stative GO_{Ext}. Also, compare the identificational cases (10.16a,b) with the spatial use of "range" (10.16c).

(10.16) a. Our clients range from psychiatrists to psychopaths.

$$[_{State} GO_{Ext,Ident} ([OUR\ CLIENTS], \begin{bmatrix} FROM_{Ident} ([PSYCHIATRISTS]) \\ TO_{Ident} ([PSYCHOPATHS]) \end{bmatrix})]$$

   b. This theory ranges from the sublime to the ridiculous.

$$[_{State} GO_{Ext,Ident} ([THEORY], \begin{bmatrix} FROM_{Ident} ([SUBLIME]) \\ TO_{Ident} ([RIDICULOUS]) \end{bmatrix})]$$

   c. Jackrabbits range from Maine to Florida.

$$[_{State} GO_{Ext} ([JACKRABBITS], \begin{bmatrix} FROM ([MAINE]) \\ TO ([FLORIDA]) \end{bmatrix})]$$

Next, compare the spatial expressions in (10.17) with the identificational ones in (10.18).

(10.17) a. The train traveled to New York.
         b. The train traveled toward New York.

(10.18) a. The balloon became small.
         b. The balloon became smaller.

In the (a) sentences, the theme achieves the goal: the train reaches New York, and the balloon ends up with the property "small." On the other hand, the (b) sentences describe the theme getting closer to the goal, without necessarily reaching it. In (10.18b), the balloon may still end up large—but it is closer to small than before. This similarity of inference patterns suggests that the comparative adjective expresses an identificational *direction,* a path whose endpoints are not specified. We therefore assign (10.18a,b) the respective representations (10.19a,b).

(10.19) a. $[GO_{Ident} ([BALLOON], [_{Path} TO_{Ident} ([_{Property} SMALL])])]$

   b. $[GO_{Ident} ([BALLOON],$
$[_{Path} TOWARD_{Ident} ([_{Property} SMALL])])]$

There is evidence that this use of identificational TOWARD is correct. Recall well-formedness rule (9.16a), which permitted the construction of places from paths, as in "He lives two miles down the road from here." If the comparative adjective expresses a direction, this explains why it can appear in constructions with analogous modifiers. (For a discussion of the syntactic parallels, see Jackendoff (1977a, chapter 6).)

(10.20) a. Sally is three inches shorter than Bill.
        b. Sally is way bigger than Bill.

In these sentences, "Bill" serves as a reference object, the comparative adjective specifies a path away from Bill along a certain scale of value, and the quantifier and measure phrases specify distance along the path. The result is an identificational [PLACE], as required by the argument structure of "be." In other words, (10.20) is a complete semantic analogue of "He lives two miles down the road from here," despite its somewhat different grammatical structure. (10.20a) therefore receives (10.21) as its representation.

(10.21) $[_{\text{State}}$ BE$_{\text{Ident}}$ ([SALLY],

$$\left[_{\text{Place}} \text{ON}_{\text{Ident}} \left(\left[_{\text{Path}} \begin{array}{l} \text{FROM ([BILL])} \\ \text{TOWARD}_{\text{Ident}} \text{ ([SHORT])} \\ [_{\text{Amount}} \text{ 3 INCHES}] \end{array} \right] \right) \right])]$$

Thus, the use of continuous identificational paths makes possible an analysis of the comparative that is in accord both with the expressive capacity of the construction and with the Thematic Relations Hypothesis.[3]

In short, adjectives express absolute properties (within syncategorematicity, of course—a small elephant is still bigger than a big mouse), while comparative adjectives express properties relative to a stipulated reference standard. In this relative sense, they act like spatial directions and can therefore undergo similar modification.

We should take note of the precise extent of the parallelism. Although all comparative adjectives can be taken to express traversal of or position on a scale, not many admit measure expressions like "three inches." We find "three inches higher/lower/longer/shorter," "three minutes earlier/later/older/younger," "three degrees hotter/colder," and a few others; but there is no unit of measurement for "big," "beautiful," "sophisticated," "wise," "tasty," "lucky," or thousands of others. Still, we do find the construction with a quantifier:

"far/much/a little bigger/wiser/tastier/luckier/more beautiful/more sophisticated," and this is sufficient for the spatial parallel. To distinguish those adjectives that allow a measure expression in the
comparative from those that do not, we will need to invoke a feature
[METRICIZABLE], which indicates the possibility of a replicable unit
of distance throughout the scale. Nonmetricizable [PROPERTIES],
which are in the great majority, will permit only a relative scale of
distance. Spatial distance, of course, is metricizable, and is thus richer
and more complex than the pseudospaces defined by most adjectives.

The next field is called *circumstantial*.

(10.22) Circumstantial field:
    a. [THINGS] appear as theme.
    b. [EVENTS] and [STATES] appear as reference objects.
    c. "*x* is a character of *y*" plays the role of spatial "*x* is at *y*."

Syntactically, circumstantial verbs always subcategorize a subordinate
clause that expresses the reference [EVENT] or [STATE]. This subordinate clause lacks a subject, and the theme of the main clause is
understood to serve in this role—that is, to be the missing character
in the reference [EVENT] or [STATE].

To make this less abstract, compare (10.23a,b) with (10.23c,d).

(10.23) a. Fred kept composing quartets.
    b. Louise kept Fred composing quartets.
    c. Fred stayed in the attic.
    d. Louise kept Fred in the attic.

In (10.23a,b), the subordinate clause "composing quartets" lacks an
overt syntactic subject; "Fred" is understood as fulfilling this function. The lexical parallel with (10.23d) suggests an analysis in which
"Louise" is agent, "Fred" is theme, and "composing quartets" serves
as a kind of [PLACE]. (10.22) defines just what kind of [PLACE] it is:
an [EVENT] in which Fred is a character. Then, just as spatial "keep"
means "maintain in a position over time," circumstantial "keep"
means "maintain in a role in an event or situation over time."

We will formalize (10.23a,b) as (10.24a,b). Since the subordinate
clause is missing its subject, its semantic structure has an open argument place, filled by the variable i. This variable is bound to the
theme of the main clause by coindexing, just as we bound [ACTORS]
to [ACTIONS] in section 9.4.[4] For convenience, the subordinate
clause has been left otherwise unanalyzed semantically.

(10.24) a. [$_\text{Event}$ STAY$_\text{Circ}$ ([Fred]$_i$,

  [$_\text{Place}$ AT$_\text{Circ}$ ([$_\text{Event}$ i COMPOSE QUARTETS])])]

   b. [CAUSE ([LOUISE], [STAY$_\text{Circ}$ ([FRED]$_i$,

  [$_\text{Place}$ AT$_\text{Circ}$ ([$_\text{Event}$ i COMPOSE QUARTETS])])])]

Thus we find the verb "keep" expressing STAY or its causative in every semantic field studied so far. That all these apparently disparate uses can be subsumed under a single semantic analysis is strong evidence for the Thematic Relations Hypothesis; under the Grammatical Constraint, this is the most general and desirable case possible.

With this analysis of "keep," it is easy to see how to analyze the aspectual verbs "start" and "stop" as circumstantial GO:

(10.25) a. Ludwig started composing quartets.

   [GO$_\text{Circ}$ ([LUDWIG]$_i$,

  [$_\text{Path}$ TO$_\text{Circ}$ ([i COMPOSE QUARTETS])])]

   b. Ludwig stopped composing quartets.

   [GO$_\text{Circ}$ ([LUDWIG]$_i$,

  [$_\text{Path}$ FROM$_\text{Circ}$ ([i COMPOSE QUARTETS])])]

These have the expected inference patterns for GO TO and GO FROM, given the definition of circumstantial location: (10.25a) asserts that at the beginning of the event Ludwig was not composing quartets and at the end he was; (10.25b) asserts the opposite—just what we want for "start" and "stop."

The missing circumstantial function is BE, and obligingly, "be" appears in a parallel construction:

(10.26) Ludwig is composing quartets.

   [$_\text{State}$ BE$_\text{Circ}$ ([LUDWIG]$_i$,

  [$_\text{Place}$ AT$_\text{Circ}$ ([i COMPOSE QUARTETS])])]

"Be" in (10.26) is of course the progressive aspect, which is ordinarily analyzed as an auxiliary rather than a main verb. On the other hand, on the strength of various syntactic parallelisms with "start," "stop," and "keep," Emonds (1976) argues that progressive "be" is indeed a main verb. Woisetschlaeger (1976) argues that there are two distinct senses of progressive aspect, only one of which patterns with "start," "stop," and "keep"; he treats this sense as a main verb and the other as an auxiliary. Without going into the details of these arguments, we may note that they support the semantic analysis of (10.26).

Let us look briefly at what the conceptual structure in (10.26) says: a situation obtains in which Ludwig is in the midst of an event of composing quartets. In effect, BE$_{Circ}$ takes a snapshot of a state in the middle of an event. This explains why progressive aspect (in this reading) is characteristic of event and not state sentences: it makes sense to freeze events in mid-course, but since states already pertain to a point in time, there is no mid-course to freeze.

A selection of causatives with circumstantial functions appears in (10.27). ((10.23b) is another example.)

(10.27) a. Sue forced/pressured/tricked/talked Jim into singing.
Sue got/forced/caused/coerced Jim to sing.
[CAUSE ([SUE], [GO$_{Circ}$ ([JIM]$_i$, [TO$_{Circ}$ ([i SING])])])]

b. Sue kept/restrained/prevented Jim from singing.
[CAUSE ([SUE], [STAY$_{Circ}$ ([JIM]$_i$,
[NOT AT$_{Circ}$ ([i SING])])])]

c. Sue allowed/permitted Jim to sing.
[LET ([SUE], [GO$_{Circ}$ ([JIM]$_i$, [TO$_{Circ}$ ([i SING])])])]

d. Sue released Jim from singing.
[LET ([SUE], [GO$_{Circ}$ ([JIM]$_i$, [FROM$_{Circ}$ ([i SING])])])]

e. Sue exempted Jim from singing.
[LET ([SUE], [STAY$_{Circ}$ ([JIM]$_i$,
[NOT AT$_{Circ}$ ([i SING])])])]

The only novel part of these representations is the representation of "from" in (10.27b,e) as NOT AT. This is parallel to the spatial sense found in "stay *away from x*" (i.e., "someplace other than at *x*"), so it is independently motivated. (However, it treats this sense of "from" as unrelated to the source-function expressed by "from," which is doubtless a mistake. For the sake of brevity, I leave the issue unexplored here.)

The familiar inference patterns for CAUSE, LET, GO, and STAY appear here as usual. In (10.27a), Sue's action results in Jim's coming to sing (note the use of spatial "come to" here in a circumstantial sense). In (10.27b), Sue's action results in Jim's continuing *not* to sing. In (10.27c), Sue could have prevented Jim from singing, but she didn't, so Jim probably sang. In (10.27d), Sue was forcing Jim to sing, and now allowed him to stop; in (10.27e), Sue could have forced Jim to sing, but chose not to. In these last two, Jim ends up probably not singing.[5]

So far, all the circumstantial expressions we have examined have the reference [EVENT] as an argument of AT, TO, or FROM. From a strictly logical point of view this is all there should be: either one is involved in an event or one is not. But evidently the projected world has more to talk about than strict logic. Consider (10.28).

(10.28)

a. You are $\left\{\begin{array}{l}\text{(nowhere) close to}\\ \text{(not) far from}\\ \text{on the verge of}\end{array}\right\}$ finishing this book.

b. You are $\left\{\begin{array}{l}\text{on the way to}\\ \text{getting close to}\end{array}\right\}$ finishing this book.

These expressions, obviously spatially inspired, show that there is a notion of circumstantial *distance*. This is a nonmetricizable sort of distance, to be sure; but, like scales of distance with nonmetricizable adjectives, it is still well-defined in a relative sense. Roughly, one is closer to a reference event if there are fewer independent steps required to bring the event about, if there are fewer places left where matters can slip up and foil one's plans. One is *traversing* a circumstantial path to a reference event if one is carrying out preliminary steps toward the bringing about of the event. (Note again the inevitability of spatial language in describing this, as for example in "steps toward . . .")

One can traverse part of a circumstantial path without reaching the reference event, as in "Gustav got close to finishing his symphony, but didn't succeed." This is entirely parallel to the spatial "Gustav got close to the house, but didn't make it all the way there." This provides an explication of the verbs "manage" and "succeed." From a logical point of view these verbs are pleonastic: (10.29a) always has the same truth value as (10.29b), and its negation (10.29c) always has the same truth value as (10.29d).

(10.29)

a. Sam $\left\{\begin{array}{l}\text{succeeded in finishing the book.}\\ \text{managed to finish the book.}\end{array}\right\}$

b. Sam finished the book.

c. Sam didn't $\left\{\begin{array}{l}\text{succeed in finishing the book.}\\ \text{manage to finish the book.}\end{array}\right\}$

d. Sam didn't finish the book.

Why do these verbs exist, if they do not alter truth values? The reason is that they express traversal of a circumstantial path to the reference event, hence allude to the presence of circumstantial obstacles that were surmounted along the way.

Circumstantial paths crop up in another class of verbs, studied by Cornu (1980). Compare the verbs in (10.27a) with those in (10.30).

(10.30) Sue urged/encouraged/pressured Jim to sing.

In (10.30), Jim's singing is not a logical inference as it was in (10.27a). It is, however, an invited inference that can be canceled by "but he didn't do it." The difference between (10.27a) and (10.30) is precisely that between spatial GO TO and GO TOWARD: the former logically implies the reaching of the reference object, but with the latter, the reaching of the reference object is only an invited inference, easily canceled. Going toward means getting closer, without necessarily guaranteeing achievement. Thus (10.31) appears to be altogether appropriate to represent (10.30).

(10.31) [CAUSE ([SUE], [GO$_{Circ}$ ([JIM]$_i$,

[TOWARD$_{Circ}$ ([i SING])])])]

This analysis is especially appealing in light of the lexical doublet "pressure NP *into*," in the class (10.27a), and "pressure NP *to*," in the class (10.30); one would like to minimize the semantic differences between them.

Analyzing (10.30) as (10.31) opens a fascinating range of verbs to analysis. "Discourage" is obviously CAUSE TO GO$_{Circ}$ AWAY-FROM$_{Circ}$, the opposite of "encourage." "Intend" is quite possibly ORIENT$_{Circ}$ TOWARD$_{Circ}$, as suggested by its synonym "aim." This leads to analyses of "persuade," "convince," and "dissuade" as causatives of ORIENT$_{Circ}$. Enterprising readers can no doubt extend the list.

Finally, consider a pseudospace so degenerate that it has only a single reference location: the *existential* field.

(10.32) Existential field:
    a. [THINGS] and [STATES] can serve as theme.
    b. There is one reference region, called [EX], expressed
       by "existence."

This gives us expressions like "be in existence," "be out of existence," "come into existence," "go out of existence," "stay in existence," "bring into existence," and "keep in existence" as obvious realizations of the fundamental state- and event-functions. Moreover, "exist," "persist," "create," and "destroy" can be seen as lexicalizations of "be in existence," "stay in existence," "cause to come into existence," and "cause to go out of existence," respectively. Even in this maximally limited field, the use of spatial language seems inevitable.

10.3 Linguistic Justification

We have demonstrated the application of the Thematic Relations Hypothesis to five fields of English verbs. While this is not insignificant, it can hardly be considered exhaustive justification of the hypothesis, which is supposed to apply to *all* fields in *all* languages. Let us therefore consider some issues of justification, first internal to English and then from the point of view of language universals.

Some fields of verbs that we have not analyzed seem to fit fairly clearly into the TRH. For example, verbs of saying and telling treat the information conveyed as theme, the speaker as source, and the hearer as goal. Some of these are analyzed in Gruber (1965), Anderson (1971), and Miller and Johnson-Laird (1976). Jackendoff (1979) analyzes expressions of temperature in terms of the TRH and proves this analysis superior to Montague's (1973) and Hacking's (1975) treatments. Jackendoff (1977b) suggests an analysis of logical predicates such as "necessary" and "possible" in terms of nontemporal causation. Finally, perception verbs, like "see," if analyzed along the lines suggested in section 8.6, fall under the TRH.

On the other hand, there are fairly common verbs, such as "use," "try," "like," "want," and "need," that have no obvious thematic analysis. In particular, "want" and "need" pattern syntactically much like "keep," appearing in many semantic fields:

(10.33) a. Spatial:
Bill kept the book on the shelf.
Bill wants the book on the shelf.
We need you in here.

b. Possessive:
Bill kept the book.
Bill wants the book.
Bill needs the book.

c. Identificational:
Bill kept Harry angry.
Bill wants Harry upset.
Bill needs his steak well-done.

d. Circumstantial:
Bill kept Harry working.
Bill wants Harry working/to work.
Bill needs Harry working/to work.

This suggests that "want" and "need" express rather general functions that have not played a role in our analysis, possibly acting as alternatives to CAUSE and LET in well-formedness rule (9.35). Similarly, it is not implausible that there are other functions we have missed. The important thing is that there should be a rather small set of state- and event-functions and a rather small set of place- and path-functions involved in the description of any semantic field of events and states, among which are the fundamental functions GO, STAY, and BE.

Suppose that in examining other languages, we failed to find the sort of lexical generalizations that we have used in English to support the TRH. A number of different cases arise. First, we should of course not expect the very same lexical items to generalize across fields as in English; the essential arbitrariness of the sound-sense relation makes this highly unlikely. Rather, the TRH predicts that there will be some tendency toward cross-field lexical generalization, governed along thematic lines, and that this tendency will create patterns that stand out against the patchwork character of the lexicon.

What *would* count as evidence from another language against the TRH would be a set of lexical generalizations that cut across the grain of the thematic generalizations in English. For instance, the verb "keep" in English expresses STAY or its causative in every field we have examined. Suppose that in this other language, each use of "keep" translated into a different lexical item; and that the translation of "keep$_{Poss}$" also meant "travel" (GO), the translation of "keep$_{Ident}$" also meant "reside" (BE), and the translation of "keep$_{Circ}$" also meant "want" (WANT). If these exemplified a typical situation, then the lexical patterns of this language would be entirely at odds with the thematic analysis of English. I would consider such a language reason to question the universal validity of the TRH; but I also tend to doubt that such a language exists.

Another way in which languages might be found to differ is in their choice of semantic fields. For example, English normally ascribes a property to a thing by making the thing theme and the property location. However, there are marginal patterns such as "Darkness descended on us," "Redness suffused his face," and "Old age overtook him," in which the property is theme and the thing serves as location. Similarly, the circumstantial field defines the person as moving to the reference event; but there are expressions like "My car broke down on me" and "A funny thing happened to me," in which the event is conceived of as coming to the person (see Jackendoff (1976, section 6.1)). Now it could be that some other language reverses the primacy of these two possible ways of expressing ascription and circumstance, so that expressions like (10.34a) would be literal translations of the normal way of saying (10.34b).

(10.34) a. Staleness came to the bread.
        The tallness in Bill exceeds the tallness in Harry.
        Sue kept anger in Bill.
        Singing began in Bill.
        Working stayed with Bill.
        Sue forced singing onto Bill.

     b. The bread got stale.
        Bill is taller than Harry.
        Sue kept Bill angry.
        Bill began singing.
        Bill kept working.
        Sue forced Bill to sing.

While such a language might seem picturesque to English speakers, and while it might be quite difficult to translate consistently into idiomatic English, it would nevertheless conform to the TRH—just in a different way than English.

I do not know whether there are such languages as this. If there are, they show the extent to which conceptualization is malleable and therefore subject to cultural influence. If there are not, this is evidence for substantive constraints on conceptual structure beyond those imposed by the TRH. In general, I would expect more variability in cognitively more peripheral fields.

In addition to lexical generalization, there is another sort of linguistic evidence for the Thematic Relations Hypothesis: the usefulness of thematic relations for explaining grammatical phenomena that lack a structural basis. I will mention three examples. (Anderson (1977) mentions further possibilities.) First, Postal (1971) enumerates a number of cases in which reflexive pronouns should apparently be acceptable on structural grounds, but are not. (10.35) presents two minimal pairs.

(10.35) a. John is angry at himself.
            John regards himself as stupid.
        b. ?John is pleasing to himself.
            ?John strikes himself as stupid.

These have the same syntactic structure, yet only (10.35) is fully acceptable (stress on "himself" in (10.35b) improves matters somewhat). They differ in thematic structure, though. In (10.35a) the person holding the opinion is subject, and the person of whom the opinion is held is postverbal; in (10.35b) the opposite matching obtains. Jackendoff (1972, chapter 4) argues therefore that the structural conditions of reflexivization must be supplemented by a condition on the relation between the thematic role of the reflexive pronoun and that of its antecedent, and shows that this condition can be formulated to deal with all of Postal's cases. Ruwet (1972) reinforces this analysis with parallel evidence from French.[6]

A second such phenomenon, discussed in Jackendoff (1974), concerns sentences like (10.36a–d).

(10.36) a. John gave Bill orders to leave.
        b. John got from Bill orders to leave.
        c. John gave Bill a promise to leave.
        d. John got from Bill a promise to leave.

There is no significant syntactic difference among these four sentences; but in (10.36a,d) Bill is understood as the person who is to leave, while in (10.36b,c) that person is John. This difference is apparently due to the thematic relations imposed by "give," "get," "order," and "promise." The one who receives an order is the one who carries it out: in (10.36a) it is "Bill," while in (10.36b) it is "John." By contrast, the person who *gives* a promise is the one who carries it out, for the benefit of the receiver of the promise. Hence, in (10.36c) "John" is the person who leaves, and in (10.36d) it is "Bill." Jackendoff (1974) works out a number of cases like this, showing how the

understood subject of the infinitive depends on the thematic relations of both the main verb and the noun that governs the infinitive.[7]

Finally, for fans of quantification, here is a little-known puzzle from
Gruber (1965).

(10.37) a. Every oak grew out of an acorn.
        b. Every acorn grew into an oak.
        c. An oak grew out of every acorn.
        d. *An acorn grew into every oak.

(10.38) a. Bill carved every clown out of a piece of wood.
        b. Bill carved every piece of wood into a clown.
        c. Bill carved a clown out of every piece of wood.
        d. *Bill carved a piece of wood into every clown.

Grammaticality in these sentences depends in part on the indefinite
NP being included within the scope of the quantifier. Apparently, if
the indefinite NP follows the quantifier, it can be within its scope,
whatever the semantic relations. If the indefinite NP precedes the
quantifier, though, thematic relations somehow come into play: when
the quantified NP is source, as in the (c) cases, quantification is acceptable; but when the quantified NP is goal, as in the (d) cases,
quantification is not possible. Thus appropriate scope of quantification can be achieved only if either the syntactic condition of ordering
or the semantic condition on source-goal relations is satisfied.

I know of no treatment of this problem in the literature. It shows
very dramatically that scope of quantification cannot be determined
on syntactic grounds alone, but must depend in part on thematic
structure. What seems to be crucial in the semantic structure of these
examples is that, because of the particular verbs used in these sentences, source-goal relations correspond to temporally dependent
ascriptions of identity; first the objects in question were acorns and
pieces of wood, then they became oaks and clowns. How this plays a
principled role in quantification, however, is a mystery. (I am grateful
to Edwin Williams for some help in laying out this problem.)

We have seen, therefore, that thematic structure is motivated not
only on grounds of lexical generalization, but also by its contribution
to linguistic phenomena loosely grouped under the rubric of "binding and control," an area of great significance in current syntactic
theory. It strikes me that this semantic contribution has been largely
overlooked. How seriously it affects the formulation of current theories remains to be seen.

10.4 Significance for Semantics

The theory of thematic relations provides a plethora of arguments that undermine the putative autonomy of semantics (the theory of logical inference) from pragmatics (the theory of invited inference, relation to discourse, and relation to the world). Thus the material developed in this chapter supports the claim of chapter 6 that the semantics-pragmatics distinction is artificial and should be abandoned.

Perhaps the simplest evidence concerns the behavior of TO and TOWARD. Every time TO appears as a path-function, there is a logical inference that the goal is attained. On the other hand, when TOWARD appears as a path-function, the attainment of the goal is only an invited inference, which can be canceled by a following clause introduced by "but." This difference underlies contrasts in a variety of semantic fields, as reviewed in (10.39).

(10.39) a. Max went to the store. (TO)
   Max went toward the store (but didn't reach it). (TOWARD)

   b. The balloon got large. (TO)
   The balloon got larger (but still wasn't very big). (TOWARD)

   c. Sue pressured Jim into singing. (TO)
   Sue pressured Jim to sing (but he still refused). (TOWARD)

Traditional autonomous semantics claims responsibility for the inferences of the TO examples but not the TOWARD examples. But why should there be separate components, operating according to separate principles, for dealing with examples as grammatically and semantically close as these pairs? More likely, given this kind of evidence, is that there is a unified system of principles of inference, some of which produce logical inferences and some invited inferences—that is, "semantic" principles are thoroughly interwoven with "pragmatic" ones and apply to the same level of representation.

There is a more fundamental objection. Without notions of [PATH], [PLACE], [EVENT], and so forth, and without a notation that treats ontological categories as formally parallel, we could not even state thematic analyses, much less draw out the similarities among fields by using different ontological categories for theme and for reference object. Thus the theory of thematic relations depends crucially on the enriched ontology and the notational innovations developed in chapters 3 and 4. However, as argued there, these proposals are antithetical to one of the most basic assumptions of traditional semantics, namely, that a principal goal of semantics is discovering how to determine the truth-value and reference of linguistic expressions vis-à-vis the real world. In other words, the theory of thematic relations cannot be regarded as an interesting gadget to be added as an improvement to truth-functional semantics. The two are profoundly incompatible.

10.5 Significance for Cognition

Chapter 6 also argued that semantic structure is the same level of representation as conceptual structure. Therefore, any theory of the semantic structure of language is ipso facto a theory of the structure of thought. Seen in this light, the Thematic Relations Hypothesis is a claim that all [EVENTS] and [STATES] in conceptual structure are organized according to a very limited set of principles, drawn primarily from the conceptualization of space. What are we to make of this claim from the point of view of the theory of cognition?

A facile response, one that I have often encountered in discussion, is to say that the theory of thematic relations reveals widespread systems of metaphor in our language and thought. But I think this debases both the theory of thematic relations and the concept of metaphor, for, unlike metaphor, thematic parallels are not used for artistic or picturesque effect. Rather, thematic structure is the only means available to organize a semantic field of events and states coherently—it is an indispensable element of everyday thought. Moreover, the most remarkable aspect of metaphor is its variety, the possibility of using practically any semantic field as a metaphor for any other. By contrast, thematic relations disclose the same analogy over and over again: time is location, being possessed is a location, properties are locations, events are locations. That is, the theory of thematic relations claims not just that some fields are structured in terms of other fields, but that all fields have essentially the *same* structure. This structure is cognitively induced: one could not decide to abandon thematic structure for some other organization. It defines the terms in which any kind of discourse, literal or metaphorical, must be framed.

I am inclined to think of thematic structure not as spatial metaphor but as an abstract organization that can be applied with suitable specialization to any field. If there is any primacy to the spatial field, it is because this field is so strongly supported by nonlinguistic cognition; it is the common ground for the essential faculties of vision, touch, and action. From an evolutionary perspective, spatial organization had to exist long before language. One can imagine the development of thematic structure in less concrete fields as a consequence of evolutionary conservatism in cognition—the adaptation of existing structure to new purposes rather than the development of entirely novel mechanisms.

From the point of view of conceptual development in the individual organism, of course, evolutionary considerations are beside the point. But at this level, it can be claimed that thematic structure is an innate organization with which the organism structures its experience. At most, the developing organism must learn the definition of location in a particular field in order to be able to develop a full range of event- and state-concepts in that field. This may be what happens in the more abstract fields such as the temporal and the circumstantial: a child may be able to acquire an abstract field on the basis of figuring out the meaning of a few words that have spatial parallels. On the other hand, some fields may be given innately and thus do not have to be learned; this seems more likely of the possessive and identificational fields, which appear early in the child's repertoire.

Whatever the resolution of these high-level issues, the material developed in these last two chapters has important consequences for the methodology of cognitive psychology. We have been able to show that detailed examination of lexical and grammatical patterns of natural language leads to highly structured hypotheses about the structure of thought. In the spatial field, we potentially have an independent source of confirmation for these hypotheses, since the visual system must interact with the linguistic faculty at this level of representation. On the other hand, the degree of detail in the language-derived theory is far beyond our present understanding of visual cognition, so for the moment the linguistic evidence provides a source of hypotheses for research in vision, perhaps satisfying the sort of need expressed by Marr (1982, 313) with respect to his 3D model representation. Moreover, we have no nonlinguistic source of evidence for the nonsensory fields, so crucial to the theory of memory and reasoning. Thus, while in the earlier part of this book we used the Cognitive Constraint to marshal nonlinguistic evidence for the theory of semantics, we have now succeeded in turning the Constraint on its head and using linguistic evidence to develop theories of cognition. I take this as the most important advance of the present work, for it integrates linguistic theory and methodology fully into the fabric of cognitive psychology.

Chapter 11
Theory of #Representation#

This chapter develops another case study in the application of the present theory to semantic description, this time in a much more well-trodden area. I will show that the Grammatical Constraint and the Cognitive Constraint motivate a solution significantly different from and more revealing than standard approaches.[1]

11.1 Problems with Belief-Contexts

A puzzle of long standing for philosophers and linguists alike has been the semantics of subordinate clauses following verbs like "believe," "think," and "imagine." Here are some of the problems these constructions present.

First, the substitution of equals for equals, which normally preserves truth value, does not in belief-contexts. Why is the syllogism in (11.1) invalid?

(11.1) a. Ralph thinks that the number of planets is seven.
       b. The number of planets is nine.
       c. Therefore, Ralph thinks that seven is nine.

Second, existential generalization into belief-contexts is invalid. Though one can make an inference from "A man walked in" to "There is a man such that he walked in," one cannot go from "Ralph believes that a man walked in" to "There is a man such that Ralph believes that he walked in."

Third, certain sentences such as (11.2) that are contradictory in isolation are sensical and in fact ambiguous as complements of "believe," as shown in (11.3).

(11.2) a. Your dead uncle is alive.
　　　 b. Susan isn't as old as she is. (where "she" = "Susan")

(11.3) a. Ralph believes that your dead uncle is alive.
　　　 b. Ralph believes that Susan isn't as old as she is. (where "she" = "Susan")

On one reading of (11.3), a mistaken belief is attributed to Ralph; on the other reading, a contradictory belief. (In (11.3a), the contradictory belief might be reconciled as a belief in reincarnation.)

Fourth, the substitution of coreferential terms into belief-contexts reveals an ambiguity pointed out by Russell (1905), which is related to that in (11.3). A standard example is due to Quine (1956). The background story is that Ralph believes a certain person he has seen lurking on the beach to be a spy. Though Ralph is not aware of it, this person happens to be Ortcutt. Relative to these assumptions, one reading of (11.4a) is true and one false. The false reading results from illegitimately substituting "Ortcutt" into (11.4b) for the coreferential phrase "the person he (Ralph) saw on the beach."

(11.4) a. Ralph believes that Ortcutt is a spy.
　　　 b. Ralph believes that the person he saw on the beach is a spy.

The false reading of (11.4a), in which substitution is illegitimate, is termed by Russell a *secondary occurrence* of "Ortcutt," and by Quine an *opaque* reading (it is "opaque" to substitution). The true reading of (11.4a) is termed by Russell a *primary occurrence* of "Ortcutt," and by Quine a *transparent* reading.

Intuitively, what lies behind these apparent anomalies is the arbitrariness of belief. One may maintain false beliefs, and (as Mates (1950) points out) if one is demented (or not logically sophisticated) enough, one may even maintain contradictory beliefs. Hence, the description of someone's incorrect beliefs should not necessarily be subject to normal laws of logic such as substitution of equals for equals and existential generalization.

However, this intuition about belief-sentences does not alone account for the ambiguities in (11.3)–(11.4). For this we need a further observation, which I will state in preliminary form as the *Opacity Principle*.

Opacity Principle

Suppose that a person P holds a belief B about some entity E. In describing B, a speaker may describe E either

a. in terms of P's internal representation of E (opaque description), or

b. in terms of a representation that adequately identifies E for the speaker and hearer, though not necessarily for P (transparent description).

If "your dead uncle" in (11.3a) is understood as an opaque description, then Ralph is taken to subscribe to this description, and he must therefore hold a contradictory belief. On the other hand, if "your dead uncle" is read as a transparent description, then Ralph is taken to believe that some entity E is dead, and "your dead uncle" is a description that identifies E for the speaker and hearer, though probably not for Ralph; this is therefore the "mistaken" reading of (11.3a). Similarly, if "not as old as she is" in (11.3b) is read as an opaque description, then Ralph is taken to ascribe to Susan a contradictory property. If it is read as a transparent description, then Ralph is taken to ascribe to Susan a property that can be identified by the speaker and hearer, but not Ralph, as "not as old as she is"; Ralph is mistaken about Susan's age. The opaque description in (11.4a), in which Ralph ascribes spyhood to someone whom he would describe as "Ortcutt," is false relative to the background assumptions; the transparent description, in which Ralph ascribes spyhood to someone whom the speaker and the hearer can identify by the description "Ortcutt," is true.

It is important to observe the different status of these two observations about belief-contexts. The arbitrariness of belief, which permits the suspension of logical principles, is an intuition about beliefs themselves. The Opacity Principle, which leads to transparent-opaque ambiguities, is a principle about the *description* of beliefs; it is a fact about language. The choice of opaque or transparent description has no grammatical reflection in English; it is a pragmatic matter for the hearer to decide which interpretation the speaker intends. However, Keenan and Ebert (1973) report that Malagasy (the language of Madagascar) has a special grammatical morpheme to distinguish transparent readings, and that Fering (a North Frisian dialect) has one that distinguishes opaque readings. This supports the claim that semantic structure must mark the difference between them.

11.2 The Scope Theory

The problem in accounting for belief-contexts is in reconciling arbitrariness of belief with the Opacity Principle. Suppose that one tries to account for the arbitrariness of belief by semantically sealing off the belief-context from logical inference. This is the approach of Carnap (1956), for example, who translates "John believes that the earth is round" as "John has the relation B to 'the earth is round' as a sentence in English" (pp. 230–232). But then, as Quine (1956) points out, this theory permits only opaque descriptions; we are never entitled to infer that there is something that John has a belief about. A more adequate theory must permit semantic connections between the content of a belief and the rest of the sentence.

Most approaches to belief-contexts embody these connections in what might be called a *scope theory*. The formal principle behind a scope theory is that material to be understood opaquely appears in semantic structure within the belief-context, but material to be understood transparently appears outside the belief-context and binds a variable within it. Versions of the scope theory appear in Russell (1905), Quine (1956), Kaplan (1969), Montague (1973), Bach (1968), McCawley (1971), Postal (1974), and Dresher (1977), to mention only a few. The respects in which they differ, though considerable, are immaterial for present concerns; a simplified version of Russell's proposal will do for now. (11.5) presents the logical expressions corresponding to (11.3) and (11.4a). The expressions prefixed with T are transparent readings; those prefixed with O are opaque readings. Both readings produce egregious violations of the Grammatical Constraint.

(11.5) a. T: $\exists x((x = $ your dead uncle) and (Ralph believes that (x is alive)))

O: Ralph believes that ($\exists x((x = $ your dead uncle) and (x is alive)))

b. T: $\exists x((\text{Susan is } x \text{ old})$ and (Ralph believes that (Susan isn't x old)))

O: Ralph believes that ($\exists x((\text{Susan is } x \text{ old})$ and (Susan isn't x old)))

c. T: $\exists x((x = $ Ortcutt) and (Ralph believes that (x is a spy)))

O: Ralph believes that ($\exists x((x = $ Ortcutt) and (x is a spy)))

The scope theory as usually stated suffers from the technical deficiencies of standard quantificational notation discussed in section 4.1. For instance, the examples that normally appear in discussions of opacity involve an ambiguity in the reading of an NP, where the mechanism of variable-binding is quite at home. In the case of comparative sentences such as (11.3b), though, the phrase bound by the quantifier is syntactically a degree phrase, which is not normally treated as a bindable position. Thus, instead of (11.5b), which already does violence to the syntax of the sentence it is supposed to express, one often sees a treatment like (11.6), an even worse violation of the Grammatical Constraint.

(11.6) $\exists x((x =$ the degree to which Susan is old) and (Ralph believes that (Susan is not old to degree x)))

Still worse is a case that has consistently been overlooked: the entire complement of "believe" may be read transparently, particularly if the main clause contains some modifier such as "in effect" or "in essence." For instance, suppose that Ralph is learning traditional chemistry but has never heard of atomic physics. Relative to these assumptions, the opaque reading of (11.7b) may be true and that of (11.7a) (omitting "in effect") false. However, (11.7b) and (11.7a) have the same truth value on their transparent readings. Thus (11.7a) may be false on the opaque reading and true on the transparent.

(11.7) a. Ralph believes (in effect) that a carbon atom has two electrons in the outer shell.

b. Ralph believes that the element carbon has a valence of +2.

We see, then, that (11.7) is analogous to (11.4), except that the terms that can be substituted on the transparent reading are entire complement sentences, not just a constituent NP.

Another such case is suggested by Partee (1973):[2]

(11.8) My dog thinks that Ortcutt is a burglar.

There is no way in which we could ascribe this belief to my dog in the form in which it is couched. Thus the description of the belief must be totally transparent.

In order to assimilate such examples to the scope theory, we must permit variables to stand for sentences as well as for NPs, so that (11.9) can formalize the readings of (11.7a).

(11.9) a. T: $\exists x((x$ = a carbon atom has two electrons in its outer shell) and (Ralph believes in effect $(x)))$

b. O: Ralph believes $(\exists x(x$ = a carbon atom has two electrons in its outer shell) and $x)$

These examples provide additional evidence for the argument in section 4.1 that quantification over sentences is necessary in a standard logical syntax. Even with such an extension, though, it is hard to justify (11.9b) as the opaque reading of (11.7a): Ralph does not believe in the *existence* of the proposition, but in the proposition itself. (Quine's, Kaplan's, and Postal's analyses, which differ in some details from Russell's, fare no better with these examples.)

Russell's version of the scope theory predicts that formal manipulations like those in (11.5) can be performed on any subordinate clause, and claims that these formal manipulations alone are the source of the referential ambiguities of belief-contexts. In fact, however, the kind of ambiguity possible in embedded clauses depends heavily on the choice of verb or adjective that subcategorizes the clause. For example, a great number of predicates do not sensibly admit contradictions within their complements:

(11.10)

a. ? $\begin{Bmatrix} \text{It is odd that} \\ \text{Ralph realizes that} \end{Bmatrix}$ $\begin{Bmatrix} \text{your dead uncle is alive.} \\ \text{Susan is older than she is.} \end{Bmatrix}$

b. ? $\begin{Bmatrix} \text{Ralph forced} \\ \text{It is useless for} \end{Bmatrix}$ $\begin{Bmatrix} \text{your dead uncle to be alive.} \\ \text{Susan to be older than she is.} \end{Bmatrix}$

c. ?Ralph is keeping $\begin{Bmatrix} \text{your dead uncle alive.} \\ \text{Susan older than she is.} \end{Bmatrix}$

(compare to "Ralph treats $\begin{Bmatrix} \text{your dead uncle as alive.} \\ \text{Susan as older than she is.} \end{Bmatrix}$")

In addition, of the verbs and adjectives in (11.10), only "realize" produces a transparent-opaque ambiguity; for instance, "Ralph realizes that Ortcutt is a spy" is ambiguous, but "Ralph forced Ortcutt to be a spy" is not.

Postal (1974) points out that "prevent" permits a contradiction to be used sensically in its complement, as in "The storm prevented it from being hotter than it was." He therefore argues that its analysis should be parallel to that of (11.3).[3] But again there is no transparent-opaque ambiguity; "Ralph prevented the cops from arresting Ortcutt" does not have a reading that depends on Ralph's calling the person arrested "Ortcutt." Thus the referential phenomena in belief-contexts are quite different from those in the complements of other verbs and adjectives, at odds with the homogeneous application of the scope theory.

To make matters worse, there is a class of verbs that create a different ambiguity in their subordinate clause.

(11.11) a. Ralph wants to catch a unicorn.
       b. Ralph is hunting for a unicorn.

There may be a specific unicorn that Ralph wants to catch—say, the one that has been terrorizing the neighborhood lately and is known as The White Fury. Or Ralph may be satisfied with any old unicorn; he is out unicorn-hunting. These two readings are called *specific* and *nonspecific* readings, respectively. Such an ambiguity also surfaces in sentences about future time: "Ralph will bring a pretty girl to the party" may intend a particular girl; or it may be a prediction, based on Ralph's pretty-girl-bringing habits, that whomever he brings, she will be pretty. This ambiguity too has been treated by means of a scope theory, so that (11.11a), for example, receives the two representations in (11.12).

(11.12) a. $\exists x$(Ralph wants (Ralph catch x))   (specific)
       b. Ralph wants ($\exists x$(Ralph catch x))   (nonspecific)

However, as pointed out by Janet D. Fodor (1970), the specific-nonspecific distinction is independent of the transparent-opaque distinction. (11.13) has four readings, not just two.

(11.13) John wants a coat like Bill's.

First consider the specific reading, where John has a particular coat in mind. He may describe his desire as "I want a coat like Bill's" (opaque description); or he may know nothing at all about Bill's coat, in which case "like Bill's" simply expresses the speaker's interpretation of John's desire (transparent description). In the nonspecific reading, where John is coat-hunting, the same opaque-transparent ambiguity obtains. However, the scope theory allows formally for only two readings; there is no room for another pair of quantifier positions. Fodor, to my knowledge the only author to have even noticed this double ambiguity and the difficulty it raises for the scope theory, proposes an analysis of want-contexts in which two distinct quantifiers bind the ambiguous phrase at once, each accounting for a different ambiguity. But then the same problem arises as with the quantification for belief-contexts: why does "believe" produce ambiguities only with one of these quantifiers, future tense only with the other, and "want" with both?

What becomes clear from all these differences among verbs is that the kind of ambiguity possible in a subordinate clause is not predictable on the basis of syntactic structure alone. Rather, the verb or adjective that subcategorizes the clause must play a role in determining the semantics of the clause. Thus Russell's purely structural theory and its descendants (e.g., McCawley, Postal) must be rejected.[4]

To make the structure of the problem clearer, consider verbs such as "imply" and "convince" that subcategorize two clauses at once. It turns out that the two may have different logical properties. A clause preceding "imply" does not permit a contradiction sensically, but a clause following "imply" does; neither clause permits a transparent-opaque ambiguity.[5] For instance, (11.14a) is acceptable and unambiguous with respect to the interpretation of "Ortcutt is a spy." But (11.14b) is unacceptable because "your dead uncle is alive" is contradictory; it too has no ambiguity with respect to "Ortcutt is a spy." The clause after "convince" behaves like a standard belief-context, so that "Ortcutt is a spy" is ambiguous in (11.14c) and "your dead uncle is alive" is acceptable and ambiguous in (11.14d). On the other hand, the clause preceding "convince" is factive, like the complement of "odd" in (11.10a): it neither accepts contradictions sensically (thus (11.14c) is unacceptable) nor creates transparent-opaque ambiguities (thus "Ortcutt is a spy" is not ambiguous in (11.14d)).

(11.14) a. That Ortcutt is a spy implies that your dead uncle is alive.
         b. ?That your dead uncle is alive implies that Ortcutt is a spy.
         c. ?That your dead uncle is alive has convinced Ralph that Ortcutt is a spy.
         d. That Ortcutt is a spy has convinced Ralph that your dead uncle is alive.

These examples show that the verb affects the semantics of its subordinate clauses not indiscriminately (e.g., by a simple feature [±opaque]), but in terms of the argument positions assigned to the clauses.

The standard approach to the altered semantics of belief-contexts is due to Frege (1892), who proposes that "believe" stipulates for its subordinate clause (and its parts) a reference different from normal reference. The problem then becomes: what choice of nonstandard reference will account for the apparent anomalies of belief-contexts?

The ontologically most narrow version of Frege's approach is an *inscriptional* theory like that of Carnap (1956), who claims that a belief is a tendency to assent to a sentence. Hence the clause following "believe" can be taken to refer to itself, parallel to the reference of "Harry" in "We named him Harry." But this theory is subject to Quine's objection mentioned above, in that it seals off the belief-context from any logical inference at all. In addition, Church (1950) points out that a description of a belief had better not be dependent on the language the believer speaks, since it is felicitous to say "Helmut believes that snow is white" even if Helmut speaks only German and would never assent to an English sentence.[6] Thus the inscriptional theory is decidedly unsatisfactory (even if hardly forgotten).

Frege's own position is that the subordinate clause refers to its normal *sense* (or *intension*). This approach accounts for some of the restrictions on substitution into belief-contexts. According to Frege, what counts as a coreferential expression in a belief-context is something with the same sense; therefore only synonymous expressions are substitutable. This position unfortunately is open to Mates's (1950) objection, mentioned above: if the subject of the sentence lacks linguistic or logical insight, he may not recognize two expressions as synonymous. Hence, on the opaque reading even substitution of synonymous expressions may not be legitimate.

Quine (1956) goes along with Frege, though he grumbles about the obscurity of intensions and flirts with returning to an inscriptional theory like Carnap's. He and Kaplan (1969) are concerned with the problem of how a quantifier outside an intensional context binds a variable within it, and they propose different formal solutions. Montague (1973) also adopts the theory that "believe" creates an intensional context; he rationalizes the (to him) suspicious notion of intension by treating it as the set of extensions in all possible worlds. But Partee (1978) and Bowers and Reichenbach (1979) essentially raise Mates's objection again with respect to Montague's notion of intension, concluding that the problems of incorporating someone else's perverted logic into semantic structure are severely damaging to possible worlds semantics.[7]

The rest of this chapter will show that Frege was correct in claiming that reference in belief-contexts is not ordinary reference, but that he was incorrect in identifying the abnormal reference with the ordinary sense. To begin with, we must brush away ontological scruples. We must not be concerned with what belief is, i.e., with truth-conditions for belief in the real world. Indeed, as observed in section 2.3, there may be no coherent notion of (real-world) belief. Rather, we are concerned with what #belief# is—what structure a speaker projects on a person (or animal) in saying "He believes that such-and-such is the case." It could be any kind of abstract #entity#, and the range of possibilities must be determined empirically, without an overzealous use of Occam's razor in advance of serious investigation.

I will show that #beliefs# are a species of #representation#, a class that also contains #pictures# and #sentences#. By examining #pictures#, which unlike #beliefs# are open to observation, we will develop the general properties of #representations#. Then, exploiting the grammatical parallels between the description of #pictures# and the description of #sentences# and #beliefs#, we will extend the theory of #representation# to include indirect discourse and belief-contexts.[8]

11.3 Characters in #Pictures#

Compare the senses of (11.15a) and (11.15b).

(11.15) a. John put Mary in the garbage can.
         b. John put Mary in the picture.

(11.15a) is a normal sentence of spatial motion, with "Mary" as theme. But (11.15b) does not describe a physical motion of Mary's body; it describes John placing an image or representation of Mary in the picture he is creating. If (11.16) follows (11.15b) in discourse, it is ambiguous.

(11.16) She looked terrible.

On one reading, "she" refers to Mary, the person who is being drawn, painted, or photographed. On the other reading, "she" refers to the representation of Mary in the picture; the real Mary may not look terrible at all. In fact, "She hates the way she looks" offers the possibility of one pronoun referring to each.

This ambiguity in (11.16) shows that, as a result of the use of (11.15b), there come to be two distinct individuals in the discourse, both referred to by the word "Mary": Mary-in-the-real-world and Mary-in-the-picture. In the metalanguage, we will call these two individuals #Real-Mary# and #Image-Mary#, respectively. Significantly, ordinary language does not directly distinguish the two.

What is the semantic factor that distinguishes (11.15b) from (11.15a), leading to the reference to #Image-Mary#? Clearly the key is in the word "picture." A #picture# is an #object# which has two alternative analyses: as a #physical object# just like any other, or as a conglomeration of #images# which, like #Image-Mary#, are somehow related to other #things# in the world. Let us call any #entity# with this dual analysis a "representational object"; among such objects are #pictures#, #statues#, #maps#, and #models#.

The status of some #object# as a #picture# rather than as a mere #design# or #pattern# is purely intensional; it is an analysis imposed by the observer. After all, #Image-Mary# is physically just some paint on a canvas. To express the relation between #Image-Mary# and #Real-Mary#, we will introduce the conceptual function *REP,* which maps conceptual structures for #things# into conceptual structures for their #images#. For example, if #Real-Mary# is projected by the conceptual structure [MARY], #Image-Mary# will be projected by [REP ([MARY])].

Let us investigate the relation between #Real-Mary# and #Image-Mary#. Formally this amounts to exploring the internal structure of the function REP. A necessary condition of REP is that the #Image-entity# be discriminable as an #entity# within the #representational object#; a nondiscriminable pattern or a pattern outside the frame of the #representational object# cannot serve as an #Image-entity#. In addition, there are two main preference rules on REP, each of which divides into various subconditions.

The first preference rule is that the creator of the #picture# has stipulated the #entity# in question as an #Image-Mary#, by some such statement as "Let this [*pointing*] stand for Mary." There need be no resemblance at all between #Real-Mary# and #Image-Mary# for this principle of *dubbing* to apply. We see it in situations as diverse as a very young child's drawing of Mommy, the *x*'s and *o*'s in a football strategy diagram, and a hunter's notches on his rifle ("This notch is the grizzly bear I shot last year up in Liberty, Maine"). It is also a commonplace in charts and graphs that represent numerosity rather than identity: "Each oil barrel in the chart stands for 10 oil spills." We may have access to the creator's dubbing either first-hand, or through a chain of informants, or through an inscription associated with the

#representational object#, such as "(Portrait of) Thomas Jefferson," "(Map of) Liberty, Maine," or "(Plans for) Octagonal Post Office."

The second preference rule is an elaboration of the idea that #Image-Mary# must somehow look like #Real-Mary#. As we have just seen, this is not a necessary condition, but in the absence of any information about how the #picture# was dubbed, resemblance is sufficient reason for a judgment. Moreover, interesting interactions take place when both conditions apply. In a picture of identical twins, we must rely on information from dubbing to tell us which is which. Or consider a case where the two conditions conflict: it would seem odd for someone to paint what he called a portrait of Eisenhower such that it looked like Churchill. We might call the figure either "Eisenhower" or "Churchill," but not without misgivings either way.[9] Thus the two conditions of correspondence interact in characteristic preference rule fashion.

To elaborate the preference rule of resemblance, we must invoke the notion of a set of *correspondence rules,* or a *normative mapping,* that applies to the #picture# to say how its #constituents# are to correspond to #Real-entities#. The rules for traditional representational painting involve correspondence in shape, proportion, color, shading, and perspective, but not in actual three-dimensionality. However, these are not the only possible correspondence rules, and different choices create different *media of representation.* The rules for black-and-white photographs omit color; colors in false-color infrared photographs correspond in a different way than usual (vegetation shows as red, for instance). Line drawings omit shading; isometric blueprints eliminate perspective. In ancient Egyptian art, relative sizes of #Image-figures# corresponded not to #Real-size# but to #Real-social status#. #Image-distances# in different map projections correspond to #Real-distances# in different ways, and one must know which projection is intended in order to use a map correctly. In short, in order to judge whether an #entity in the picture# is an #Image-X#, one must know (or guess) what correspondence rules are appropriate for the #picture# in question.

There are at least four ways in which a medium of representation can fail to provide a *complete* mapping between every aspect of #Image-X# and #Real-X#. First, it may simply fail to specify certain aspects of the represented #Real-X#. For instance, an ordinary photograph tells us nothing about the condition of #Real-Mary's liver# or the price of her car. Second, the medium may resort to dubbing for certain aspects of the representation—for instance, in the football diagram that represents the relative position of players geometrically (i.e., by rule), but represents the players only by x's and o's. Third, the "graininess" of the medium of representation may preclude correspondence down to the last detail: paintings don't depict every #Real-hair# and maps don't usually depict every #Real-house#. Finally, the correspondence rules themselves may sanction a further degree of graininess or fuzziness, so that exact tolerances are eliminated, as for example in impressionistic painting.

These four factors plus accidental wear or defacement of the representational object all can contribute to what Kaplan (1969) calls a lack of *vividness* in the image—a degree of indeterminacy in the correspondence between #Image-X# and #Real-X#. Depending on our purpose, we may be able to tolerate a certain lack of vividness and still judge some #entity in the picture# to be an #Image-X#. For instance, a rough sketch map may suffice to pick out #Real-landmarks# and get us to our friend's party. On the other hand, a much more vivid representation is necessary if we are surveying property lines. The way in which correspondence rules are applied is therefore in part task-dependent.

As has already been intimated, the correspondence rules are not used only for judging a match between #entities in the picture# and #Real-entities#: they can also be used to project a stipulated #Image-X# into a hypothetical #Real-X#. This procedure is what enables us to make plans of buildings yet to be built and to use the plans to direct construction. It is also what enables us to place an #Image-unicorn# in an otherwise realistic #Image-scene# and thereby imagine what it would be like to have a #Real-unicorn# around. Thus the correspondence rules have the power to cut a medium of representation loose from strict imaging of #reality#: within limits, the observer can impose a meaningful analysis on arbitrary #entities in the picture#.

The arbitrariness of the #image#, however, leads to the possibility of an *unfaithful* #Image-X#, some of whose details do not correspond to #Real-X# in the way they should. Unfaithfulness is different from lack of vividness, in that details are not missing but actually discrepant. A #representation# may be unfaithful either by mistake (because of its creator's misperception) or by design (because of the creator's whim or artistic license). Despite the infidelity, the #picture# can often still be considered an #Image-X#, either because of the artist's stipulation or simply because it is a good enough approximation to suit its purpose. (If the #picture# in question were used as a map or blueprint, such approximation might not be good enough.)

To sum up, an #entity in a picture# can be judged an #Image-X# if (preferably) it has been so dubbed by its creator, or if (preferably), according to the correspondence rules appropriate for the #picture# in question, it is mapped with a sufficient degree of accuracy into #Real-X#, where "sufficient degree" is in part task-dependent. As a side effect of the correspondence rules, it is possible to meaningfully depict nonexistent #Real-entities#; thus #pictures# have much the same property of arbitrariness as #beliefs#. To push the analogy further, we now turn to sentences that describe #pictures#.

11.4 The Description of #Pictures#

First let us develop formal machinery to account for the reading of "John put Mary in the picture" (11.15b). To distinguish "picture" from "garbage can" in (11.15), we will introduce a feature *REPRESENTATIONAL,* which will be present in the conceptual structure of words that denote #representational objects#. With this feature and the function REP, we can state the following rule:

(11.17) *Representation Rule*
         If a sentence S (or sequence of sentences) expresses or
         implies

$$[\text{BE} ([X], [\text{IN} (\begin{bmatrix} Y \\ \text{REPRESENTATIONAL} \end{bmatrix})]],$$

         optionally replace every occurrence of [X] in the
         interpretation of S by [REP ([X])].

(11.17) is part of the correspondence rule system; that is, it is one of the rules that construct interpretations from syntactic structures. The normal correspondence rules for thematic structure produce the readings (11.18a,b) for (11.15a,b), respectively.

(11.18) a. [CAUSE ([JOHN], [GO ([MARY],
                       [TO ([IN ([GARBAGE CAN])])])])]

         b. [CAUSE ([JOHN], [GO ([MARY],
                       [TO ([IN ($\begin{bmatrix} \text{PICTURE} \\ \text{REPRESENTATIONAL} \end{bmatrix}$)])])])]

Then (11.17) optionally converts (11.18b) into (11.19).

(11.19) [CAUSE ([JOHN], [GO ([REP ([MARY])],

$$[\text{TO} ([\text{IN} (\begin{bmatrix} \text{PICTURE} \\ \text{REPRESENTATIONAL} \end{bmatrix})])])])]$$

This is read as the creation of an #Image-Mary#. (We will see shortly how it manages to refer to both #Image-Mary# and #Real-Mary#.)

(11.17) is stipulated as optional because, under certain pragmatic conditions such as those in (11.20), one can put a #Real-object# into an #Image-object#.

(11.20) a. John put Mary in the sculpture.
        b. John put a scratch in the picture.

(11.20a) can be read like either (11.15a) or (11.15b): John picked Mary up and put her among the statues, or he produced a statue of Mary. Similarly, (11.20b) can be read as John scratching the picture or as John painting a scratch. The former reading in each case results from not applying (11.17). (Notice that on this reading of (11.20a), "she looked terrible" following it is unambiguous: [REP ([MARY])] is not introduced in conceptual structure, so there is no #Image-Mary# to refer to.) Thus the introduction of REP on any particular occasion of uttering (11.20a) or (11.20b) depends on the pragmatics of the situation.

Another syntactic construction that introduces the function REP is (11.21).

(11.21) In that picture, Mary is wearing a hat.

The introductory PP in (11.21) is syntactically parallel to that of "In Ottawa, John wore long underwear"; it locates the entire situation expressed by the main clause. Thus rule (11.17) creates the conceptual structure [REP ([MARY IS WEARING A HAT])], which projects into #Image-Mary-wearing-a-hat#, an #Image-state#.[10]

Using this construction, we can create contrasts like the following.

(11.22) a. Unicorns don't exist.
        b. Unicorns exist only in Ottawa.
        c. Unicorns exist only in pictures.

(11.22b) contradicts (11.22a); but (11.22c) does not, since by virtue of rule (11.17), (11.22c) asserts only the existence of #Image-unicorns#.

REP is introduced more directly in (11.23).

(11.23) a. John has a picture of Mary.
        b. John drew Mary.

"Picture," like all words for #representational objects#, occurs in the construction "picture of *x*." Its conceptual structure incorporates this possibility roughly as shown in (11.24).

(11.24)
"picture ⟨of *x*⟩":
$$\begin{bmatrix} \text{THING} \\ \text{REPRESENTATIONAL} \\ \langle\text{CONTAINS [REP ([X])]}\rangle \end{bmatrix}$$

Similarly, the construction "*x* draw *y*" expresses roughly [CREATE ([X], [REP ([Y])])]; the function REP is lexicalized with the verb. Given the right pragmatics, we can refer to either #Real-Mary# or #Image-Mary# after (11.23a) or (11.23b).

As we have seen, an #Image-entity# receives a linguistic description that is appropriate for the #Real-entity# it represents, even if, as in the case of unicorns, the #Real-entity# is only hypothetical. In other words, the argument position of REP is an exception to our general condition that conceptual constituents are referential. As a result, existential generalization fails for this position; though there is an #Image-unicorn#, there need be no #Real-unicorn#. Moreover, its nonreferentiality makes this position immune to substitution of equals for equals, just like belief-contexts. Compare (11.25) to (11.1): the syllogisms are invalid in exactly the same way.

(11.25) a. In that old diagram of the solar system, the number of planets is seven.
        b. The number of planets is nine.
        c. Therefore, in that old diagram of the solar system, seven is nine.

Now consider some sentences that describe unfaithful #images#.

(11.26) a. John incorrectly painted Mary with brown eyes.
        b. John painted Mary, who has blue eyes, with brown eyes.
        c. John painted the blue-eyed girl with brown eyes.
        d. In John's painting, the blue-eyed girl has brown eyes.
        e. In John's painting, Mary is taller than she (really) is.

These examples, especially the last two, parallel the belief-sentences (11.3a,b), in which an embedded clause is contradictory in isolation.

But the sentences are not contradictory. John has created some #Image-entity# x, which by virtue either of John's stipulation or of sufficient resemblance according to the correspondence rules represents some #Real-entity# y. On the sensical reading of (11.26b,c,d), x has #Image-brown-eyes#, and y has #Real-blue-eyes#.

Similarly, given the situation described in (11.26b,c,d), the following sentence has a true reading and a false reading.

(11.27) John painted a blue-eyed girl.

This parallels the two readings of (11.4a), "Ralph believes that Ortcutt is a spy." On the true reading, "a blue-eyed girl" is a description of the #Real-girl# depicted in the painting; this is like the transparent reading of (11.4a). On the other reading, "a blue-eyed girl" is taken as a description of what the correspondence rules map the #Image-entity# into, if taken literally; this reading, like the opaque reading of (11.4a), is false. Conversely, "John painted a brown-eyed girl" is false on the transparent reading and true on the opaque.

We thus find in the description of #pictures# the same constellation of puzzling characteristics that we found in the description of #beliefs#. We may state the principle behind the interpretation of (11.26) and (11.27) as follows:

Opacity Principle (generalized)
Suppose that a #representational object# P contains an #Image-entity# E. In describing P, a speaker may describe E either

a. in terms of the correspondence rules' projection of E (opaque description), or

b. if there is a #Real-X# of which E is an #Image-X#, in terms of the characteristics of #Real-X# (transparent description).

There is an important asymmetry between opaque and transparent description. Suppose that E is described opaquely, but one of its parts that is mentioned in the description projects into a #Real-entity#. Then this part presents the possibility of a transparent description that does not further involve characteristics of E. The result is a transparent description embedded as part of an opaque description. For example, consider "In that picture, my sister is riding a unicorn." Obviously the situation as a whole is described opaquely, since there are no #Real-people-riding-unicorns#. But the phrase "my sister" must be taken as a transparent description of some constituent of the #Image-situation#, since #pictures# cannot depict kinship relations.

By contrast, it is impossible to embed an opaque description as part of a transparent one. Once we choose to describe an #Image-entity# E in terms of the characteristics of the #Real-X# it represents, we have lost contact with the characteristics of the #picture# itself. On the other hand, having made contact with #reality#, all constituents of a transparent description are referential in the normal way.

These considerations suggest the following formalization of the opaque-transparent distinction for #pictures# in conceptual structure. Suppose that all the material in the argument of REP is taken as opaque description, hence nonreferential, unless otherwise marked. Then let us introduce an operator *TR*, which, when applied to a constituent of [REP ([X])], converts that constituent into a transparent description, in effect undoing the referential effects of REP. (11.28) then expresses the sensical reading of the main clause of (11.26d), in which the description of the girl is transparent, but the brown eyes and her relation to them are opaque.

(11.28) [REP ([BE$_{Poss}$ ([BROWN EYES],

[AT ([TR ([BLUE-EYED GIRL])])])])]

Let us specify a little more clearly how TR works. In (11.28), the #Image-brown-eyes# are attributed to the #Image-girl#. There must therefore be a constituent that refers to the #Image-girl#; this is [TR ([BLUE-EYED GIRL])]. At the same time, since the #Image-girl# is described transparently, there must be a constituent that refers to the #Real-girl#; this is [BLUE-EYED GIRL]. Hence there are two distinct conceptual constituents corresponding to the phrase "the blue-eyed girl" in (11.26d), both of them referential. This formalism thus provides a way to express the dual referentiality of "John put Mary in the picture," the initial observation that motivated this approach.

In English, the application of TR to any constituent within REP is optional, resulting in a systematic ambiguity between opaque and transparent readings that must be resolved pragmatically. In languages that grammatically distinguish opaque from transparent readings, the relevant grammatical morphemes will affect the placement of TR in conceptual structure.

This formalization of the transparent-opaque distinction bears an interesting relation to the formalization of belief-contexts in terms of quantifier scope. The material within REP that is *not* within TR corresponds to the material that the scope theory retains within the belief-context; the material within both REP and TR corresponds to the material that the scope theory exports outside the belief-context and binds to a variable within it. One might therefore think of TR as a sort of "inside-out" quantifier.[11]

The scope theory and the REP-TR formalization will be more directly comparable after we extend the theory of #pictures# to the treatment of #beliefs#, to which we now turn.

11.5 Treatment of Indirect Discourse and Belief-Contexts

We will reach #beliefs# via an intermediate topic, the treatment of indirect discourse, which has a philosophical history similar to that of belief-contexts. Suppose that we consider #sentences# and #stories# as a kind of #representational object# in an auditory medium of representation (written language is best considered as a visual representation of spoken language). The Grammatical Constraint strongly supports such a hypothesis, for the grammatical paradigms describing verbal representation are practically identical to those for pictorial representation. Compare (11.29) with (11.15)–(11.16).

(11.29) a. John put Mary in his story.
        b. She was indignant.

"She" in (11.29b) is ambiguous between #Real-Mary# and #Mary-in-the-story#. Hence we must consider the noise #"Mary"#, occurring in the #story#, as an #Image-Mary#. The conceptual structure that permits this noise to be perceived as a #word# rather than just a #sound# must include the information [REP ([MARY])]. (This conceptual structure is of course the lexical entry for the word "Mary.") It goes without saying that a #word#, like a #picture#, is an *intensional* #object#; it acquires its value as representation only by virtue of its human users. Just as we say an #entity in the picture# *depicts* #Real-Mary#, we say that an #entity in the story# (qua noise) *refers to* #Real-Mary#.

The preference rules for depiction, which tell us when we are entitled to call an #entity in the representational object# an #Image-X# that corresponds to a #Real-X#, carry over without difficulty to the case of #verbal representation#. The dubbing–causal chain source of correspondence—"Call her [*pointing*] 'Mary'," "Call that stuff [*pointing*] 'gold' "—is the *rigid designator* theory of reference worked out in Kripke (1972): an arbitrary #noise# is stipulated to be an #Image-X# by fiat, and this correspondence is handed down by custom from language user to language user. The other source of reference is of course through the compositional rules of the language, which play the role of the correspondence rules in the pictorial theory. These two sources of reference are intertwined in any particular utterance in much the way that dubbing and correspondence rules can interact in the interpretation of #pictures#.

Like #pictures#, #verbal representations# can suffer from lack of vividness. The medium of representation is more flexible than #pictures#; but it too has its inherent limitations (recall the discussion of effability in section 5.2), and any particular #sentence# or #story# may of course lack detail. Paralleling loss of vividness from defacement of #pictures# is loss of detail in a heard #utterance# due to background noise or the like.

Using the combinatorial rules of the language, one can of course build up arbitrary #entities in the representation# that do not refer to any #Real-X#. Among such #entities#, for example, are #commands#, which like #blueprints# are used to construct a corresponding #Real-entity#, in this case an #action#. This arbitrariness leads to the possibility of discrepancy as well—for example, Donnellan's (1966) case of using the phrase "the man drinking a martini" in a way that successfully refers to a #man drinking water#. As in #pictures#, the creation of an unfaithful #Image-X# may be a result of the creator's misperception (a descriptive error) or design (a lie or fiction, depending on the creator's motives).

The treatment of #utterances# as #representational objects# thus parallels that of #pictures# exactly, differing only in the inherent properties of the medium of representation. Similarly, sentences *describing* #verbal representations# parallel in nearly all respects descriptions of #pictures#. To account for the presence of #Image-Mary# in (11.29a), we invoke the Representation Rule (11.17). As in picture-sentences, the rule is optional, though it is difficult to find examples of its nonapplication that are pragmatically acceptable. One possibility is (11.30), paralleling (11.20b).

(11.30) John put a long pause in (the middle of) his story.

This can mean either that John paused in the middle of his story or that the plot of the story somehow involved a pause.

The other syntactic sources of REP in picture-descriptions have parallels here too. Like (11.21) is (11.31a); like (11.23a,b) are (11.31b,c).

(11.31) a. $\begin{cases} \text{In John's story,} \\ \text{According to John,} \end{cases}$ Mary is fun to be with.

    b. John heard a story about Mary.

    c. John described/mentioned Mary.

Conceptual structures are derived from these in exactly the same way as with #pictures#. (11.32a) is another syntactic construction that introduces #verbal representations#. It is not paralleled by a construction for #pictures# such as (11.32b), for reasons unknown to me. However, it is easily incorporated into the analysis by applying REP to the [EVENT] or [STATE] expressed by the subordinate clause, just as it applies to a [THING] in (11.31c).

(11.32) a. John said/mentioned that Mary is fun to be with.

    b. *John drew that Mary is/was wearing a hat.

As is well known, existential generalization into #verbal representation# fails. "John talked about a unicorn" does not entail that there is a #Real-unicorn# John is talking about, only that there is an #Image-unicorn# contained in John's discourse. And of course, substitution of equals for equals fails:

(11.33) a. $\begin{cases} \text{In John's science-fiction novel,} \\ \text{According to John,} \\ \text{John said that} \end{cases}$ the number of planets is twelve.

    b. The number of planets is nine.

    c. Therefore, $\begin{cases} \text{in John's science-fiction novel,} \\ \text{according to John,} \\ \text{John said that} \end{cases}$ nine is twelve.

Paralleling (11.26) is (11.34).

(11.34) a. John incorrectly described Mary with brown eyes.

    b. John described Mary, who has blue eyes, with brown eyes.

    c. John described the blue-eyed girl $\begin{cases} \text{with} \\ \text{as having} \end{cases}$ brown eyes.

$$\text{d. } \left\{ \begin{array}{l} \text{In John's story,} \\ \text{According to John,} \\ \text{John said that} \end{array} \right\} \text{ the blue-eyed girl has brown eyes.}$$

$$\text{e. } \left\{ \begin{array}{l} \text{In John's story,} \\ \text{According to John,} \\ \text{John said that} \end{array} \right\} \text{ Mary is taller than she (really) is.}$$

Finally, given the situation described in (11.34), (11.35) has a true (transparent) reading and a false (opaque) reading.

(11.35) John described/mentioned/talked about a blue-eyed girl.

Thus the conceptual and grammatical phenomena characteristic of #pictures# and their descriptions all generalize fully to #verbal representations# and their descriptions. The Cognitive Constraint, which addresses the generalization of conceptual structures, and the Grammatical Constraint, which marshals the linguistic descriptions, would both be strongly violated if the same formal approach were not applied to both systems of representation.

#Beliefs#, being unobservable, cannot be freely examined to see if they decompose into #entities in the belief# that can be identified, by dubbing or correspondence rules, with #Real-entities#. Nevertheless, the numerous grammatical parallels between the description of #pictures#, #utterances#, and #beliefs# are strong evidence for treating a #belief# as a #representational object#, a *#mental* representation# this time. This position accords with the common-sense notion that a #belief# is something in someone's head, and thus, unlike an inscriptional or intensional theory, it seems a reasonable explication of our everyday intuitions about #beliefs#.

#Mental representations# are of course subject to lack of vividness, if the possessor lacks certain information. Parallel to wear or defacement of a #picture#, I suppose, is forgetting aspects of an #idea#. And of course, a #belief# may be an unfaithful representation of #reality#, either by mistake or on purpose (in the latter case we call it a "fantasy" instead). Thus, all the ways that #pictures# can fail to correspond completely also appear with #beliefs#.

#Mental representations# can be referred to in a discourse by means of most of the grammatical devices available for describing #pictures# and #verbal representations#. The only dubious parallels are for (11.15) and (11.29), for which we have only the idioms in (11.36).

(11.36) a. John kept Mary in mind.

b. John put Mary out of his $\begin{Bmatrix} \text{mind.} \\ \text{thoughts.} \end{Bmatrix}$

The forms in (11.37) are syntactic and semantic parallels for the rest of the constructions discussed above.

(11.37)

a. $\begin{Bmatrix} \text{In John's mind,} \\ \text{In John's opinion,} \end{Bmatrix}$ Mary is fun to be with.

b. John has $\begin{Bmatrix} \text{an idea} \\ \text{a fantasy} \\ \text{a misconception} \end{Bmatrix}$ about Mary.

c. John $\begin{Bmatrix} \text{imagined} \\ \text{thought of} \end{Bmatrix}$ Mary.

d. John $\begin{Bmatrix} \text{thought} \\ \text{believed} \\ \text{imagined} \end{Bmatrix}$ that Mary was fun to be with.

To tie the three kinds of #representation# together, notice that (11.38) is ambiguous with respect whether John drew, described, or imagined Mary; the verb "picture" is neutral with respect to the mode of representation.

(11.38) John pictured Mary as fun to be with.

Only in a theory that accords parallel structure to all three modes is it possible to account for this generalization.

11.6 Comparison to the Scope Theory

There are two major differences between the theory of belief-contexts as #mental representations# and the theories discussed in section 11.2. In assimilating the analysis of #beliefs# and #descriptions# to that of #pictures#, we are giving them a quite different ontological status than does Carnap's inscriptional theory or Frege's intensional theory. Besides corresponding more closely to the intuitive notion of #belief#, this analysis frees #beliefs# of any obligations to logic other than those imposed by the holder of the #belief# himself. It thus disposes of Mates's objection and its descendants, which are serious stumbling blocks to previous theories.

The other innovation is in the formal representation. Compare (11.39) to (11.5) as representations of (11.3) and (11.4). T and O stand for transparent and opaque readings, respectively. We treat "believe" very provisionally as "have in mind"; further research is necessary to differentiate the thematic analyses of "believe," "imagine," "remember," and so forth.

(11.39) a. Ralph believes your dead uncle is alive.
       T (mistaken reading):
       [BE ([REP ([BE$_{Ident}$ ([TR ([YOUR DEAD UNCLE])],
                  [AT ALIVE])])], [IN ([RALPH'S MIND])])]
       O (contradictory reading):
       [BE ([REP ([BE$_{Ident}$ ([YOUR DEAD UNCLE],
                  [AT ALIVE])])], [IN ([RALPH'S MIND])])]

     b. Ralph believes that Susan isn't as old as she is.
       T:
       [BE ([REP (NOT[BE$_{Ident}$ ([SUSAN], [TR ([AS OLD
                  AS SHE IS])])])], [IN ([RALPH'S MIND])])]
       O:
       [BE ([REP (NOT[BE$_{Ident}$ ([SUSAN],
            [AS OLD AS SHE IS])])], [IN ([RALPH'S MIND])])]

     c. Ralph believes that Ortcutt is a spy.
       T (true reading):
       [BE ([REP ([BE$_{Ident}$ ([TR ([ORTCUTT])],
                  [AT ([$_{Type}$ SPY])])])], [IN ([RALPH'S MIND])])]
       O (false reading):
       [BE ([REP ([BE$_{Ident}$ ([ORTCUTT], [AT ([$_{Type}$ SPY])])])],
                  [IN ([RALPH'S MIND])])]

As in the descriptions of #pictures#, the parts of the sentence referring to the contents of the #belief# are contained in the argument of REP, and those parts of the #belief# that are described transparently are in the argument of TR as well.

These representations, unlike those of the scope theory, eminently satisfy the Grammatical Constraint: the embeddings in conceptual structure correspond closely to those in syntactic structure, instead of grossly distorting them. Moreover, recall that the limitations of standard quantificational notation prevent the scope theory from expressing the transparent-opaque distinction for anything other than NPs, without resorting to ad hoc adjustments that only violate the Grammatical Constraint further. By contrast, since the operators REP and TR can be applied to any conceptual constituent, there is no difficulty in treating the AP "as old as she is" as varying in opacity.

Quantificational formalism also restricts opacity phenomena to within subordinate clauses, since the scope of a quantifier must always be a sentence (or proposition). But REP can be applied to a main clause or just to an NP, correctly making opacity phenomena possible in (11.37a,b) without difficulty. (11.40) gives the conceptual structures.

(11.40) a. $\begin{bmatrix} \text{REP ([MARY IS FUN TO BE WITH])} \\ [_{\text{Place}} \text{ IN ([JOHN'S MIND])}] \end{bmatrix}$

b. $[\text{BE } (\begin{bmatrix} \text{MENTAL REPRESENTATION} \\ \text{CONTAINS [REP ([MARY])]} \end{bmatrix},$
$\qquad\qquad\qquad\qquad [\text{IN ([JOHN'S MIND])])])}]$

The case of an entirely transparent complement, also problematic for the scope theory, is easily represented as well. (11.41) shows how to ascribe a transparent #belief# to a dog (quite a reasonable thing to do in a theory of #beliefs# as #mental representations#).

(11.41) My dog thinks Ortcutt is a burglar.
$\quad$ [BE ([REP ([TR ([BE$_{\text{Ident}}$ ([ORTCUTT],
$\quad\quad$ [AT ([$_{\text{Type}}$ BURGLAR])])])])], [IN ([MY DOG'S MIND])])])]

Note that REP and TR do not just "cancel each other out" here. The presence of REP creates reference to an additional #entity# in the sentence, the #belief#, which would not be present if the two operators were absent.

This theory accounts quite naturally for the fact that only certain verbs create the constellation of grammatical characteristics found in belief-contexts: it is just these verbs that introduce REP, and it is the internal structure of REP that gives these verbs much of their meaning. Other ambiguities, such as the specific-nonspecific distinction introduced by "want," are due to other operators with their own characteristics.[12]

Beyond the immediate concerns of belief-contexts, the Grammatical Constraint forces us to find an analysis that generalizes to the analysis of #pictures#. Yet this is clearly impossible for the inscriptional and intensional theories of belief-contexts, since #pictures# have no analogous sentence-like structure. Moreover, the only syntactic structure in which the quantificational formalism is at home— "NP Vs that S"—is conspicuously lacking in the description of #pictures#, as seen in (11.32b). Thus generalizing the scope analysis to #pictures# would require ad hoc grammatical distortions for *every* syntactic environment, beyond those the analysis already imposes on the "simple" case. By contrast, the representational theory of #belief# accounts naturally for the relation of #beliefs# to #pictures# in both ontological and formal respects.

Some readers may object that treating #beliefs# as #mental representations# is too high an ontological price to pay for the formal advantages of the representational theory. Even if such an objection is little but an assertion of prejudice, it is worth considering for a moment: how much does the representational theory really add to the ontology?

Intuition takes for granted the interpretation of #pictures# and #sentences# as representations of #Real-entities#, because we learn and use the correspondence rules for such representations unconsciously. #Pictures# and #sentences# are taken to be natural kinds in the #world#, little different from, say, #tigers#. #Language# is even perceived as having a quasi-Platonic existence independent of its speakers. But this intuitive view cannot withstand scientific scrutiny, and it is clear that #pictures# and #sentences# must be regarded as intensional objects: a #tiger-picture# and the word #"tiger"# resemble a #tiger# in no physical sense, but only through the mind of an observer. Cognitive theory must therefore in any event include a theory of #representation# that accounts for these relationships.

Thus the only ontological expansion in the representational theory of #belief# is the introduction of a new species of #representation#, namely, #mental representation#. Intuitively this is not implausible, inasmuch as we commonly experience our own #beliefs# as #mental images#, either visual or sentential. In fact, the representational theory accounts for the persistent difficulty psychologists and philosophers have had in shaking imagistic and propositional theories of #belief#: according to the representational theory, our conceptual structure makes such views far more salient than any possible alternative.

Like the theory of thematic relations, the representational theory of #belief# is a vindication of the assumptions and methodology proposed in the earlier part of this study. Through detailed grammatical analysis and strict attention to the Grammatical Constraint, we have been able to construct a theory of conceptual structure that accounts not only for grammatical phenomena, but also for many characteristics (and even foibles) of common-sense intuition. A cornerstone of the approach is the distinction between the theory of

#belief#—what we intuitively think beliefs are and what the word "belief" refers to—and the theory of belief—cognitive psychology. Just as we saw in section 2.3 in the discussion of #color#, there is a profound difference between the two, and this difference is precisely the disparity between common sense and science.

11.7 #Truth#

Early in this study we argued that semantic theory must not take as its primary goal the explication of truth in the Tarskian sense. Along the way, we have observed on many occasions that truth, purportedly a relationship between language and reality, has little relevance to the nature of linguistic and cognitive judgments, if it can be defined at all. However, the theory of #representation# allows us to provide a preliminary theory of #truth#—the projected #characteristic# that people attribute to certain #sentences#. Consider what kind of #object# can be described as a "true picture of X": it is a #picture# sufficiently vivid to serve its intended purpose, in which, following the correspondence rules, all the #parts# of #Image-X# and the #relationships# among them correspond to the #Real-parts# of #Real-X# and their #relationships#. More intuitively, a #true picture# gives enough information to be useful, and will not lead the user astray. By simply changing the mode of representation, this sense of "true picture" extends without difficulty to "true sentence/ description/story" and "true belief" as well.

Like all other words, "true" tends to be conceived of as absolute: common sense tells us that a #sentence# must be either #true# or #false#, and if we can't tell which, it's our fault. But experience proves otherwise. For every category judgment "X is a Y" that is inherently dubious, ambiguous, or fuzzy, the judgment " 'X is a Y' is true" is likewise dubious, ambiguous, or fuzzy. The trouble is that intuition, in quest of salience and stability, strongly prefers to disregard marginal cases. As a result, we tend to think about #true sentences# in the same way we tend to thing about #dogs#—in terms of stereotypical exemplars—and we assume that dubious cases will someday, somehow, disappear. This sort of wishful thinking is what gives truth-conditional semantics its fatal attraction. Perhaps the strong dose of data administered here will have begun to dispel the illusion.

In a sense, this study has come full circle: we began by rejecting the concept of truth in natural language semantics, and now, through the theory of #representation#, we have come to understand something about #truth#. In the process, we have developed cognitively plausible approaches to many traditional problems of semantics. It is to be hoped that the methodology and conclusions of this study have shown how semantic theory can effect a reconciliation of philosophical concerns with the empirical demands of linguistics and psychology.

Notes

Chapter 1

1. These are the *computational* and *algorithmic* levels of Marr (1982). Marr too emphasizes the futility of pursuing physiological and process models without an adequate theory of structure.

2. An early example of this problem arises in Chomsky and Miller's (1963) treatment of center-embedded sentences. For more recent and much more complex cases, see Janet D. Fodor (1978) and references therein.

3. This paragraph will be recognizable as a distillation of many discussions on this topic by Chomsky, especially Chomsky (1965).

4. Many people have failed to see the importance of universal grammar as distinct from general cognitive capacity, believing that children can learn language on the basis of general-purpose learning strategies alone. I suspect they have taken this position because they have drastically underestimated the complexity and abstractness of linguistic structure. A serious look at any issue of the major journals of linguistic theory, with attention to the empirical evidence for which explanations are sought, ought to dispel this misconception. For work specifically on the problems the child faces in learning syntax, see Wexler and Culicover (1980), Tavakolian (1980), Baker and McCarthy (1981), Macnamara (1982).

5. Lerdahl and Jackendoff (1982, section 12.3) present a possible example of a general-purpose abstract structure common to language and music. However, it grew not out of an attempt to look for general-purpose strategies, but out of a comparison of detailed theories of specific capacities. This appears to be a more fruitful approach methodologically.

6. This theory is so-called interpretive semantics, with an autonomous syntactic component. An alternative popular during the early 1970s was generative semantics, in which syntactic and semantic structures intermingled freely in syntactic derivations (Lakoff (1971)). But this alternative failed for two reasons. One difficulty was technical: the proposed analyses were by and large shown to be syntactically and/or semantically incorrect. More importantly, the theory led to far too unconstrained a theory of universal gram-

mar; the language learner's choices were so vast as to render language learning impossible (cf. Chomsky (1972)).

7. This position became influential in linguistics at just about the time that generative linguistics itself gained greater recognition among philosophers and psychologists, and it is thus the view that appears in many popularizations of the results of generative linguistics. It often takes the form "Deep structure determines meanings" or even, inaccurately, "Deep structure is meaning." There has moreover been an unfortunate tendency to confuse deep syntactic structure—a level of derivation—with innate universal grammar—which helps determine the nature of rules applying to all levels of derivation. Thus one sometimes encounters statements like "Chomsky posits an abstract 'deep structure' in language which is universal and innate." Such statements have often led to serious misconceptions of linguistic theory among nonlinguists.

8. A striking illustration of this problem has been pointed out by John Lisman (personal communication). Consider the task faced by a baseball player trying to hit a pitched ball. Between the time the ball leaves the pitcher's hand and the time the batter must decide whether to swing, there is time for fewer than twenty sequential neural firings. Even granted the effects of practice and information derived from watching the pitcher's windup, it is hard to imagine the necessary information processing taking place within a chain twenty neurons long unless the chain is also hundreds or thousands of neurons wide.

9. See Vendler (1967) for arguments to this effect with respect to natural language quantifiers; Goldsmith and Woisetschlaeger (1982) with respect to progressive aspect; Jackendoff (1979) with respect to sentences about temperatures.

10. For readers conversant in syntactic theory, the argument can be sharpened. There do exist syntactic constructions in natural language that have roughly the form of restricted quantifiers like (1.2b). Two well-known examples are questions and relative clauses, in which a preposed *wh*-phrase binds a trace, a gap, or a resumptive pronoun within a clause. On the other hand, there seem to be no natural languages in which an *indefinite article* triggers such a syntactic construction. The question about (1.2b) thus becomes: If indefinite articles and *wh* are logically parallel, why is there no pressure for them to be syntactically parallel as well?

11. Montague grammar is a notable exception among logically based theories of semantics, in that it takes something like the Grammatical Constraint as a fundamental tenet.

12. The grammatical and lexical choices of one's native language quite possibly help shape the relative salience of concepts one develops, so there is room in the theory for a certain amount of "Whorfian" variation in concepts due to linguistic experience if that should prove necessary. See section 10.3 for a possible example.

13. Diagrams (1.3) and (1.4) represent explicitly only the linguistic components of a full theory of mind. Each of the other systems can be expected to decompose similarly into various levels of representation. For instance, Marr's (1982) theory of the visual system posits at least three levels of representation beyond the retinal image: the primal sketch, the 2 1/2D sketch, and the 3D model. Only the last of these interacts directly with conceptual structure.

A further complication omitted in these diagrams is the fact that phonetic representation itself is fairly abstract, and that it is related on the one hand to some level of representation in the auditory system and on the other to some level of representation in the motor system. As representation, it must of course be neutral between the two modalities, although, as is well known, it shows influences of both.

The theory of Chomsky (1975, 1981) interposes a level of "logical form" between syntactic structure and semantic structure (his "meaning"). But this level is not the one responsible for linguistic inference; it is thus to be regarded as an internal elaboration of the correspondence rule component rather than as the semantic structure level of (1.3).

Whatever these extra complications, they do not affect the question at hand—the decision for or against an autonomous level of semantic representation.

Chapter 2

1. Some readers may be disturbed by my reliance here and elsewhere in the book on results of the Gestalt school of psychology, which is often taken to be thoroughly discredited. While the Gestalt theorists' attempts at psychological explanation ultimately failed, their observations regarding the nature of the problems to be solved are often precisely to the point. In fact, Neisser (1967, 245–248) observes that the viewpoint of the Gestalt school is remarkably similar to that of generative grammar, particularly in its reasons for rejecting associationist explanations. Marr (1982, 8) points out that "with the death of the school, many of its early and genuine insights were unfortunately lost to the mainstream of experimental psychology." For more detailed remarks on Gestalt psychology and its demise, see Marr (1982, 186–187) and Lerdahl and Jackendoff (1982, section 12.1).

2. For instance, Goodman (1968) claims that a piece of music is the set of performances in exact conformance with the score. From my experience as a performer, I can attest that many pieces, by Goodman's definition, would have to consist of the null set.

3. One can see in Beethoven's sketchbooks his painstaking efforts to fit the notes intuitively to an underlying conception that is unstated but evidently clear to him. See also Arnheim (1974), who develops essentially this view with respect to the visual arts.

4. This is not to say that one should not distinguish cases where projection leads one astray, as in paranoia or hallucination; we may speak of such cases as "illegitimate projection."

5. It is interesting that Tarski himself (1956b) recognized the difficulty of a recursive theory of truth for natural languages. Citing, among other things, the inevitable appearance of antinomies in natural language, he concludes,

... *the very possibility of a consistent use of the expression 'true sentence' which is in harmony with the laws of logic and the spirit of everyday language seems to be very questionable, and consequently the same doubt attaches to the possibility of constructing a correct definition of this expression.* [Tarski's italics—RJ] For [these] reasons ... I now abandon the attempt to solve our problem for the language of everyday life and restrict myself henceforth entirely to *formalized languages.*

Tarski's pessimistic view notwithstanding, the attempt to apply his approach to natural language has flourished. We will see that there are many reasons besides Tarski's to give it up.

6. Though this has been known for a long time, it has been driven home in especially striking fashion by Land (1959, 1977), who shows how to generate full projected #color# from only two wavelengths of light.

7. Perhaps, in the interest of clarity, it would be well to drop the term *knowledge* for the former case, adopting the more technical term *cognition.* Chomsky (1975) suggests the term *cognizing* for this case, then reverts back to *knowing.* This is also the enterprise for which Fodor (1980) suggests the strategy of *methodological solipsism,* a point of view not unlike that adopted here. We differ principally (I think) in that the present account incorporates awareness as an integral part of the theory.

8. Some people in artificial intelligence (e.g., Hofstadter (1979)) speculate confidently that consciousness arises automatically out of sufficiently complex principles of computation. But this is a category error. Though it may well be that a certain degree of complexity, including self-reference, is a necessary precondition of consciousness, computations, no matter how many, simply are not experiences.

9. And it is not necessary that this class of inputs be especially natural from a physical point of view. See the work along these lines by Michotte (1954), for example.

Chapter 3

1. On facial recognition, see Carey (1979), Carey and Diamond (1980), and also Helmholtz's (1885, 369) brief but insightful remarks.

2. Shiman (1975) presents mathematical criteria relevant to this case, among a wide range of others. In his account, the circular boundary is treated as a boundary of the shaded region; the circular unshaded region, lacking its own boundary, becomes background.

3. Of course there are good reasons for us to make the judgments we do. Real objects are often occluded by other objects so that the field they present to the eye is discontinuous; hence one's experience can be more unified (or predictable) if one is prepared to make hypotheses about #things# that incorporate this possibility. However, such functional justifications of our cognitive capacity do not explain the existence of the capacity itself. (It would be

useful to us to be able to fly and read minds, too, but we have not managed to develop these abilities.) The best we can say is that our evolutionary history luckily has provided us with a source of useful hypotheses about the world, some of which emerge into consciousness as #things#. But the individual's behavior does not explicitly take into account his evolutionary history, and is certainly not explained by invoking it.

4. Note that "it" alone cannot be replaced by anything but abstract NPs like "the job" in this context, except in such expressions as "do the dishes/laundry/puzzle," which are lexically and semantically distinct from (3.7b).

5. For example, Michotte (1954) on causation; Jenkins, Wald, and Pittenger (1978) on event-perception; remarks of Köhler (1929) on temporal grouping; Lerdahl and Jackendoff (1982) on musical structure; and of course the entire literature on phonetic and syntactic perception.

6. One might speculate whether organisms differ in the ontological categories that their minds provide. Note however that this is a different issue from the question of what sensory apparatus provides evidence for which ontological categories. For instance, both sight and touch provide us evidence about #things#, but a bat can use sonar as well. I would guess that this would not make the ontological category [THING] itself different for a bat—though the permissible internal structure of a [THING] could be different, possibly changing the holistic character of experience in ways unimaginable to a human. See Nagel (1974).

7. One might question whether some of the sentences in (3.11) assert *token-* or *type*-identity (some are probably ambiguous, as well). Either reading is sufficient for present purposes, though, for an assertion of type-identity presupposes individuation of tokens.

Here is a bit of evidence that one can identify #actions# occurring on different occasions as token-identical, contrary to most received philosophical intuition. As we have just noted, "the same" can be read as token- or type-identity, and the particular reading chosen can often be forced by pragmatic considerations. For example, (i) is probably taken to assert token-identity of the hat; whereas (ii) is probably taken to assert type-identity of the sandwich ("the same *kind* of sandwich")—the token-identity reading would entail regurgitation.

(i) Sam wore the same hat he always wears.

(ii) Sam ate the same sandwich he always eats.

However, there is an English construction that appears to *require* the token-identity reading, involving the verbal prefix "re-": (iii) has only the regurgitation reading that was rejected for (ii).

(iii) Sam re-ate the sandwich.

Given the Grammatical Constraint, this difference between "the same" and "re-" suggests that (iv) asserts token-identity of the trick (an #action#) on its second occurrence.

(iv) Sam re-performed the trick.

This fragmentary evidence is hardly conclusive, but it is indicative of the sort of linguistic phenomena that are worthy of exploration in dealing with problems of identity and individuation.

8. An interesting case is the identity of #sounds# or #sequences of sounds#. As mentioned in section 2.1, Goodman (1968) forces himself to regard a piece of music as a set of performances in compliance with the score. Thus each individual performance is regarded as a separate token belonging to the set "performances of piece X." But this goes against the linguistic evidence. We say of the *Eroica* "I heard *it* on the radio last night," not "I heard *one of them* (a member of the set of performances) last night." This suggests that we intuitively think of the *Eroica* as a single #entity# (a complex #sound# or #group of sounds#) that may be heard on various occasions—just as, for instance, the morning star is a #thing# that may be seen on various occasions.

9. We have ignored an important enrichment of the structure [THING]: the distinction between what might be called bounded and unbounded #things#. A physical #object# has spatial boundaries; however, one can refer to #substances# in such a way that the existence of spatial boundaries is not part of the picture being conveyed. Contrast (i) and (ii).

(i) Oil was leaking $\begin{Bmatrix} \text{onto} \\ \text{all over} \end{Bmatrix}$ the floor.

(ii) Some oil was leaking $\begin{Bmatrix} \text{onto} \\ \text{??all over} \end{Bmatrix}$ the floor.

(i) presents the oil as a more or less continuous stream, of unbounded quantity within the time-frame described by the utterance. By contrast, (ii) presents the oil as a bounded quantity. This difference is related to the oddness of "all over" in (ii).

Another direction in which [THING] must be extended is to the grouping of a number of [THINGS] into a unit, as expressed by pluralization of NPs in English. Plural NPs are also subject to the bounded/unbounded distinction, as shown by (iii)–(iv).

(iii) People were running all over the place. (unbounded)
(iv) Some people were running all over the place. (bounded)

In (iii), the number of people is potentially unlimited; they are treated as uncountable. There are people "all over." In (iv) there is a bounded number of people, each of whom is running "all over." (As is well known, there are strong syntactic parallels between mass nouns and plural count nouns.)

Interesting discussions of these dimensions of conceptual structure are found in Talmy (1978) and Platzack (1979). What is significant about both these treatments is that they extend both dimensions to [EVENT]. For instance, (v) describes a temporally bounded #event#, while (vi) describes a temporarily unbounded #event#, or #process#. The addition of certain modifiers to (vi), as in (vii), places temporal bounds on the #process#, making it a bounded #event#.

(v)   Max sneezed.

(vi)   Max slept.

(vii)   Max slept for three hours.

In addition, #events# are subject to iteration, paralleling pluralization in NPs:

(viii)   Max sneezed three times.

Talmy shows that iteration and bounding can be recursively embedded in each other, as in (ix)–(x):

(ix)   In NP:

three groups of four men

(iteration of "man," bounded by "four," the whole iterated by "groups," bounded by "three")

(x)   In S:

The light kept flashing three times for four hours.

(iteration and bounding of "flash" by "three times," the whole iterated by "kept" and bounded by "for three hours")

What this parallelism shows is that the two ontological categories [THING] and [EVENT] share some of the same possibilities for internal structure. Anticipating section 9.1, it is worth pointing out that [PATH] is also differentiated in the bounded/unbounded dimension: "to the house" specifies a [PATH] that attains a goal (bounded), while "toward the house" leaves the endpoint of the [PATH] unspecified (unbounded). It is this latter type of [PATH] that we have called in this chapter a [DIRECTION].

The grammatical devices used to express bounding and iteration are complex, and they interact with each other in ways as yet only little explored (though Platzack proposes some formal rules that cover certain cases; see also Jackendoff (1972, section 7.4.4), Declerck (1979), Mittwoch (1982)).

Chapter 4

1. The inclusion of preposition here may warrant comment, in light of the fact that prepositions are normally considered as part of the set of "closed-class" items, along with auxiliary verbs, pronouns, and inflectional affixes (Kean (1980), Bradley, Garrett, and Zurif (1980)). My understanding of this classification is that it is not relevant to formal syntax as such, since the closed-class items form such a grammatically heterogeneous collection. Rather, these items mark obligatory but relatively limited semantic oppositions, and are therefore relatively common, short, and susceptible to phonological reduction. As a result, these items appear to trigger specialized processing mechanisms that are used as grammatical shortcuts. According to Bradley, Garrett, and Zurif, these processing mechanisms are lost in Broca's aphasia. The point is that the open/closed-class distinction is more significant to processing than to syntactic structure.

2. In fact, there is a sense in which English syntax is *less* general than the semantic form it expresses: it lacks simple proforms for [ACTION] and [EVENT], resorting to "do it/that/what/something" and "it/that/what/some-

thing . . . happen" as the simplest expressions for these types. Despite the absence of simplex forms, the generality of the semantics shines clearly through in the paradigms of chapter 3.

3. That #event# and #action# must be represented separately follows from the existence of sentences that express an #event# but not the performance of an #action#. See section 9.4 for discussion.

4. The examples in (4.3e) are somewhat controversial cases. In one school of thought, these VPs are represented syntactically as subjectless sentences; in another, they are bare VPs. On the perception verbs, see Akmajian (1977); on "try" see Bresnan (1978), Brame (1978).

5. Traditional grammar usually calls the forms in (4.6a) *adverbs* and those in (4.6e) *subordinating conjunctions*. The lexical parallelism of both of these with standard prepositions, along with their dissimilarity from -*ly* adverbs on the one hand and coordinating conjunctions on the other, justifies their treatment as prepositions. See Jackendoff (1977a) and references there.

6. The treatment of "on" as a two-place predicate ON (x,y), "x is on y," appears in Davidson (1967a) and is one of the two possible analyses suggested by Miller and Johnson-Laird (1976). Anderson (1976) adopts a similar treatment without justification or even comment. Miller and Johnson-Laird in fact present the only serious attempt I have seen to deal with prepositions in a quasi–predicate logic format.

7. One such alternative of some importance is the logical syntax of Montague grammar (Montague (1973), Partee (1975)), which requires more extended discussion than I can provide here.

Those familiar with the history of generative linguistics may have found the arguments of this section reminiscent of certain lexicalist arguments against the generative semantics position of the early 1970s. The reason for this is that generative semantics essentially incorporated the assumptions of first-order logic into the theory of syntactic underlying structure. Thus we find in generative semantics a theory of quantifiers as outermost predicates (Lakoff (1970), McCawley (1971)), of "be" as transformationally inserted (Bach (1967)), of adjectives as underlying verbs (Lakoff (1970)), of nouns as underlying predicates (McCawley (1971), Bach (1968)), of adjectives as referential and hence NPs (Ross (1969)), of prepositions as underlying verbs (Becker and Arms (1969)), and of relative clauses as underlying conjoined propositions (Ross (1967), Bach (1968)). The syntactic difficulties of these positions (Chomsky (1970, 1972), Jackendoff (1971, 1972), Schachter (1973), Bowers (1975)) led to the richer lexicalist theory of underlying syntactic structure. The message of the present section is that, given the Grammatical Constraint, these arguments apply to the standard assumptions about predication and referentiality, whether they are regarded as assumptions about syntax or about semantics.

8. My treatment of grammatical subjects might be open to question at this point in the exposition. For one thing, the Grammatical Constraint suggests that there should be a division in conceptual structure corresponding to the

syntactic division of the sentence into subject and predicate. The present treatment rejects such a division, and my treatment of compositionality in section 4.4 takes this into account rather naturally. On the other hand, a reflex of the subject-predicate distinction appears in the treatment of [ACTIONS] in section 9.4, and further refinements along such lines are not excluded by the formalization adopted in the present chapter.

There is also a debate about whether grammatical subjects are within the domain of subcategorization, as I have assumed. Chomsky (1965, 1981) has treated subcategorization as confined to the sisters of the head (direct and indirect objects, etc.), leaving the subject as an "external argument" to the verb. By contrast, I have argued (Jackendoff (1974)) that the subject of *nominals* must be subcategorized, so that one can distinguish "the/Bill's criticism" from "the/*Bill's blame." By extension, the subjects of verbs must be subcategorized as well. There may be, however, mitigating semantic factors that I did not observe; if these could be specified clearly, my argument would be weakened. In any event, it does not seem difficult to adapt the proposals here to Chomsky's theory of subcategorization; the requisite changes would likely mesh nicely with the considerations of the preceding paragraph.

9. What is to be done with languages that lack an overt verb "be"? In cases such as Russian and Hebrew, which lack it only in the present tense, but in which it is overt in past and future tenses, the proper solution is probably a simple deletion or a morphological zero form. For a language like Papago that really has no verb "be" (Kenneth Hale (personal communication)), one might take a different approach. The semantic function BE is the least informative, or the least highly marked, among EVENT- and STATE-functions. There are typically two strategies for a language to express an opposition: by having distinct expressions for each member of the opposition, or by expressing only the marked member(s) of the opposition. An example of the latter strategy is the singular-plural opposition in English nouns, where there is a marker only for the plural, the marked member of the opposition. A language that lacks "be" could be said to be choosing this strategy for the expression of STATE-functions. (See Woisetschlaeger (1976) for an extensive treatment of tense and aspect based on this premise about markedness.)

10. Two well-known classes of cases should be mentioned that do not conform to this generalization. The first class is *idioms:* in "Sam kicked the bucket" ("Sam died"), for example, we do not expect the NP "the bucket" to correspond to a conceptual constituent. The second class consists of constituents whose heads are *grammatical morphemes* — words that are present to satisfy the exigencies of syntax but do not carry an interpretation. One clear example is the NP dominating the pleonastic "it" in sentences such as "It is raining" and "It is obvious that the Reds will win." This NP is present just to fill the obligatory subject position of English, and does not correspond to an argument position of the verb. Another example is the PP headed by "of" in phrases like "the destruction of the city" and "afraid of Bill." This "of" is present because English nouns and adjectives cannot be followed by a direct object (see Chomsky (1970), Jackendoff (1977a, chapter 4)); the corre-

sponding verbal expressions "destroy the city" and "fear Bill" lack it, with no apparent difference in the semantic relation expressed. Thus it seems reasonable to claim that the "of" is meaningless, that the NPs "the city" and "Bill" appear directly as arguments of "destruction" and "afraid," respectively, and hence that the PPs "of the city" and "of Bill" do not correspond to any constituent of the interpretation.

These two classes of exceptions do not, I should think, constitute defects in my theory. Their properties have long been recognized, and, as far as I know, they will emerge as special cases in any reasonable theory of compositionality. They are places where the syntax-semantics match is inescapably less than ideal.

Chapter 5

1. If I may be permitted a speculation here, it seems plausible to attribute the bizarre behavior of autism to a severe limitation in the ability to form categories and to make sufficiently general categorization judgments. Such a view would account for three important characteristics of this disability. First, if one could not go beyond #individual tokens# to the #similarities# among them, one could neither form stable categories of #objects in the world# nor categorize #utterances# as sequences of repeated #words#. Thus language would be extremely difficult at both the semantic and the phonological level. Second, since only small differences among #tokens# could be accommodated in the categorization process, stabilization of the projected #world# could be achieved only under very limited conditions of variation. Hence the autistic would be badly confused by even moderate changes in the environment. Third, since [TOKENS] would be subject to only minimal categorization, their internal structure would be left basically at the initial level of perception, accounting for the autistic's quasi-eidetic memory.

These speculations seem to be supported by recent research, which suggests that autism is not merely a social or linguistic deficit but in fact a central cognitive one:

It has been suggested . . . that the autistic child's stereotyped behavior and insistence on sameness in his environment may reflect the same underlying deficit as is revealed in echolalia, namely an inability to segment or break down patterns . . . When given a list of items to recall, normals will tend to group these into semantic categories, whereas the autistic children failed to do this.

(Baker et al. (1976, 144))

No abnormalities were found in primary perceptual processing per se; the data suggested, however, that the autistic children were unable to generate modality-independent rules by which features of external stimuli were processed or "understood." This deficit in creating rules for dealing with perceptual information is a useful explanation for many of the apparent incongruities and discrepancies revealed during psychological testing of autistic children . . . Persistent rejection of external sensory stimulation implies, not inability to perceive stimuli, but, rather, abnormal processing and impaired coding. . . . The autistic children's failure in social development may be seen, in some ways, as a symptom of their inability to make sense of the world and the people in it.

(Caparulo and Cohen (1977, 625–626, 630, 641))

(I am grateful to Laura Meyers for her help with this note.)

2. Strictly speaking, this is Katz's account of *analytic* truth; he consigns synthetic truth to the theory of pragmatics, which is none of his concern. However, the inclusion of markers (or attributes) is a characteristic conception of the criterion for categorization within decompositional theories of meaning such as Katz's.

3. Or, in possible worlds semantics, between sentences and the set of possible worlds, one of which is the real world. The same objections obtain.

4. Such an account of [TOKENS] is assumed by Montague semantics. See Partee (1975).

5. It is interesting to compare these statements with Katz's (1972) discussion of effability. Citing principles of Frege, Searle, and Tarski as antecedents, Katz says (p. 19), ". . . anything which is thinkable is communicable through some sentence of a natural language. . . . It would clearly be absurd for anyone to assert that he cannot communicate one of his thoughts because English has no sentence that expresses it. . . ." As the quotations above show, it is not absurd at all. At best, one might claim that anything which is *projectable* is communicable through some sentence of a natural language. But even this is doubtful if we consider thoughts about, say, music, dance, or art, particularly from the point of view of creation or production rather than merely appreciation.

6. Most studies of [TYPE] acquisition have involved perception, where the output of the acquisition process can be studied only through further categorization judgments. However, Polanyi (1958, chapter 4) emphasizes the strict cognitive parity between perceptual [TYPES] and motor skill [TYPES]. The latter are learned by following someone's example and practicing. Think of how inadequate verbal instructions alone would be for teaching someone to drive a car or play the piano or paint; one cannot learn these skills by merely reading a book or seeing someone else perform them. If the skill is not too hard, there is a point where practice pays off and we "get it"—we have formed a motor skill [TYPE] for which we can summon up exemplars at will.

If Polanyi's argument is correct (and I see no reason to doubt it), the unconscious processes behind motor skill acquisition are very much like those behind learning perceptual [TYPES] from exemplars. In the case of motor skills, though, we have a highly structured motor output to study during the acquisition process—potentially a much richer source of information than perceptual judgments. Thus Polanyi's hypothesis suggests that the study of motor skills is of great importance to cognitive theory and, in the present framework, to semantics as well.

7. This is not the problem of learning in general, where one is not even presented with discrete stipulated examples. The general case involves the

prior (and probably even more serious) problem of noticing that there is a generalization to be made, hence deciding to construct a [TYPE] in the first place.

8. The theory of language acquisition would by contrast appear not to conform to this generalization, since rules of grammar, the output of the acquisition process, are not apparently of the same formal nature as sentences, the #tokens# from which the rules are constructed. However, I think this appearance is merely a consequence of common notational practice in linguistics. For example, phrase structure rules and the trees they describe look entirely different. When treated formally, however, both are descriptions of structures whose elements are syntactic categories and whose principles of combination are daughter-dependency and linear order. It is simply that the internal structure of particular [SENTENCE TOKENS] is much more specific than [SENTENCE TYPE] (the phrase structure grammar) about the relationships among its syntactic categories. A similar construal can be placed on the relationship of transformations to transformational derivations and on the relationship of phonological rules to phonological derivations—though perhaps less transparently. If this is so, the generalization stands that the internal structure of [TYPES] is in large part formally undistinguished from that of [TOKENS].

9. (5.12c) is deliberately reminiscent of Donnellan's (1966) much-discussed distinction between *referential* (here, token-identity) and *attributive* (categorization) readings for definite NPs. Kripke (1977) shows that this distinction cannot be expressed by quantifier scope, and that the choice between the two readings is pragmatic. Such an analysis seems appropriate to the treatment here. The referential-attributive distinction does not always lead to a [TOKEN]-[TYPE] difference, as it does in (5.12), but it will in many of the examples to follow in this section.

10. That is, there are specific individuals picked out by these NPs. However, it may be (as Donnellan believed) that the definite NPs here still display the referential-attributive distinction (see note 9).

11. This sort of interaction is explicitly denied in the traditional logical approach to reference, where scope differences of various sorts are the only source of nonreferentiality. In a critique of Jackendoff (1975b), Abbott (1979) takes the verb's lack of influence on referentiality as a virtue of the traditional scope analysis of belief-contexts; Jackendoff (1980) argues that in fact it is a liability. Similarly, Aune (1975) expresses amazement that Vendler (1975) could propose that subordinate clauses have different referential properties depending on what verb they are subordinate to. I agree with Vendler in seeing this interaction as an inescapable fact. See also chapter 11.

12. It might be objected that these functions cannot be identical, since IS TOKEN-IDENTICAL TO is symmetrical and IS AN INSTANCE OF is not. But I think the symmetry of IS TOKEN-IDENTICAL TO is an artifact of comparing two [TOKENS]: identity is the only way for one [TOKEN] to be "included in" another in the requisite sense.

13. It is interesting that the division between [TOKEN] and [TYPE] readings falls at a different point with these than with "be": here indefinite NPs are ambiguous, rather than expressing only [TYPES]. Moreover, my intuition is that definite NPs in the object of "resemble" allow only a [TOKEN] reading, but are ambiguous in the object of "seek." I have no explanation for these differences, but they make impossible any simple-minded reduction of one of these classes of verbs to another. The ambiguity with "seek" is usually attributed to differences in quantifier scope; for arguments against this, see Jackendoff (1972, chapter 7; 1980).

14. This point is already recognized by Frege (1892), who unlike Putnam is not disturbed by it:

The sense of a proper name is grasped by everybody who is sufficiently familiar with the language. . . . Comprehensive knowledge of the reference would require us to be able to say immediately whether any given sense belongs to it. To such knowledge we never attain.

15. To say with Putnam that word meanings are spread over the society won't work either—they still must be in *somebody's* mind. See section 7.1.

Chapter 6

1. I am not sure whether (6.3) should be a [SITUATION TOKEN] or a [SITUATION TYPE], so I leave the feature unspecified. Nothing in this chapter appears to depend on the choice, though a general theory of generic sentences would have to address it. I lean toward the [TYPE] alternative.

2. For treatments of the artificial intelligence approach, see Jerry A. Fodor's (1978) discussion of Winograd (1972), Weizenbaum's (1976, 178–179) discussion of Newell and Simon's General Problem Solver, and Dreyfus (1981) and Marr (1982, 344–345) on microworlds.

3. A typical strategy for getting a strong judgment in an otherwise indeterminate case is to give the right-hand relatum a stipulated definition that addresses the particularities of the case at hand. For example, one may claim that a language must meet a certain set of criterial conditions, then argue that (6.14c) is true only if Washoe's signs have these properties. Or one switches the question to another generic categorization from which the point at hand may be deductively derived; nowadays the dispute on (6.14d) has been pushed back to the equally indeterminate "A fertilized human egg is a person." In effect, one sets up meaning postulates that replace an intuitive judgment with a deductive one. Of course, two can play that game, and the opposing sides typically set up their own definitions to make things come out the way they want. (It gets dangerous when one side can stipulate its definition as law.) But all of this pseudodeductive maneuvering never really resolves the original question. Usually it only serves to divert attention from the motives that lead the disputants to want the outcome one way or the other.

4. The contrast also appears in the distinction between the "spirit" and the "letter" of the law, where the latter is commonly acknowledged to underspecify or even misrepresent the former; one relies on intuitions about the

categorization of precedents to justify an interpretation of the written law's stipulative definition.

5. Katz (1966) makes essentially the same reduction that I do here, though it emerges formally in terms of inclusion of semantic markers. One of the virtues of Katz's theory is this formal unification of a diverse set of semantic properties, and any semantic theory must relate them along similar lines. However, since Katz's theory of semantic markers will be shown inadequate in chapter 7, I have stated the argument here informally in terms of intuitions about GCSs.

6. I distinguish "nontrue" from "false" so as to include anomaly in the former; my use of "nontrue" is thus equivalent to Russell's (1905) use of "false" when he says that "The present king of France is bald" is false.

7. Katz's (1980) defense, for example, is insupportable; see Jackendoff (1981). Gazdar (1979, 164–168) observes that while he, along with most logicians, assumes an autonomous truth-conditional semantics, one can cite some rather convincing evidence against it. Moreover, Gazdar's notion of pragmatics is more limited than mine.

Chapter 7

1. Note that the "expert" need not be expert. A jury is a panel of *non*experts appointed to make a categorization judgment of an #event# as, say, #instance of murder#. Similarly, a baseball umpire's judgments *stipulate* the categorization of #events# as #balls# or #strikes#—whether or not his judgment is borne out by the instant replay. Such examples seem to me to show that Putnam's division of linguistic labor is not a matter of semantics, but a matter of whom you choose to trust with what decisions, and why.

2. Accordingly, distinguishers disappeared from Katz's analyses by Katz (1966). Fodor, on the other hand, came to question the enterprise of decomposition altogether, as we will see in section 7.5.

3. In fact, Mervis and Roth (1981) argue that fuzzy set theory does not provide an adequate account of the *observations*, even in so elementary a domain as color terms.

   Note 5 to chapter 8 will suggest how Lakoff's uses of fuzzy sets for "hedge" terms can be accommodated in the present theory.

4. Katz (1977) purports specifically to address Labov's cup-bowl case. He claims that one of Labov's factors, having a handle (which we address in section 8.3), is encyclopedia information and hence nonsemantic. However, he deals with the height-width ratio by specifying a semantic marker "height about equal to top diameter," and it is precisely the interpretation of "about equal" that gives rise to the gradation of judgments we are concerned with here. Since Katz proposes this marker without comment, I cannot evaluate the degree to which he appreciates the significance of this implicit concession.

5. I cannot resist quoting Wittgenstein (1953, 44):

We are under the illusion that what is peculiar, profound, essential, in our investigation, resides in its trying to grasp the incomparable essence of language. That is, the order existing between the concepts of proposition, word, proof, truth, experience, and so on. . . . Whereas, of course, if the words "language," "experience," "world," have a use, it must be as humble a one as that of the words "table," "lamp," "door."

Katz's attack on Quine's premises again appeals to the distinction between dictionary and encyclopedia information. He claims that analyticity can be defined precisely, in terms of inclusion of semantic (dictionary) markers in lexical entries, whereas encyclopedia information is synthetic. Katz's criterion for an attribute to be a semantic marker is that semantic properties of the lexical item depend on it. However, since all the semantic properties are interdependent (as Katz himself works out—see section 6.3), Katz begs the question. See Bar-Hillel (1970, chapters 15 and 31) for further discussion of Katz's views on analyticity.

6. Armstrong, Gleitman, and Gleitman (AGG) (1983) present evidence that has been widely interpreted as vitiating Rosch's arguments for family resemblance ("cluster") concepts. They show that certain of Rosch's typicality effects appear even with concepts like "even number" and "female" that should be absolutely categorical: subjects judge 18 and 42 more typical even numbers than 34 and 106, and mothers and sisters more typical females than comediennes and cowgirls. Moreover, verification times for "better" exemplars are faster than for "poorer" exemplars, just as with Rosch's alleged cluster categories such as "fruit" and "vehicle." The conclusion that AGG draw is that category exemplariness is not psychologically equivalent to category membership, as has generally been assumed. Hence experimental results that bear on exemplariness reveal nothing about the mental representation of category membership.

The treatment of categorization in the present study is, I believe, immune to AGG's objection to Rosch. The crucial issue here has not been gradation of typicality, but the gradation of uncertain category judgments, which involves a narrower class of cases. For instance, "even number," while subject to typicality effects, does not produce uncertain judgments. By contrast, "fruit" not only has gradations in typicality, from cases like "apple" (most typical) to cases like "fig" (less typical), but also has uncertain cases like "tomato," which is conflicted between "fruit" and "vegetable" (would a tomato go in a fruit bowl?). Even "female," which AGG treat as well defined, has its uncertain cases. To be sure, "comedienne" unquestionably is a subcategory of "female," though an atypical exemplar. But "transsexual" presents real conflicts of judgment, which may be resolved differently depending on one's purpose: apparently, transsexuals count as females for legal marriage, but not for competition on the women's professional tennis circuit. It is this narrower class of cases, those that produce uncertain or conflicted judgments, that is crucial to the argument against necessary and sufficient conditions for category membership. The value of AGG's results, therefore, is in showing the importance of distinguishing this class of cases from the wider class of atypical exemplars. That is, the argument against necessary and sufficient conditions must be pursued more carefully than it often has been in the literature.

One further remark on AGG's analysis. They observe that a theory of cluster concepts makes the process of semantic composition far more difficult computationally: how is one to construe the combination of the two cluster concepts "foolish" and "bird" into a single cluster concept "foolish bird"? They take this complexity as reason to avoid a theory of cluster concepts if at all possible. While this observation is methodologically sound, it lacks empirical force. The formidable problems of semantic composition in a cluster theory in no way diminish the weight of evidence against necessary and sufficient conditions. Rather, this just seems to be one of those times when the theorist has to bite the bullet.

7. As I have encountered no explicit discussion of network theory in relation to the general issues raised here, I rely on Fodor's treatment, especially Fodor (1975). Nonetheless, the arguments apply equally to network theory.

8. I should also discuss the experiments of Fodor, Garrett, Walker, and Parkes (1980) very briefly. Sensitive to criticisms that the earlier experiments involved chronometric measurements exclusively, they attempt to find a nonchronometric test for semantic decomposition, and claim to have found one in Levelt's (1970) test of intuitive "relatedness" among pairs of lexical items in a sentence. They find that there is no difference between the relatedness of items in the causative "John killed Mary" and of those in the (probably) noncausative "John bit Mary," while a variety of other pairs of constructions do show differences. However, as they themselves point out, four of the six pairs of constructions they test have differences in underlying grammatical relations, whereas this is not the case in the causative-noncausative pair (assuming the sort of interpretive semantic theory we are maintaining here). Thus it could be the case that Levelt's test is sensitive to underlying grammatical relations rather than semantic decomposition. The remaining two control cases are designed to eliminate this possibility. These both involve constructions that disturb referentiality—negation and intensional verbs such as "want"—and Fodor et al. test these only in a forced-choice paradigm. Such cases, however, like the other cases of negation, involve the interaction of scopes and therefore are not, strictly speaking, comparable with cases such as causatives, which involve only item-internal composition. Since no argument is given that such cases *ought* to be comparable, I think it is safe to treat the results of these experiments as interesting in general but not necessarily pertinent to the point they are intended to prove.

Chapter 8

1. Needless to say, these organizations are projected on the presented field. To avoid unnecessary typographical clutter, I will for the time being ignore the need for ## in the metalanguage, trusting the reader to keep track of the necessary distinctions.

2. As a hint toward the argument there, notice that we use words such as "distance" and "spacing" to speak of either spatial or temporal relations. If

this is not to be attributed to sheer coincidence, we must claim that spatial and temporal organization are encoded in conceptual structure in similar terms. Lashley (1951) argues persuasively that this should not be surprising, since a temporal pattern, to be stored in its entirety, must somehow be stored spatially in the brain (think of memory for songs, for example).

3. Despite the apparently perceptual character of many of these conditions, they must be stated over *conceptual* structure, according to the arguments of the previous section. Thus they are at the appropriate level to appear in a word meaning.

4. As Rosch and Mervis (1975) point out, this account of family resemblances helps account for some experimental results in which subjects had to learn an artificial category. When the exemplars presented had characteristics overlapping in a family resemblance pattern, subjects often mistakenly remembered seeing stereotypical items that were not actually presented. Assuming that subjects are trying to maximize normality (see the next section), this outcome is not surprising.

5. The measure of stability thus can play the role that Lakoff (1972) assigns to degree of fuzzy set membership in discussing the meaning of "hedge" terms. Something that is judged "rather large," for example, is judged large, but with an analysis at the outer limits of stability; a penguin is judged "sort of a bird" because it fails many of the typicality conditions for "bird" and thus receives a relatively unstable analysis.

6. This approach makes the interesting claim that among *auditory* concepts, "flute-sound" would be a basic concept, since one can form a unitary image, but "song" would not be, since the preference rules for musical structure do not converge on a unified stereotype. Perhaps auditory images merit investigation along these lines. My own intuitions in such cases are much less secure than in Rosch's visual examples.

7. The analysis to follow was suggested in part by the treatment of "see" in Miller and Johnson-Laird (1976, 583ff.). Another such case is the verb "lie" ("tell a lie"), discussed in Coleman and Kay (1981).

8. Actually, the framework of section 9.2 will suggest that "see$_b$" is a verb of extent. This may help defuse some of VanDevelde's criticisms of Gruber, but it is immaterial to the present argument.

Chapter 9

1. This chapter and the next present a revised version of material originally published in Jackendoff (1976, 1977b, 1978).

2. The three readings of "between" illustrate the possibility of embedding expansion (9.13a) within (9.12). One reading of "John ran between the houses" involves the path expressed by "from one house to the other." "John is between the houses" locates John at a place on this path. Finally, another reading of "John ran between the houses" involves John traveling, say, from the front to the back, passing through the space between the houses, i.e., along the path in (i).

(i) [Path VIA([Place ON([Path FROM ONE HOUSE TO THE OTHER])])]

(I am indebted to Janice Broder for this observation.)

3. There is a slight hint (p. 225) that Schank intends to treat the distinction between bounded paths and directions by means of an operator "t$_f$", but the hint is nowhere followed up.

4. This use of "theme" is not to be confused with Halliday's (1967) use of the term to stand roughly for *topic*. The topic-comment distinction (Halliday's theme-rheme) is orthogonal to the thematic structure discussed here, and also to the subject-predicate distinction. For discussion, see Jackendoff (1972, chapter 6).

5. It has sometimes been suggested that the inventory of event-functions could be simplified by decomposing STAY as NOT GO FROM, yielding (i) in the present notation.

(i) [Event NOT GO ([Thing x], [Path FROM ([Place y])])]

While not implausible, this analysis leads to certain technical problems in the correspondence rules for prepositions. Given that there is no lexical generalization that this reduction captures, I will retain the notation (9.23). The interested reader is invited to substitute (i) throughout the exposition, and see how well it works.

6. Whether rule (9.42) is applicable to cases other than pseudocleft constructions like (9.37) depends in part on one's syntactic treatment of sentences like "We saw the moon rise over the mountain" and "Max tried to eat." If the surface VPs "rise over the mountain" and "eat" have underlying (or PRO) subjects, as in Chomsky's treatments over the years, the rule is unnecessary. On the other hand, Bresnan's (1978, 1982) and Brame's (1978) theories sanction underlying bare VPs not dominated by S, and rule (9.42) plus various principles of control would account for the interpretation of these examples.

7. This is the analysis proposed in Jackendoff (1976). It entails that the willful reading of (9.43b) be [CAUSE ([JOHN], [GO ([JOHN], [DOWN THE HILL])])], i.e., "John rolled *himself* down the hill." But this claims that intransitive "roll" and a host of other such verbs are lexically ambiguous, a conclusion avoided in the present analysis.

8. The semantic analysis of [EVENTS] and [ACTOR]-[ACTION] pairs helps differentiate various syntactic and semantic classes of adverbs described in Jackendoff (1972, chapter 3). *Manner* adverbs, which appear in VP, are modifiers of [ACTIONS]; WILLFUL is just one case of such a modifier. *Subject-oriented* adverbs are attached to S and refer to some property of the [ACTOR], as in "Slowly John counted the beans." *Neutral* and *speaker-oriented* adverbs, such as "fortunately" and "frankly," are also attached to S but are modifiers of the whole [EVENT] or [STATE]. This treatment meets Fodor's (1972) objection to Davidson's (1967a) analysis of manner adverbs, in that their semantic structure is clearly distinguished from that of sentential adverbs.

This proposal also helps to explain some disputes in syntactic theory about whether S or VP is the major phrasal category corresponding to the lexical category V. The claim made here is that S is indeed the major phrasal category. However, VP alone among nonmajor phrasal categories may correspond to a conceptual constituent. By virtue of this, VP acquires certain distributional properties otherwise restricted to major phrasal categories: it may be used referentially; it may be the antecedent of appositives; it may be strictly subcategorized. The viability of this explanation rests on the claim that the VPs with these special properties all express [ACTIONS]. My impression is that on the whole this is indeed the case. Should it prove false, one might want to introduce other conceptual constituents such as [PREDICATE] to correspond to other sorts of VP, as suggested by Williams (1980). I leave the question open.

9. In present terminology we do not want to call "the room" a goal, since a goal is the end of a path rather than a thing. So for precision I deviate from common usage, including my own usage in earlier work.

10. For cognoscenti, I should point out that there are some interesting potential counterexamples to the Lexical Variable Principle (LVP), falling into three classes exemplified by (i)–(iii).

(i)   Mary is easy to please.
(ii) John is handsome to look at.
(iii) We chose Bill to pick on.

"Easy," "handsome," and "choose" all require infinitival complements that lack one internal NP, superficially violating the LVP. Standard generative analyses have always filled this NP position in underlying structure with either lexical material or an anaphoric expression, then moved or deleted this material. (See for instance Lasnik and Fiengo (1974) and references there; also Chomsky (1977, especially pp. 102–108).) In effect, these analyses have assumed the LVP, then accounted for the surface deviance by means of transformational processes or requirements on variable binding. So far as I know, no one has explored the possibility that these predicates simply require semantically incomplete arguments, in violation of the LVP (though such an analysis might be fairly natural in a framework like that of Brame (1978) or Gazdar (1981), for instance). The problem in any case would be to appropriately constrain the possible violations of the LVP so as to produce only these cases. One important difference between these and the examples in the text is that the missing NP appears elsewhere in the sentence, rather than being lexicalized within the verb as in "bread" and "trentertain"; this might be a crucial consideration.

Chapter 10

1. A third conceptualization of time appears in the tense and aspect system of language, a system grammatically quite different from those we have been investigating in this chapter. As Talmy (1978) points out, it is also semantically different, in that it cannot be metricized: whenever one wishes to speak of absolute location or duration in time, one cannot use the tense-aspect sys-

tem but must resort to the thematic system defined by (10.3). Thus it is unclear whether the semantics of tense and aspect should fall under the Thematic Relations Hypothesis, Anderson's (1971) attempt notwithstanding. For an analysis of tense and aspect in tune with the goals of the present work, see Woisetschlaeger (1976).

2. "Melt" must specify its beginning-state as well as its end-state, since a gas becomes a liquid by condensing, not by melting. As Dick Carter has pointed out (personal communication), the verbs expressing change between solid, liquid, and gaseous states are extremely unusual in having to specify a beginning state; there are not special verbs, for example, meaning "change from yellow to red," "change from green to red," and the like.

There appear to be few inchoative verbs in English derived from nouns, such as a verb "endoctor" meaning "make someone into a doctor." The only examples I have found are "knight" and "enslave." I do not know whether this gap is accidental or systematic.

As a bit of evidence for the interchangeability of [TYPES] and [PROPERTIES] as identificational reference objects, notice that there are a few colloquial nouns in English that can be used only in predicate nominal position: for instance, "a drag," "a gas," "a bummer." We can say "Bill, who is a drag, walked in," but not *"A drag walked in." In present terms, we can account for these exceptional nouns by claiming that they express [PROPERTIES] rather than [THINGS]. Thus they can occur only in positions both where NPs are syntactically possible (i.e., not as prenominal modifiers) and where [PROPERTIES] are semantically appropriate. Such a confluence occurs only in predicate nominal position. These nouns can only have developed because of the close relationship between [TYPES] and [PROPERTIES] in this position.

Maling (1982) points out that there are also idiomatic PPs that express [PROPERTIES]: for instance, "out of shape," "out of his mind," "in good health."

3. This analysis supports Hankamer's (1973) claim that the simplex comparative "John is taller than Bill" is not derived by reduction from the comparative with a sentential complement "John is taller than Bill is"; the theory provides different semantic representations for the two constructions. The former represents the expansion of (9.16a) with a reference [THING] as argument of FROM and parallels the spatial phrase "two miles down the road from Bill." The latter represents the expansion with a reference [PLACE], parallel to "two miles down the road from where Bill is." The syntactic similarities between "than Bill is" and "where Bill is" are well documented (Chomsky (1977)) and support the semantics.

4. In fact, it might be reasonable to regard the reference object as an [ACTION] or a [PREDICATE] rather than an [EVENT] or a [STATE], since its formal structure corresponds precisely to the former. I leave the question open.

5. See Jackendoff (1976, sections 4.1 and 4.5) for more detailed discussion of the inferences and invited inferences of CAUSE and LET. In present terms, an invited inference is the result of a preference rule (see sections 8.4–5).

6. Admittedly, a number of the thematic analyses in Jackendoff (1972) are not as strongly justified as they might be. It was an effort to strengthen these analyses that led me to the work presented here, which has still not reached the stage of being able to formally express all the necessary predicates. On the other hand, I know of no alternative accounts for these facts within the framework of the extended standard theory.

It is interesting that minimal pairs involving "regard" and "strike" serve as Chomsky's (1980, 17–18) motivation for positing structure-building rules in logical form, which seem rather makeshift within his system. In Chomsky (1981), a different explanation is proposed in terms of "small clauses," which present their own syntactic problems. The account of (10.35) in terms of thematic relations suggests a parallel account for the related phenomena that Chomsky is concerned with, since the structural distinctions he desires are present in thematic structure in any event.

7. Actually, the story is somewhat more complicated. In an interesting discussion of this phenomenon, Oehrle (to appear) presents some further cases. For example, (ia) can be interpreted as (ib), (ic), or (id).

(i) a. The dancer gave the director a kick.
   b. The dancer kicked the director.
   c. The dancer let the director take a kick.
   d. The dancer performed a kick for the director.

The (ib) interpretation treats "kick" as a two-place function, whose places are filled by NPs in the main clause according to the same matching of thematic relations exhibited in (10.36). But in the other two interpretations, "kick" is treated as a one-place function, and either NP in the main clause can serve as its argument. Thus, only when the number of NPs matches in main and subordinate functions are the thematic relations called into play. However, notice that (iia) also has three interpretations, corresponding to those of (ia) but with the roles of "the dancer" and "the director" reversed.

(ii) a. The dancer got a kick from the director.
    b. The director kicked the dancer.
    c. The director let the dancer take a kick.
    d. The director performed a kick for the dancer.

This shows that, whatever else is going on, the switch of source and goal when we change from "give" to "get from" is playing a part in the interpretation of these examples.

Hust and Brame (1976) present a counterexample that has been widely cited (for instance by Chomsky (1981)) as refuting my claim (Jackendoff (1972, section 5.11)) that lexically induced control is mediated through thematic relations. This is the case of "promise," which I analyzed as specifying that its Source (which normally falls in subject position) controls the complement subject, as in (iii).

(iii) Bill promised Harry to leave.

My analysis predicts, incorrectly, that (iv) will be acceptable and synonymous with (iii), and that (v) will be interpreted as Bill, not Harry, being allowed to leave.

(iv) *Harry was promised by Bill to leave.

(v) Harry was promised (by Bill) to be allowed to leave.

While I cannot propose a definitive solution here, I should point out that the facts are extremely curious, in that the range of acceptable complements in (v) is restricted to passives of verbs such as "allow" and "permit." To my knowledge, no one has explained this restriction. However, rather similar though less restricted behavior appears with verbs of communication such as "beg," "ask," "tell," and "scream," suggesting the possibility of an analysis of "promise" along related lines. These verbs are discussed in Jackendoff (1972, section 5.12), immediately following the discussion of "promise," and it is odd that Hust and Brame do not notice the similarity. They also do not take notice of Jackendoff (1974), which discusses examples like (10.36) involving thematic relations and control, and which was in print before the cited date of submission of their review.

Chapter 11

1. This chapter is largely a recasting of material in Jackendoff (1975b, 1980).

2. Partee is hesitant about ascribing beliefs to dogs, but in fact we do so routinely and nonmetaphorically. Her hesitation most likely comes from the reluctance of traditional philosophical treatments of belief to come to terms with such examples.

3. Postal claims that this sentence is (subtly) ambiguous, as the scope theory would predict. I suspect that the ambiguity, if it exists, is a referential-attributive ambiguity (see note 9 to chapter 5), which is available even in main clauses. This distinction is not the same as transparent-opaque, though they are linked: an opaque description must be attributive, but a transparent description may be either attributive or referential (I think).

4. We encountered a similar conclusion with respect to the interpretation of subcategorized NPs in section 5.3. See especially note 11.

5. Postal (1974) argues against "assertor" theories of belief-contexts—essentially theories that incorporate what is called here the Opacity Principle—on the grounds that "imply" produces ambiguities similar to belief-contexts and involves no one other than the speaker to whom a description could be attributed. I now think that I was wrong to accept his argument in Jackendoff (1975b): it is precisely the fact that "imply" *cannot* attribute a description to someone else that accounts for its not producing transparent-opaque ambiguities. The ambiguity Postal discusses is probably referential-attributive, like that of "prevent" (see note 3).

6. Church is criticizing the theory in the original edition of Carnap (1956), dating from 1947. In the 1956 edition, Carnap adds an appendix replying to

Church, in which he retreats from the behaviorist interpretation to a much less explicit position.

7. I have hardly done justice here to a vast and complex literature. Yet I find it remarkable that no one author seems to pay attention to the whole constellation of phenomena characteristic of belief-contexts. Logicians tend to be concerned with quantification and inference, while linguists tend to be concerned with ambiguity. I know of no study of the complex interaction of the transparent-opaque, specific-nonspecific, and referential-attributive distinctions (with the exception of Janet D. Fodor (1970)). Indeed, these three phenomena are often erroneously conflated (for example, see my comments on Abbott (1979) in Jackendoff (1980)). Failing to recognize ambiguity, people sometimes "refute" arguments concerning opaque readings on the basis of evidence from transparent readings (I think this is true of Katz's (1972) reply to Mates, for instance). All of this makes perspicuous and brief commentary on the literature virtually impossible, and I beg the reader's indulgence.

8. The generalization between #pictures# and #beliefs# is hinted at by Kaplan (1969) in his discussion of "vividness." My theory of #representation# owes a great deal to Goodman (1968), particularly in the relativization of representation to the medium of imagery. Wittgenstein (1953) and Fodor (1975) also make suggestive remarks on these matters.

9. A nonhypothetical instance of this situation is the Magritte painting of a pipe above the inscription "Ceci n'est pas une pipe," which derives its wit from the conflict of these two rules, as well as from a further ambiguity: is the inscription a #Real-inscription# or an #Image-inscription#?

10. Fauconnier (1979) points out that "In reality" can be used as a converse of "In that picture," to designate unambiguously that a *non*-image reading is intended.

11. To handle multiple embeddings, TR needs to be bound in some fashion to the particular occurrence of REP that it "undoes." The treatment is fairly obvious and I omit it here.

12. The REP-TR formalism appears to generalize readily to all the phenomena treated under the theory of "modal structure" of Jackendoff (1972, chapter 7; 1975b). This theory, proposed as an alternative to standard quantificational logic, accounts for the properties and interactions of all manner of scope phenomena, including nonspecificity, possibility, quantification, negation, and *wh*-questions, as well as opacity. It also may apply to the wider range of referential phenomena studied in Fauconnier (1979); each REP operator sets up a "mental space" in Fauconnier's sense, and TR would return reference to the previous space of discourse. The REP-TR formalism is a distinct improvement on the notation devised in Jackendoff (1972); the semantic effect is the same, but achieved with a much simpler representation.

Bibliography

Abbott, Barbara (1979). Remarks on "On Belief-Contexts." *Linguistic Inquiry* 10.1, 143–149.

Akmajian, Adrian (1977). The Complement Structure of Perception Verbs in an Autonomous Syntax Framework. In Culicover, Wasow, and Akmajian (1977), 427–460.

Anderson, John M. (1971). *The Grammar of Case: Towards a Localistic Theory.* Cambridge University Press, Cambridge.

Anderson, John R. (1976). *Language, Memory, and Thought.* Wiley, New York.

Anderson, John R., and Gordon H. Bower (1973). *Human Associative Memory.* Wiley, New York.

Anderson, Stephen R. (1977). Comments on Wasow (1977). In Culicover, Wasow, and Akmajian (1977), 361–377.

Armstrong, Sharon Lee, Lila R. Gleitman, and Henry Gleitman (1983). On What Some Concepts Might Not Be. *Cognition* 13, 263–308.

Arnheim, Rudolf (1974). *Art and Visual Perception (The New Version).* University of California Press, Berkeley.

Aronoff, Mark (1976). *Word Formation in Generative Grammar.* MIT Press, Cambridge.

Aune, Bruce (1975). Vendler on Knowledge and Belief. In Gunderson (1975), 391–399.

Bach, Emmon (1967). *Have* and *Be* in English Syntax. *Language* 43.2, 462–485.

Bach, Emmon (1968). Nouns and Noun Phrases. In Bach and Harms (1968), 91–124.

Bach, Emmon, and Robert T. Harms, eds. (1968). *Universals in Linguistic Theory.* Holt, Rinehart and Winston, New York.

Bach, Kent, and Robert M. Harnish (1979). *Linguistic Communication and Speech Acts.* MIT Press, Cambridge.

Baker, C. L. (1979). Syntactic Theory and the Projection Problem. *Linguistic Inquiry* 10.4, 533–581.

Baker, C. L., and John McCarthy, eds. (1981). *The Logical Problem of Language Acquisition.* MIT Press, Cambridge.

Baker, L., D. Cantwell, M. Rutter, and L. Bartak (1976). Language and Autism. In E. Ritvo, ed., *Autism: Diagnosis, Current Research, and Management.* Spectrum, New York, 121–149.

Bar-Hillel, Yehoshua (1967). Dictionaries and Meaning Rules. *Foundations of Language* 3, 409–414.

Bar-Hillel, Yehoshua (1970). *Aspects of Language.* Magnes Press, Jerusalem.

Becker, A. L., and D. G. Arms (1969). Prepositions as Predicates. In R. I. Binnick et al., *Papers from the Fifth Regional Meeting of the Chicago Linguistic Society.* Department of Linguistics, University of Chicago, Chicago.

Bierwisch, Manfred (1981). Basic Issues in the Development of Word Meaning. In Werner Deutsch, ed., *The Child's Construction of Language.* Academic Press, New York, 341–380.

Bolinger, Dwight (1965). The Atomization of Meaning. *Language* 41.4, 555–573.

Borkin, Ann (1973). To Be and Not To Be. In C. Corum, T. Smith-Stark, and A. Weiser, eds., *Papers from the Ninth Regional Meeting of the Chicago Linguistic Society.* Department of Linguistics, University of Chicago, Chicago.

Bower, T. G. R. (1977). *A Primer of Infant Development.* Freeman, San Francisco.

Bowers, John S. (1975). Adjectives and Adverbs in English. *Foundations of Language* 13, 529–562.

Bowers, John S., and U. K. H. Reichenbach (1979). Montague Grammar and Transformational Grammar: A Review of *Formal Philosophy: Selected Papers of Richard Montague. Linguistic Analysis* 5.2, 195–248.

Bradley, Dianne, Merrill Garrett, and Edgar Zurif (1980). Syntactic Deficits in Broca's Aphasia. In Caplan (1980), 269–286.

Brame, Michael (1976). *Conjectures and Refutations in Syntax and Semantics.* Elsevier-North-Holland, New York.

Brame, Michael (1978). *Base Generated Syntax.* Noit Amrofer, Seattle.

Bresnan, Joan (1978). A Realistic Transformational Grammar. In Halle, Bresnan, and Miller (1978), 1–59.

Bresnan, Joan, ed. (1982). *The Mental Representation of Grammatical Relations.* MIT Press, Cambridge.

Caparulo, B. K., and D. J. Cohen (1977). Cognitive Structures, Language, and Emerging Social Competence in Autistic and Aphasic Children. *Journal of Child Psychiatry* 16.4, 620–645.

Caplan, David, ed. (1980). *Biological Studies of Mental Processes*. MIT Press, Cambridge.

Carey, Susan (1979). A Case Study: Face Recognition. In E. Walker, ed., *Explorations in the Biology of Language*. Bradford/MIT Press, Cambridge, 175–202.

Carey, Susan, and Rhea Diamond (1980). Maturational Determination of the Developmental Course of Face Encoding. In Caplan (1980), 60–93.

Carnap, Rudolf (1956). *Meaning and Necessity*. University of Chicago Press, Chicago.

Charniak, E. (1972). *Toward a Model of Children's Story Comprehension*. Report AI–TR266, MIT Artificial Intelligence Laboratory, Cambridge.

Chomsky, Noam (1965). *Aspects of the Theory of Syntax*. MIT Press, Cambridge.

Chomsky, Noam (1970). Remarks on Nominalization. In R. Jacobs and P. Rosenbaum, eds., *Readings in English Transformational Grammar*. Ginn, Waltham, Mass., 184–221; also in Chomsky (1972), 11–61.

Chomsky, Noam (1972). *Studies on Semantics in Generative Grammar*. Mouton, The Hague.

Chomsky, Noam (1975). *Reflections on Language*. Pantheon, New York.

Chomsky, Noam (1977). On Wh-Movement. In Culicover, Wasow, and Akmajian (1977), 71–132.

Chomsky, Noam (1980). On Binding. *Linguistic Inquiry* 11.1, 1–46.

Chomsky, Noam (1981). *Lectures on Government and Binding*. Foris, Dordrecht.

Chomsky, Noam, and Morris Halle (1968). *The Sound Pattern of English*. Harper & Row, New York.

Chomsky, Noam, and George Miller (1963). Introduction to the Formal Analysis of Natural Languages. In R. D. Luce, R. Bush, and E. Galanter, *Handbook of Mathematical Psychology*, Vol. II. Wiley, New York.

Church, Alonzo (1950). On Carnap's Analysis of Statements of Assertion and Belief. *Analysis* 10, 97–99; reprinted in Davidson and Harman (1975), 129–131.

Clark, Herbert H. (1973). Space, Time, Semantics, and the Child. In T. E. Moore, ed., *Cognitive Development and the Acquisition of Language*. Academic Press, New York, 27–64.

Clark, Herbert H., and William G. Chase (1972). On the Process of Comparing Sentences against Pictures. *Cognitive Psychology* 3.3, 472–517.

Coleman, Linda, and Paul Kay (1981). Prototype Semantics: The English Verb *Lie. Language* 57.1, 26–44.

Collins, A., and M. Quillian (1969). Retrieval Time from Semantic Memory. *Journal of Verbal Learning and Verbal Behavior* 9, 240–247.

Cornu, Anne-marie (1980). *On the Meanings of "Force," "Encourage," and Related Verbs.* Doctoral dissertation, Katholieke Universiteit Leuven, Belgium.

Culicover, Peter, Thomas Wasow, and Adrian Akmajian, eds. (1977). *Formal Syntax.* Academic Press, New York.

Davidson, Donald (1967a). The Logical Form of Action Sentences. In N. Rescher, ed., *The Logic of Decision and Action.* University of Pittsburgh Press, Pittsburgh.

Davidson, Donald (1967b). Causal Relations. *Journal of Philosophy* 64, 691–703.

Davidson, Donald (1969). The Individuation of Events. In N. Rescher et al., eds., *Essays in Honor of Carl G. Hempel.* Reidel, Dordrecht, 216–234.

Davidson, Donald (1970). Semantics for Natural Languages. Reprinted in Davidson and Harman (1975), 18–24.

Davidson, Donald, and Gilbert Harman, eds. (1972). *Semantics of Natural Language.* Reidel, Dordrecht.

Davidson, Donald, and Gilbert Harman, eds. (1975). *The Logic of Grammar.* Dickenson, Encino, Calif.

Declerck, Renaat (1979). Aspect and the Bounded/Unbounded (Telic/Atelic) Distinction. *Linguistics* 17, 761–794.

Donnellan, Keith (1966). Reference and Definite Descriptions. *Philosophical Review* 75, 281–304.

Dresher, Elan (1977). Logical Representations and Linguistic Theory. *Linguistic Inquiry* 8.2, 351–378.

Dreyfus, Hubert L. (1981). From Micro-Worlds to Knowledge Representation: AI at an Impasse. In J. Haugeland, ed., *Mind Design.* Bradford/MIT Press, Cambridge, 161–204.

Ellis, Willis D., ed. (1938). *A Source Book of Gestalt Psychology.* Routledge & Kegan Paul, London.

Emonds, Joseph E. (1970). *Root and Structure-Preserving Transformations.* Doctoral dissertation, MIT, Cambridge.

Emonds, Joseph E. (1976). *A Transformational Approach to English Syntax.* Academic Press, New York.

Fauconnier, Gilles (1979). Mental Spaces: A Discourse-Processing Approach to Natural Language Logic. Unpublished mimeo, Université de Paris VIII.

Published in part as Espaces référentiels, in *Sulli anafora,* Firenze-Presso l'Accademia della Crusca, 1981.

Fillmore, Charles (1968). The Case for Case. In Bach and Harms (1968), 1–90.

Fodor, Janet D. (1970). *The Linguistic Description of Opaque Contexts.* Doctoral dissertation, MIT, Cambridge; Garland Publishing Co., New York, 1979.

Fodor, Janet D. (1978). Parsing Strategies and Constraints on Transformations. *Linguistic Inquiry* 9.3, 427–474.

Fodor, Janet D., Jerry A. Fodor, and Merrill Garrett (1975). The Psychological Unreality of Semantic Representations. *Linguistic Inquiry* 6.4, 515–532.

Fodor, Jerry A. (1970). Three Reasons for Not Deriving "Kill" from "Cause to Die." *Linguistic Inquiry* 1.4, 429–438.

Fodor, Jerry A. (1972). Troubles about Actions. In Davidson and Harman (1972), 48–69.

Fodor, Jerry A. (1975). *The Language of Thought.* Harvard University Press, Cambridge.

Fodor, Jerry A. (1978). Tom Swift and his Procedural Grandmother. *Cognition* 6, 229–247.

Fodor, Jerry A. (1980). Methodological Solipsism Considered as a Research Strategy in Cognitive Psychology. *Behavioral and Brain Sciences* 3.1, 63–73.

Fodor, Jerry A., Thomas Bever, and Merrill Garrett (1974). *The Psychology of Language.* McGraw-Hill, New York.

Fodor, Jerry A., Merrill Garrett, E. Walker, and C. Parkes (1980). Against Definitions. *Cognition* 8, 263–367.

Frege, Gottlob (1892). On Sense and Reference. Reprinted in Davidson and Harman (1975), 116–128.

Gazdar, Gerald (1979). *Pragmatics.* Academic Press, New York.

Gazdar, Gerald (1981). Unbounded Dependencies and Coordinate Structure. *Linguistic Inquiry* 12.2, 155–184.

Gleitman, Lila, and Eric Wanner (1982). The State of the State of the Art. In E. Wanner and L. Gleitman, eds., *Language Acquisition: The State of the Art.* Cambridge University Press, New York.

Goffman, Erving (1974). *Frame Analysis.* Harvard University Press, Cambridge.

Goldsmith, John (1979). On the Thematic Nature of *See. Linguistic Inquiry* 10.2, 347–352.

Goldsmith, John, and Erich Woisetschlaeger (1982). The Logic of the English Progressive. *Linguistic Inquiry* 13.1, 79–90.

Goodman, Nelson (1968). *Languages of Art*. Bobbs-Merrill, New York.

Grice, Paul (1975). Logic and Conversation. In P. Cole and J. Morgan, eds., *Syntax and Semantics*. Vol. 3. Academic Press, New York, 41–58.

Grimshaw, Jane B. (1981). Form, Function, and the Language Acquisition Device. In Baker and McCarthy (1981), 165–182.

Gruber, Jeffrey S. (1965). *Studies in Lexical Relations*. Doctoral dissertation, MIT, Cambridge; Indiana University Linguistics Club, Bloomington, Ind. Reprinted as part of *Lexical Structures in Syntax and Semantics*, North-Holland, Amsterdam, 1976.

Gruber, Jeffrey S. (1967). Look and See. *Language* 43.4, 937–947.

Gunderson, Keith, ed. (1975). *Language, Mind, and Knowledge*. (Minnesota Studies in the Philosophy of Science, Vol. 7). University of Minnesota Press, Minneapolis.

Hacking, Ian (1975). All Kinds of Possibility. *Philosophical Review* 84.3, 321–337.

Halle, Morris (1973). Prolegomena to a Theory of Word Formation. *Linguistic Inquiry* 4.1, 3–16.

Halle, Morris, Joan Bresnan, and George Miller, eds. (1978). *Linguistic Theory and Psychological Reality*. MIT Press, Cambridge.

Halliday, M. A. K. (1967). Notes on Transitivity and Theme in English. *Journal of Linguistics* 3.2, 199–244.

Hankamer, Jorge (1973). Why There Are Two *Than*'s in English. In C. Corum, T. Smith-Stark, and A. Weiser, eds., *Papers from the Ninth Regional Meeting of the Chicago Linguistic Society*. Department of Linguistics, University of Chicago, Chicago, 179–191.

Hankamer, Jorge, and Ivan Sag (1976). Deep and Surface Anaphora. *Linguistic Inquiry* 7.3, 391–428.

Helmholtz, Hermann (1885). *On the Sensations of Tone*. Dover reprint, New York, 1954.

Hintikka, K. J. J., J. M. E. Moravcsik, and P. Suppes, eds. (1973). *Approaches to Natural Language*. Reidel, Dordrecht.

Hochberg, Julian (1974). Organization and the Gestalt Tradition. In E. C. Carterette and M. P. Friedman, eds., *Handbook of Perception*. Vol. 1. Academic Press, New York, 179–210.

Hofstadter, Douglas (1979). *Gödel, Escher, Bach: An Eternal Golden Braid*. Basic Books, New York.

Hust, Joel, and Michael Brame (1976). Jackendoff on Interpretive Semantics [review of Jackendoff (1972)]. *Linguistic Analysis* 2.3, 243–277.

Ioup, Georgette (1975). Some Universals for Quantifier Scope. In J. Kimball, ed., *Syntax and Semantics*. Vol. 4. Academic Press, New York, 37–58.

Jackendoff, Ray (1971). On Some Questionable Arguments about Quantifiers and Negation. *Language* 47.2, 282–297.

Jackendoff, Ray (1972). *Semantic Interpretation in Generative Grammar*. MIT Press, Cambridge.

Jackendoff, Ray (1974). A Deep Structure Projection Rule. *Linguistic Inquiry* 5.4, 481–506.

Jackendoff, Ray (1975a). Morphological and Semantic Regularities in the Lexicon. *Language* 51.3, 639–671.

Jackendoff, Ray (1975b). On Belief-Contexts. *Linguistic Inquiry* 6.1, 53–93.

Jackendoff, Ray (1976). Toward an Explanatory Semantic Representation. *Linguistic Inquiry* 7.1, 89–150.

Jackendoff, Ray (1977a). *X̄ Syntax: A Study of Phrase Structure*. MIT Press, Cambridge.

Jackendoff, Ray (1977b). Toward a Cognitively Viable Semantics. In C. Rameh, ed., *Georgetown University Round Table on Languages and Linguistics*. Georgetown University Press, Washington, 59–80.

Jackendoff, Ray (1978). Grammar as Evidence for Conceptual Structure. In Halle, Bresnan, and Miller (1978), 201–228.

Jackendoff, Ray (1979). How to Keep Ninety from Rising. *Linguistic Inquiry* 10.1, 172–177.

Jackendoff, Ray (1980). Belief-Contexts Revisited. *Linguistic Inquiry* 11.2, 395–414.

Jackendoff, Ray (1981). On Katz's Autonomous Semantics. *Language* 57.2, 425–435.

Jackendoff, Ray, and Fred Lerdahl (1981). Generative Music Theory and Its Relation to Psychology. *Journal of Music Theory* 25.1, 45–90.

Jenkins, James J., Jerry Wald, and John B. Pittenger (1978). Apprehending Pictorial Events: An Instance of Psychological Cohesion. In C. Wade Savage, ed., *Perception and Cognition: Issues in the Foundations of Psychology*. (Minnesota Studies in the Philosophy of Science, Vol. 9). University of Minnesota Press, Minneapolis, 129–164.

Kaplan, David (1969). Quantifying In. In D. Davidson and J. Hintikka, eds., *Words and Objections: Essays on the Work of W. V. Quine.* Reidel, Dordrecht, 178–214.

Katz, Jerrold J. (1966). *The Philosophy of Language*. Harper & Row, New York.

Katz, Jerrold J. (1972). *Semantic Theory*. Harper & Row, New York.

Katz, Jerrold J. (1974). Where Things Stand with the Analytic-Synthetic Distinction. *Synthese* 28, 283–319.

Katz, Jerrold J. (1975). Logic and Language: An Examination of Recent Criticisms of Intensionalism. In Gunderson (1975), 36–130.

Katz, Jerrold J. (1977). A Proper Theory of Names. *Philosophical Studies* 31.1, 1–80.

Katz, Jerrold J. (1980). Chomsky on Meaning. *Language* 56.1, 1–41.

Katz, Jerrold J., and Jerry Fodor (1963). The Structure of a Semantic Theory. *Language* 39.2, 170–210.

Katz, Jerrold J., and Paul Postal (1964). *An Integrated Theory of Linguistic Descriptions.* MIT Press, Cambridge.

Kean, Mary-Louise (1980). Grammatical Representations and the Description of Language Processing. In Caplan (1980), 239–268.

Keenan, Edward, and Karen H. Ebert (1973). A Note on Marking Transparency and Opacity. *Linguistic Inquiry* 4.3, 420–424.

Keil, Frank C. (1979). *Semantic and Conceptual Development: An Ontological Perspective.* Harvard University Press, Cambridge.

Kimball, John (1973). Seven Principles of Surface Structure Parsing in Natural Language. *Cognition* 2, 15–47.

Kintsch, Walter (1974). *The Representation of Meaning in Memory.* Wiley, New York.

Klima, Edward S. (1964). Negation in English. In J. Fodor and J. Katz, eds., *The Structure of Language.* Prentice-Hall, Englewood Cliffs, N.J., 246–323.

Klima, Edward S. (1965). *Studies in Diachronic Syntax.* Doctoral dissertation, Harvard University, Cambridge.

Koffka, Kurt (1935). *Principles of Gestalt Psychology.* Harcourt, Brace & World, New York.

Köhler, Wolfgang (1920). Physical Gestalten. In Ellis (1938), 17–54.

Köhler, Wolfgang (1927). *The Mentality of Apes.* Routledge & Kegan Paul, London.

Köhler, Wolfgang (1929). *Gestalt Psychology.* Liveright, New York.

Köhler, Wolfgang (1940). *Dynamics in Psychology.* Liveright, New York.

Kosslyn, Stephen M. (1980). *Image and Mind.* Harvard University Press, Cambridge.

Kripke, Saul (1972). Naming and Necessity. In Davidson and Harman (1972), 253–355.

Kripke, Saul (1977). Speaker's Reference and Semantic Reference. *Midwest Studies in Philosophy* 2, 28–41.

Labov, William (1973). The Boundaries of Words and Their Meanings. In C.-J. N. Bailey and R. W. Shuy, eds., *New Ways of Analyzing Variation in English.* Vol. 1. Georgetown University Press, Washington.

Lakoff, George (1970). *Irregularity in Syntax.* Holt, Rinehart and Winston, New York.

Lakoff, George (1971). On Generative Semantics. In Steinberg and Jakobovits (1971), 232–296.

Lakoff, George (1972). Hedges: A Study in Meaning Criteria and the Logic of Fuzzy Concepts. In P. Peranteau, J. Levi, and G. Phares, eds., *Papers from the Eighth Regional Meeting of the Chicago Linguistic Society.* Department of Linguistics, University of Chicago, Chicago.

Land, Edwin (1959). Experiments in Color Vision. *Scientific American* 200.5 (May), 84–99.

Land, Edwin (1977). The Retinex Theory of Color Vision. *Scientific American* 237.6 (December), 108–128.

Lashley, Karl (1951). The Problem of Serial Order in Behavior. In L. A. Jeffress, ed., *Cerebral Mechanisms in Behavior.* Wiley, New York, 112–136.

Lasnik, Howard, and Robert Fiengo (1974). Complement Object Deletion. *Linguistic Inquiry* 5.4, 535–572.

Lerdahl, Fred, and Ray Jackendoff (1982). *A Generative Theory of Tonal Music.* MIT Press, Cambridge.

Levelt, W. J. M. (1970). A Scaling Approach to the Study of Syntactic Relations. In G. B. Flores d'Arcair and W. J. M. Levelt, eds., *Advances in Psycholinguistics.* North-Holland, Amsterdam.

Lewis, David (1972). General Semantics. In Davidson and Harman (1972), 169–218.

Liberman, Alvin, and Michael Studdert-Kennedy (1977). Phonetic Perception. In R. Held, H. Leibowitz, and H.-L. Teuber, eds., *Handbook of Sensory Physiology, Vol. VIII, Perception.* Springer-Verlag, Heidelberg.

Liberman, Mark, and Alan Prince (1977). On Stress and Linguistic Rhythm. *Linguistic Inquiry* 8.2, 249–336.

McCawley, James D. (1968). Lexical Insertion in a Transformational Grammar without Deep Structure. In B. Darden, C.-J. N. Bailey, and A. Davison, eds., *Papers from the Fourth Meeting of the Chicago Linguistic Society.* Department of Linguistics, University of Chicago, Chicago.

McCawley, James D. (1971). Where Do Noun Phrases Come From? In Steinberg and Jakobovits (1971), 217–231.

McCawley, James D. (1978). Conversational Implicature and the Lexicon. In Peter Cole, ed., *Syntax and Semantics.* Vol. 9. Academic Press, New York, 245–259.

McCulloch, Warren S., and Walter H. Pitts (1943). A Logical Calculus of the Ideas Immanent in Nervous Activity. Reprinted in *Embodiments of Mind*. MIT Press, Cambridge, 19–39.

Macnamara, John (1978). How Do We Talk about What We See? Unpublished mimeo, McGill University, Montreal.

Macnamara, John (1982). *Names for Things*. Bradford/MIT Press, Cambridge.

Maling, Joan (1982). Transitive Adjectives: A Case of Categorial Reanalysis. In F. Heny, ed., *Linguistic Categories*. Reidel, Dordrecht.

Marcus, Mitchell (1980). *A Theory of Syntactic Recognition for Natural Language*. MIT Press, Cambridge.

Marr, David (1982). *Vision*. Freeman, San Francisco.

Marr, David, and H. K. Nishihara (1978). Visual Information Processing: Artificial Intelligence and the Sensorium of Sight. *Technology Review* 81 (October), 28–49.

Mates, Benson (1950). Synonymity. In *Meaning and Interpretation*. Berkeley, 201–226.

Mervis, Carolyn, and John Pani (1980). Acquisition of Basic Object Categories. *Cognitive Psychology* 12, 496–522.

Mervis, Carolyn, and Emilie M. Roth (1981). The Internal Structure of Basic and Non-basic Color Categories. *Language* 57.2, 383–405.

Michotte, A. (1954). La perception de la causalité. 2nd ed. Publications Universitaires de Louvain, Louvain.

Miller, George (1978). Semantic Relations among Words. In Halle, Bresnan, and Miller (1978), 60–118.

Miller, George, and Philip Johnson-Laird (1976). *Language and Perception*. Harvard University Press, Cambridge.

Minsky, Marvin (1975). A Framework for Representing Knowledge. In P. H. Winston, ed., *The Psychology of Computer Vision*. McGraw-Hill, New York.

Mittwoch, Anita (1982). On the Difference between *Eating* and *Eating Something*: Activities versus Accomplishments. *Linguistic Inquiry* 13.1, 113–121.

Montague, Richard (1973). The Proper Treatment of Quantification in Ordinary English. In Hintikka, Moravcsik, and Suppes (1973), 221–242.

Nagel, Thomas (1974). What Is It Like to Be a Bat? *Philosophical Review* 83, 435–450.

Neisser, Ulric (1967). *Cognitive Psychology*. Prentice-Hall, Englewood Cliffs, N.J.

Norman, D. A., D. E. Rumelhart, and the LNR Research Group (1975). *Explorations in Cognition*. Freeman, San Francisco.

Oehrle, Richard (to appear). *The English 'Dative' Constructions: Form and Interpretation.* Synthese Language Library. Reidel, Dordrecht.

Parsons, Terence (1972). Some Problems Concerning the Logic of Grammatical Modifiers. In Davidson and Harman (1972), 127–141.

Partee, Barbara (1973). The Semantics of Belief-Sentences. In Hintikka, Moravcsik, and Suppes (1973), 309–336.

Partee, Barbara (1975). Montague Grammar and Transformational Grammar. *Linguistic Inquiry* 6.2, 203–300.

Partee, Barbara (1978). Semantics: Mathematics or Psychology? In R. Bäuerle, U. Egli, and A. von Stechow, eds., *Semantics from Different Points of View.* Springer-Verlag, Berlin.

Perls, Frederick S. (1947). *Ego, Hunger, and Aggression.* Vintage Books, New York.

Platzack, Christer (1979). *The Semantic Interpretation of Aspect and Aktionsarten.* Foris, Dordrecht.

Polanyi, Michael (1958). *Personal Knowledge.* University of Chicago Press, Chicago.

Postal, Paul (1971). *Crossover Phenomena.* Holt, Rinehart and Winston, New York.

Postal, Paul (1974). On Certain Ambiguities. *Linguistic Inquiry* 5.3, 367–424.

Putnam, Hilary (1975). The Meaning of "Meaning." In Gunderson (1975), 131–193.

Pylyshyn, Zenon (1980). Computation and Cognition: Issues in the Foundation of Cognitive Science. *Behavioral and Brain Sciences* 3.1, 111–132.

Quine, W. V. (1953). *From a Logical Point of View.* Harvard University Press, Cambridge.

Quine, W. V. (1956). Quantifiers and Propositional Attitudes. *Journal of Philosophy* 53.

Quine, W. V. (1960). *Word and Object.* MIT Press, Cambridge.

Quine, W. V. (1969). Natural Kinds. In *Ontological Relativity and Other Essays.* Columbia University Press, New York, 114–138.

Raphael, Bertram (1968). SIR: A Computer Program for Semantic Information Retrieval. In Marvin Minsky, ed., *Semantic Information Processing,* MIT Press, Cambridge, 33–145.

Reed, Ann (1974). *The Structure of English Relative Clauses.* Doctoral dissertation, Brandeis University, Waltham, Mass.

Regan, David, Kenneth Beverley, and Max Cynader (1979). The Visual Perception of Motion in Depth. *Scientific American* 241.1, 136–151.

Rosch, Eleanor, and Carolyn Mervis (1975). Family Resemblances: Studies in the Internal Structure of Categories. *Cognitive Psychology* 7, 573–605.

Rosch, Eleanor, Carolyn Mervis, W. Gray, D. Johnson, and P. Boyes-Braem (1976). Basic Objects in Natural Categories. *Cognitive Psychology* 8, 382–439.

Ross, John Robert (1967). *Constraints on Variables in Syntax*. Doctoral dissertation, MIT, Cambridge.

Ross, John Robert (1969). Adjectives as Noun Phrases. In D. Reibel and S. Schane, eds., *Modern Studies in English*. Prentice-Hall, Englewood Cliffs, N.J., 352–360.

Ross, John Robert (1972). Act. In Davidson and Harman (1972), 70–126.

Russell, Bertrand (1905). On Denoting. *Mind* 14, 479–493; reprinted in Davidson and Harman (1975), 184–193.

Ruwet, Nicolas (1972). A propos d'une classe de verbes "psychologiques." In *Théorie syntaxique et syntaxe du français*. Seuil, Paris, 181–251.

Schachter, Paul (1973). On Syntactic Categories. Indiana University Linguistics Club, Bloomington, Ind.

Schank, Roger (1973). Identification of Conceptualizations underlying Natural Language. In Schank and Colby (1973), 187–248.

Schank, Roger (1975). *Conceptual Information Processing*. American Elsevier, New York.

Schank, Roger, and Robert Abelson (1975). *Scripts, Plans, Goals, and Knowledge*. Erlbaum, Hillsdale, N.J.

Schank, Roger, and Kenneth Mark Colby, eds. (1973). *Computer Models of Thought and Language*. Freeman, San Francisco.

Scragg, Greg (1976). Semantic Nets as Memory Models. In E. Charniak and Y. Wilks, eds., *Computational Semantics*. North-Holland, New York, 101–127.

Searle, John (1958). Proper Names. *Mind* 67, 166–173.

Shiman, Leon (1975). *Grammar for Vision*. Doctoral dissertation, MIT, Cambridge.

Simmons, R. F. (1973). Semantic Networks: Their Computation and Use for Understanding English Sentences. In Schank and Colby (1973), 63–113.

Smith, Edward (1978). Theories of Semantic Memory. In W. K. Estes, ed., *Handbook of Learning and Cognitive Processes*. Vol. 5. Erlbaum, Hillsdale, N.J.

Smith, Edward, and Douglas Medin (1981). *Categories and Concepts*. Harvard University Press, Cambridge.

Smith, Edward, Edward Shoben, and Lance J. Rips (1974). Structure and Process in Semantic Memory: A Featural Model for Semantic Decisions. *Psychological Review* 81.3, 214–241.

Sommers, Fred (1965). Predictability. In M. Black, ed., *Philosophy in America*. Cornell University Press, Ithaca, N.Y.

Steinberg, Danny, and Leon Jakobovits, eds. (1971). *Semantics: An Interdisciplinary Reader*. Cambridge University Press, New York.

Talmy, Leonard (1976). Semantic Causative Types. In M. Shibatani, ed., *Syntax and Semantics*. Vol. 6. Academic Press, New York.

Talmy, Leonard (1978). The Relation of Grammar to Cognition—A Synopsis. In D. Waltz, ed., *Theoretical Issues in Natural Language Processing—2*. Association for Computing Machinery, New York.

Talmy, Leonard (1980). Lexicalization Patterns: Semantic Structure in Lexical Forms. In T. Shopen et al., eds., *Language Typology and Syntactic Descriptions*. Cambridge University Press, New York.

Tarski, Alfred (1956a). *Logic, Semantics, and Metamathematics*. Oxford University Press, London.

Tarski, Alfred (1956b). The Concept of Truth in Formalized Languages. In Tarski (1956a), 152–197; reprinted in Davidson and Harman (1975), 25–49.

Tavakolian, Susan, ed. (1980). *Language Acquisition and Linguistic Theory*. MIT Press, Cambridge.

Tenney, James, with Larry Polansky (1980). Temporal Gestalt Perception in Music. *Journal of Music Theory* 24.2, 205–241.

Thomason, Richard, and Robert Stalnaker (1973). A Semantic Theory of Adverbs. *Linguistic Inquiry* 4.2, 195–220.

Trubetzkoy, N. S. (1939). *Grundzüge der Phonologie*. Trans. as *Principles of Phonology*. University of California Press, Berkeley, 1969.

VanDevelde, Robert (1977). Mistaken Views of *See*. *Linguistic Inquiry* 8.4, 767–772.

Vendler, Zeno (1967). Each and Every, Any and All. In *Linguistics in Philosophy*, Cornell University Press, Ithaca, 70–96.

Vendler, Zeno (1975). On What We Know. In Gunderson (1975), 370–390.

Wanner, Eric, and Michael Maratsos (1978). An ATN Approach to Comprehension. In Halle, Bresnan, and Miller (1978), 119–161.

Wasow, Thomas (1977). Transformations and the Lexicon. In Culicover, Wasow, and Akmajian (1977), 327–360.

Webber, Bonnie Lynn (1978). *A Formal Approach to Discourse Anaphora*. Technical Report 3761, Bolt, Beranek, and Newman, Cambridge, Mass.; Garland Publishing Co., New York, 1979.

Weinreich, Uriel (1966). Explorations in Semantic Theory. In T. Sebeok, ed., *Current Trends in Linguistics*. Vol. 3. Mouton, The Hague.

Weizenbaum, Joseph (1976). *Computer Power and Human Reason*. Freeman, San Francisco.

Wertheimer, Max (1912). Experimentelle Studien über das Sehen von Bewegung. *Z. Psychol.* 61, 161–265.

Wertheimer, Max (1922). The General Theoretical Situation. In Ellis (1938), 12–16.

Wertheimer, Max (1923). Laws of Organization in Perceptual Forms. In Ellis (1938), 71–88.

Wexler, Kenneth, and Peter Culicover (1980). *Formal Principles of Language Acquisition*. MIT Press, Cambridge.

Wexler, Kenneth, and Henry Hamburger (1973). Insufficiency of Surface Data for the Learning of Transformational Languages. In Hintikka, Moravcsik, and Suppes (1973), 167–179.

Wilks, Yorick (1973). An Artificial Intelligence Approach to Machine Translation. In Schank and Colby (1973), 114–151.

Williams, Edwin (1980). Predication. *Linguistic Inquiry* 11.1, 203–238.

Winograd, Terry (1972). *Understanding Natural Language*. Academic Press, New York.

Winston, Patrick (1970). *Learning Structural Descriptions from Examples*. MIT Project MAC, Cambridge.

Wittgenstein, Ludwig (1953). *Philosophical Investigations*, Blackwell, Oxford.

Woisetschlaeger, Erich (1976). *A Semantic Theory of the English Auxiliary System*. Doctoral dissertation, MIT, Cambridge.

Zadeh, L. (1965). Fuzzy Sets. *Information and Control* 8, 338–353.

Index